Violence and Mediation
in Contemporary Culture

SUNY Series, The Margins of Literature
Mihai I. Spariosu, Editor

Violence and Mediation in Contemporary Culture

Edited by
Ronald Bogue and
Marcel Cornis-Pope

State University of New York Press

Published by
State University of New York Press, Albany

For information, address State University of New York Press,
State University Plaza, Albany, N.Y. 12246

Production by M. R. Mulholland
Marketing by Fran Keneston

Library of Congress Cataloging-in-Publication Data

Violence and mediation in contemporary culture / edited by Ronald Bogue
and Marcel Cornis-Pope
    p.   cm. — (SUNY series, the margins of literature)
    Includes bibliographical references and index.
    Contents : Introduction : paradigms of conflict and mediation in literary and cultural
imagination / Ronald Bogue and Marcel Cornis-Pope — The melancholy object of
consumption / Stanley Corngold — On wounding : windows, screens, and desire /
Jerry Herron — The last days of Arnold Schwarzenegger / Albert Liu — The Jew as
woman's symptom : Kathlyn Bigelow's conflictive representation of feminine power /
Elisabeth Bronfen — Shattered hopes: on Blue Velvet / Susan Derwin — Murder and
mystery Mormon style : violence and mediation in American popular culture / Terryl
Givens — Revolution : hope without future or future without hope / Tonglin Lu —
What is mimetic desire? / Paisley Livingston — Murder as play : Conrad Aiken's King
Coffin / Mihal Spariosu — Contest vs. mediation : models of discursive power in
innovative fiction / Marcel Cornis-Pope
    ISBN 0-7914-2719-6. — ISBN 0-7914-2720-X (pbk.)
    1. Popular culture—History—20th century.   2. Popular culture—United States—
History—20th century. 3. Violence in literature.   4. Violence in mass media.
5. Violence in mass media—United States. I. Bogue, Ronald, 1948– . II. Pope-Cornis,
Marcel. III. Series.
CB430.V56   1995
306 .0973—dc20
                                           95-2451
                                             CIP

Contents

1

Introduction: Paradigms of Conflict and Mediation in Literary and Cultural Imagination

Ronald Bogue and Marcel Cornis-Pope

The only gain of civilization for mankind is the greater capacity for variety of sensations—and absolutely nothing more. And through the development of this manysidedness man may come to finding enjoyment in bloodshed. In fact, this has already happened to him. Have you noticed that it is the most civilized gentlemen who have been the subtlest slaughterers, to whom the Atillas and Stenka Razins could not hold a candle, and if they are not so conspicuous as the Atillas and Stenka Razins it is simply because they are so often met with, are so ordinary and have become so familiar to us. In any case civilization has made mankind if not more bloodthirsty, at least more vilely, more loathsomely bloodthirsty. In old days he saw justice in bloodshed and with his conscience at peace exterminated those he thought proper. Now we do think bloodshed abominable and yet we engage in this abomination, and with more energy than ever. Which is worse? Decide that for yourselves.

—Dostoyevsky, *Notes from Underground*[1]

The problems identified by Dostoyevsky's underground man more than a century ago, it would seem, are still with us. Our collective capacity for polymorphous sensation and cynical violence has hardly decreased, and our age of instant global communication has only made us more aware of the ubiquity of violent action. Examples of unconscionable cultural violence are readily available on every channel of mass communication. In the mid-1990s we find ourselves visually and mentally violated by images from several theaters of abomination: Waco, Bosnia, Somalia, Rwanda, Chechnya, the Middle East. They all illustrate degrees of the same model of self-reproduced conflict which expands by absorbing outside interventions into an underlying structure of conflictive differentiation, perpetuating the insidious cycle of violence.

The violence itself is nothing new, of course, as Dostoyevsky understood. But what appears to be new is the cynical self-awareness that accompanies it, a phenomenon that one can trace to a disintegration of cultural values in an age of expanding communication, a process already underway in 1864 and only accelerated in our century. The current escalation of violence reflects, ironically, both a deepening of the cultural crisis and an intensification of the communicative circuits that exhibit it. The latter contribute their own form of representational violence as they glamorize/naturalize conflict. Crude plot-driven narratives of horror collaborate with cunning postmodern re-presentations to create a permanent spectacle of violence. This theater of overstimulation has been cleverly exploited by recent "revolutions" which, as the 1989 East European upheavals can testify, have spent much of their contestatory energy in the postmodern space of television; and by the entertainment industry which has colonized our imagination with daily doses of domestic, racial, and professional violence: Amy Fischer, Lorena Bobbit, Tonya Harding, the Menendez brothers, O. J. Simpson.

Following Dostoyevsky's hints, we can link the issue of violence in contemporary culture to the ever-widening crisis of modernity. This crisis, as Nietzsche argued persuasively, affects both the system of beliefs and the discursive means that mediate them. Therefore, the study of cultural conflicts must proceed from a critical examination of the ethical, psychological, and narrative models undergirding modernity. Modern culture perpetuates the exclusionary, repressive oppositions of the ratiocentric and logocentric Platonic tradition, but in an exacerbated form, professing values that are—in Nietzsche's view—divorced from reality, predicated on arbitrary foundations and radical exclusions. One may measure a culture's movement through decadence toward nihilism by the degree of arbitrariness (or articulative violence) involved in its constructs. As John Burt Foster Jr. summarizes,

> A culture is decadent so long as it offers a system of values that can shape experience to some extent, even though its capacity to affirm life fully and directly has slipped to a marked degree or never existed. Of course Nietzsche sees all cultures as victories over chaos and hence as arbitrary. But a decadent culture represents a new level of the arbitrary, since its form giving impulse is capable of mastering only a part of the reality presented for assimilation; it operates only by virtue of a radical exclusion, and this exclusion is the measure of its decadence. The situation of nihilism arises

when the shaping principle breaks down still further, to the point where no cultural form at all is produced. In that case, people confront the essential chaos of the universe from which all meaning has disappeared, and they experience a total loss of coherence.[2]

Decadent cultures gradually lose their ability to ground their system of values, mastering only "part of reality" through their exclusionary articulations. Nihilistic cultures experience a further breakdown of the "form giving impulse," thereby losing their "capacity to affirm life fully and completely." Therefore, self-willed death ("revenge against life") is, according to Nietzsche, a natural response to the bewilderment and chaos of nihilism.[3] Modernity approaches life with an "instinct of weariness" and an endorsement of fragmentation, but this *ressentiment* against the wholeness of life is only a manifestation of the age-old "will to death" that Nietzsche traced back to the Apollonian, rationalistic side of the Hellenistic tradition and the life-denying, utopian side of Christianity. The model of tragedy that best embodies the agonistic ethos inherited by modernity from the Greeks pitted ratiocentric heroes against an array of cultural taboos. The tragic hero's transgression of boundaries ended in self-violence and cultural purging, as the two forms of mediation which recognized and tried to control the hero's antithetical identity. Nietzsche's antidote to this mentality paralysed by a conflictive rationality is, of course, the Dionysian spirit of personal vitality and political growth, a "self-overcoming" through which the "spirit who has *become free* stands amid the cosmos with a joyous and trusting fatalism, in the *faith* that only the particular is loathsome, and that all is redeemed and affirmed in the whole."[4]

Nietzsche's analysis of decadence and nihilism aptly frames the problem of cultural violence in modernity, but we must note that Nietzsche, by positing an Apollonian/Dionysian duality, elevates a structure of conflictive differentiation (which he otherwise wished to eradicate) into a global view of cultural history defined as a recurring confrontation between opposing types. Hence Nietzsche's example is instructive in at least two ways that bear directly on the essays in this collection. First, his systematic focus on cultural decadence opens an important area of investigation at the intersection of the anthropological, cultural, and political spheres. And second, his work reveals the extent to which any analysis of cultural violence becomes at least partially trapped in the system of conflictive differentiations it critiques. As Derrida and Foucault have suggested in their rereadings of Nietzsche, one cannot "do" cultural history after Nietzsche without seeking out those moments of "difference" that undermine the coherence of history and force a reevaluation of the present;[5] nor without confronting the limits and impositions of one's explanatory models. According to Derrida, Nietzsche vacillated between a semiotic understanding of "truth" as an interpretive "fiction" and as a metaphysical search for the "deeper" figurative "truth" of the will-to-power (which could occasionally turn into a search for the disciplining presence of a master-leader as in Nietzsche's 1872 lectures on education).[6] That tension sharpened Nietzsche's awareness of the ideological and rhetorical infrastructures of culture, conferring upon his work a critical-reflexive stance not unlike that of deconstruction. Nietzsche's skeptical epistemology problematized key oppositions in the Platonic tradition (metaphor and concept, mind and body, truth and language, essence and appearance), undoing their conflicting hierarchies through an intersubstituting of terms.

Nietzsche interests us today as the philosopher of modernity who first explored the complex interconnections of cultural systems to power. A work such as *On the Genealogy of Morals* (1887) suggested an intricate interplay between violence and mediation, describing a mechanism of internalized moral control through threats and violence. At the same time, Nietzsche envisioned a more positive form of mediation that emphasized individual "self-overcoming" and multiple subjectivity (a plurality of individual wills-to-power). Under his influence, the philosophers of postmodernity (Foucault, Lyotard, Deleuze, Baudrillard) have denounced the "totalizing metaphors" of our traditional ways of dispensing truth, proposing in their place self-problematized modes of semiotic interaction (e.g., Deleuze's "finding, encountering, stealing instead of regulating, recognizing and judging"[7]). For Jean-François Lyotard, as the self-questioning philosopher of a post-Auschwitz world, reality "is not what is 'given' to this or that 'subject,'" but a state of "the differend," that is an irreducible, litigious object that can only be negotiated through partial "testimonies" and questionable cognitive appropriations.[8] Our establishment procedures always involve "totalizing metaphors" that need to be foregrounded critically. Therefore, the mode of articulation he recommends is self-contradictory, combining the task of "perpetually flushing out" artifices of representation with the task of reinventing the familiar rules and categories of thought, seeking a new "realization."[9] This mode of articulation retains an agonistic, confrontational aspect: as long as "to speak is to fight, in the sense of playing" against a formidable adversary ("the accepted language, or connotation"), all acts of signification place us in the domain of "general agonistics" (*The Postmodern Condition*, p. 10). But Lyotard's postmodern dialectic of signification also has its pleasurable side, as it mediates between the contractual and the innovative facets of language games: "A move can be made for the sheer pleasure of its invention: what else is involved in that labor of language harassment undertaken by popular speech and by literature? Great joy is had in the endless invention of turns of phrase, of words and meanings, the process behind the evolution of language on the level of *parole*" (p. 10). Innovative cultural agents "can move from one game to another, and in each of these games (in the optimal situation) they try to figure out new moves. . . . What we call an 'artist' in the usual sense of the term, is someone who, in relation to a given purport, the purport of the canvas the medium of the *picta*, for example, proposes new rules of the painting game."[10]

Needless to say, the "artist's" linguistic and cultural creativity is not unbridled; even as it opens up the scene of signification to new articulatory possibilities, it cannot (should not) eradicate all sources of conflict and differentiation. Intellectual discussions of violence find themselves in a similar position: while they cannot hope to remove all traces of violence from their own discourses, they can provide a space for their critique and mediation. As Derrida wrote in the afterword to *Limited Inc.*, apropos of the violent tenor of his own controversy with Searle and Austin:

> The violence, political or otherwise, at work in academic discussions or in intellectual discussions generally, must be acknowledged. In saying this I am not advocating that such violence be unleashed or simply accepted. I am above all asking that we try to recognize and analyze it as best we can in its various forms. . . . And if, as I believe, violence remains in fact (almost) ineradicable, its analysis and the most refined, ingenious account of its conditions will be the least violent gestures, perhaps even nonviolent, and in any case those which contribute most to transforming the legal-ethical-political rules: *in* the university and *outside* the university.[11]

Postmodern feminists will concur with Derrida that the task of transforming the "legal-ethical-political rules" is essential to a rethinking of cultural practices around collaborative rather than conflictive relations. But they will also concede that even the most imaginative, subversive "semiotic" may enforce certain framings and exclusions. The "écriture feminine" advocated by Hélène Cixous can appear as both liberating and contentious: as an art of transgressive "excess" and "perverse" resistance,[12] this heterogeneous language recovers repressed desires but also unsettles the subject's illusion of stability and control. Likewise, Julia Kristeva's rhythmic, bodily "semiotic is both the precondition of symbolic functioning and its uncontrollable excess. . . . Its subversive, dispersing energies transgress the boundaries or tolerable limits of the symbolic . . . [posing] a new recodification of the symbolic."[13]

The two related concerns outlined above—one with the anthropological and ideological roots of cultural violence, the other with the discursive means (narrative, figural, political) that mediate/rearticulate conflictive mentalities—are well reflected in the articles that comprise this volume. By contrast to other thematic collections, *Violence and Mediation in Contemporary Culture* is not a mere sequence of essays but a unified collective effort organized around two issues of considerable import today: the problem of cultural violence in relation to the much-debated notions of difference, representation, and power; and the corresponding question of the role of mediation in providing a communal space for the nonconflictive play of cultural differences. Another distinctive feature of this volume is its analytical comprehensiveness: the nine contributors explore specific manifestations of violence in contemporary culture from philosophical, literary, anthropological, psychological, and sociocultural perspectives, involving their readers in an interdisciplinary dialogue among complementary approaches. Focused on topics as diverse as the semiotics of windows/TV screens, the politics of consumer culture, gender relations in contemporary film, and the dynamics of representation in the fiction of Kafka, Lu Xun, Conrad Aiken, Toni Morrison, and Ronald Sukenick, this volume foregrounds subtle relationships between literary and popular culture, or between discursive and sociocultural forms of violence. A major concern in these essays is the impact of an ethos of force and contestation upon literary and cultural imagination. A number of essays have also envisioned forms of mediation based on alternatives to an agonistic cultural ethos, applying them to fictional or real situations that require conflict resolution.

Those contributors who actively pursue such a model of mediation (Spariosu, Cornis-Pope, Givens) do not propose a simplistic eradication of difference from cultural transactions but rather a nonconflictive economy of differentiation that would take us beyond an oppositional power mentality.[14] At the same time, however, they suggest that mediation has its conceptual and pragmatic limitations, functioning frequently as an extension of violence. An important question these essays raise concerns the politics and pragmatics of mediation: Is mediation an alternative to violence or simply, like Clausewitzian politics, a way of conducting violence by other means? The *Oxford English Dictionary* offers as one definition of mediation "agency or action as a mediator; the action of mediating between parties at variance; intercession on behalf of another." But equally venerable is the now obsolete sense of mediation as "division by two; division into two equal parts; halving, bisection." To mediate is to divide *and* to bring together, to represent one of two divided parts, and hence to come between those parts and yet reconcile those parts within a whole. Etymologically, then, mediation points directly to the problem of difference in all its ramifications, and particularly as it bears on the relationship between power and representations.

Terryl Givens's discussion of popular representations of Mormonism (" 'Murder and Mystery *Mormon Style'*: Violence and Mediation in American Popular Culture") is a case in point, emphasizing the violence inherent in the acts of sociocultural and fictional mediation that have tried to contain the heretical challenge of Mormon theocracy. Mormonism has a complex cultural identity, as a religious group clearly outside the American mainstream and yet historically and ethnically American to the core. Nineteenth-century fictional representations of Mormonism tended to demonize the religion while at the same time deploring the violence of anti-Mormon bigotry; such representations mediated social violence by "orientalizing" Mormonism as culturally other and by attributing Mormon conversion to the mesmeric elimination of individual will. Givens finds in the works of two contemporary mystery writers, Robert Irvine and Cleo Jones, many of the same patterns of Mormon caricature, with the difference that the gradual assimilation of Mormons within the dominant culture has necessitated a compensatory demonization of "bourgeoisified" Mormonism as *too much* a part of the American mainstream. Through his historical overview of Mormon representations, Givens highlights the persistence of oppositional violence in our categories of otherness and difference. We have advanced beyond the nineteenth-century notions of mainstream (nativist) intolerance, but our new-found multicultural tolerance can be easily disarmed through a reification/sensationalization of differences (to wit, the recent Waco, Texas, and Rodney King dramas). There is, finally, a "close kinship of those representations which demonize the other to relive cultural anxieties and those which appropriate the other with more benevolent intentions." One can apply this conclusion not only to various forms of popular culture (TV shows, films, popular fiction) that have tried to negotiate conflictive issues such as race, AIDS, abortion, and women's politics into the mainstream but also to sophisticated theoretical discourses that have appropriated politico-discursive projects under broader agendas (male feminism, Western postcolonial studies, "straight" uses of "queer theory").

The analyses in this volume explore both ends of the discursive-cultural spectrum, moving progressively from shared practices in mass culture that enhance conflict to distinctive literary-theoretical strategies that negotiate/mediate it. The first two contributors (Stanley Corngold and Jerry Herron) concern themselves with the systemic violence of commodity exchange within consumer societies, exploring its economic and semiotic roots. Corngold's focus in "The Melancholy Object of Consumption" is the mediated violence of consumer culture, in which the mass-produced commodity, both as disenchanted simulacrum and as unit of equivalency in the universal exchange of capital, creates a melancholy void in the souls of consumers which the commodity itself paradoxically promises to fill. Depression (the "unhinging of the soul") is regularly produced in capitalism by goods that themselves pose as antidepressants, a fact that becomes particularly clear in recent efforts to commodify depression, such as those of pharmaceutical companies marketing antidepressant drugs or of mental hospitals whose experts promise to tell melancholy consumers whether their depression is genuine or not. Ultimately, these products aim not at providing cures but at creating even stronger psychological needs, trapping consumers in a melancholic carnival of consumption. Corngold's proposed repoliticization of the exchange relations, in the conclusion of his essay, is particularly fitting in view of the new acquisitive fever that has contaminated the countries of Eastern Europe and other developing nations.

In "On Wounding: Windows, Screens, and Desire," Jerry Herron proposes an analysis of the role played by windows, and subsequently by TV screens, as devices for constructing domestic, middle-class interiors. Windows are semiotically overdetermined sites for mediating certain important differences—inside/outside, private/public—that constitute a desirable life. They function like "wounds," inducing a rupture and a discovery process whereby a new class of subjectivity is born. A homologous relationship exists between windows and the screens, first of movie theaters and subsequently of TV. While windows introject, visibly and decoratively, the disciplinary time of culture into the management of private life, the TV screen carries this work further, reasserting a certain temporal sociality—but one that is a parody of social interaction. Herron's examination of home decoration manuals, together with the technoviolence of film and television, demonstrates how commercialized representations are calculated to mediate, or "cure," the wound opened by the modern window. But these examples of technoviolence could also be described as a new form of "wounding" (through disgorging, disindividualizing) that re-stage the domestic wound of spectation.

The three subsequent authors (Albert Liu, Elisabeth Bronfen, and Susan Derwin) are concerned not only with an all-too-familiar form of "technoviolence" (film) but also with popular culture in general as the site where conflictual notions of identity, gender, and race are continually raised and transacted. Albert Liu's speculations on the media, violence, and politics converge in the performative image of Schwarzenegger ("True Lies: Arnold Schwarzenegger's Life and Times"). Liu has chosen not to treat Schwarzenegger as a representative cliché of masculine identity, as have most previous commentators,[15] but explores instead his involvement in a network of effects relating technology, recent history, and the representation of violence, effects resulting in the instability of Schwarzenegger's gender configurations and his engagement in new, hypothetical forms of identity. Liu reads Schwarzenegger's image as a limit-case of cultural intelligibility whose aporias of communication contribute to a politics of the disperformative. In many of his films, especially *The Terminator* and *Terminator 2*, Schwarzenegger's inactions have extreme consequences and his actions serve primarily to prevent things from happening. His cinematic representations function as sheer displays of potentialized force and as disjunctive syntheses of irreconcilable elements. In *Terminator 2*, the aporias are exaggerated through the creation of Arnold's cybernetic antagonist/ double, the metalmorph assassin T-1000. A unit of pure self-organizing, morphogenetic matter, T-1000 is the embodiment of law as the power to give form. As simulacrum of the Oscar statue, T-1000 is also an image of filmic intelligence, a nonbiological consciousness through which film asserts its autonomy as a living being. A related point that Liu makes is that, for all its resistance to discursivity and a clear semiotics of action, the Schwarzenegger politics of the disperformative is still committed to two forms of mediated and morally sanctioned violence, euthanasia and sacrifice; and to an ambivalent "language" of bodybuilding, at once "asymbolic" and phallic, that privileges "certain kinds of physical experience over modes of identification based on semiotic or linguistic mediation."

Liu's semiotic exploration is fittingly expanded with the psychoanalytic and narratological approaches of Bronfen and Derwin. No analysis of cultural violence would be complete without the latter. In psychoanalytic terms, the mediation of violence is also directly related to the problem of desire, a consideration that is reflected in a number of the volume's contributions. Throughout Freud's writings, the enigma of sadomasochism haunts his theory, forcing him eventually to posit a death drive that is mediated through the agencies of the ego and the superego.[16] For Jacques Lacan as well, from his early essays on the mirror stage and aggressivity to his later works on feminine desire, the mediation of violence is an important concern, taking place as it does through the specular ego's transcendence of the fragmented body and through the interdiction of the "Nom du Père" which inaugurates the Symbolic.[17] Further on, in Julia Kristeva's theory of sacrifice, the parallels between social violence and the constitution of the Symbolic are made explicit, the murder of the sacrificial victim figuring the structural violence of language's transformation of the soma.[18] Kristeva's treatment of "abjection" is particularly useful for our focus: the abject, in her description, "disturbs identity, system, order," being related to that which "does not respect borders, positions, rules. The in-between, the ambiguous, the composite" (*Powers of Horror*, p. 4). By drawing us "towards the place where meaning collapses" (p. 2), foregrounding "the *want* on which any being, meaning, language, or desire is founded" (p. 5), abjection produces a major crisis in the subject (who becomes a "deject"/a "stray" [pp. 2, 8]) and in the world. On the positive side, abjection allows us to move beyond the Law of the Father into a cultural-semiotic space that disrupts the boundary between self and other, inside and outside, consciousness and subconsciousness. As such, it both challenges the prohibitive violence of the symbolic and returns us to "what existed in the archaism of pre-objectal relationship," to the "immemorial violence with which a body becomes separated from another body in order to be" (p. 10). Modern writing, in Kristeva's view, is best suited to imagine the abject by means of its complex displacements; Dostoyevsky, Lautréamont, Proust, Joyce, Artaud, Kafka, Céline, and Borges are just some of the writers who have mapped the paradoxical play of that which is "inseparable, contaminated, condemned [or unsymbolizable] at the boundary of what is assimilable, thinkable: abject" (p. 18).

For Elisabeth Bronfen ("The Jew as Woman's Symptom: Kathlyn Bigelow's Conflictive Representation of Feminine Power") and Susan Derwin ("Shattered Hopes: On *Blue Velvet*"), these psychoanalytic considerations are particularly useful in determining the role of violence in feminine desire. In Bigelow's film *Blue Steel* (1989) Bronfen finds a complex cultural representation of the relationship of woman's desire to power and violence. The film's plot operates via a logic of Kristevan sacrifice, the heroine (a New York City cop) gaining acceptance within the culture of masculine authority only through the destruction of the "internal Other," a psychopathic Jew whose death stands in for and signifies woman's violent desire, while also epitomizing the stereotypical need for scapegoating in the culture's symbolic system. The film lends itself to three complementary forms of analysis: a feminist reading, in which the patriarchal anxiety over women's access to power is mediated through the sacrificial cultural representation of the Jew; a psychoanalytic reading, in which the death drive is mediated through the

imaginary and symbolic processes of the Oedipal trajectory; and a narratological reading, in which heterogeneous scenes of violence are mediated through the hierarchical integration of the narrative elements
within a coherent diegetic structure.

Derwin's essay starts with a similar emphasis on the enmeshed
questions of longing, desire, and violence in middle-class America
which seem to bear out Kristeva's point about "want" and "aggressivity" as logically coextensive (*Powers of Horror,* p. 39). She finds in
David Lynch's movie *Blue Velvet* (1986) an uncanny reversal of the expected cultural oppositions (domestic suburbia/criminal world, sur-
face/subterranean, ordinary/exceptional), to the point where the
repressed "other" (as pathological violence and sexual perversion) becomes a heightened version of the norm accepted by contemporary society. Jeffrey Beaumont enters the subterranean spaces of middle-class
America by way of a comfortable voyeurism which finally traps him in
a violent economy of sexuality and self-engendering. Sexuality is experienced conflictually as narcissistic, self-enclosing voyeurism by the
men and as self-denying masochism by the women. In spite of the threat
posed to patriarchal authority by Dorothy's "Medusan" power, the
movie leaves undisturbed the Freudian convergence of masochism, representation, and the engendering of selfhood articulated in "A Child Is
Being Beaten" (1919). By presenting masochism as a static condition or
objective attribute unique to femininity, *Blue Velvet* encourages a certain
ethical complacency in the viewer. The troping of masochism onto femininity dissimulates a misogynistic, if more submerged, view of woman
as misandrous sadist.

By way of their discussion of popular ideologies of representations, the two essays also engage us in some rethinking of the theoretical models (psychoanalysis, narratology, and feminism) brought to bear
on this analysis of feminine power. As Bronfen pointedly asks, "Why
does an emancipatory project like feminism require the stereotyping of
the Other (the Jew, in this case), that amounts to the sacrifice of this
Other?" Derwin's analysis of *Blue Velvet*'s fetishistic structure also raises
important questions about the meaning and ideological function of key
terms in psychoanalysis (fetishization, narcissistic projection, the return
of the repressed), resituating current debates concerning violence
against women. Ultimately, the primary focus of Bronfen and Derwin is
more sociological than psychological, for their prevailing interest is in a
critique of cultural representations as social symptoms. They share this
interest with the rest of the volume's contributors. Derwin, Spariosu,
and Liu converge in their focus on the legitimation and regulation of violence within (and outside of) the social institution of law. Bronfen joins

Givens and Lu in analyzing the compensatory mechanisms of sacrificial victimage that mediate social disequilibrium. And all of the contributors, in one way or another, treat representation itself as contemporary culture's prevailing mode of mediating violence, the various signs of massmediated culture tracing the deflections, displacements, and dissimulations of power and domination.

Terryl Givens (whose essay we have already reviewed) and Tonglin Lu move the discussion from visual to print culture and from semiotic forms of violence to political-rhetorical ones. In "Destruction, Revolution, and Cultural Nihilism," Lu explores the paradoxical narrative figuration of revolution in the fiction of Lu Xun, one of China's greatest twentieth-century writers. The writer whom Mao praised as "an obliging ox for the proletarian masses" was no sycophantic propagandist, as this essay shows, but a complex artist who embraced collectivist revolution as a means of undermining feudal power relations yet who recognized the mimetic mechanisms that perpetuated past iniquities in new social structures. Lu Xun, therefore, had little faith in the free play of revolutionary forces as a means of mediating past forms of institutionalized violence. Attracted equally to the values of Confucian collectivism and Western individualism, Lu Xun finally could frame himself as revolutionary subject only in the most antithetical of terms— as fool and madman in his unavoidable commitment to social action, as loner and misanthrope in his necessary isolation from the mimetically shaped masses. Lu Xun's antithetical figuration of revolutionary change has interesting implications for Western theory and political practice, calling attention to the inherent contradictions of an ethos of contestation and transformation. A Western reader will experience these agonic structures both at a philosophic-metaphoric level ("dead fire," "high wall," and "shadow" are Lu Xun's tropes for violence and uncertainty in revolution) and at a semantic level (the neologistic phrases that name the writer's vision of "new life" are devoid of meaning in common language).

Most of the essays in this volume critique the various means whereby mediation functions as an extension of violence. The final two studies, however, attempt to envision forms of mediation that are true alternatives to an ethos of force and contestation and test them against specific cultural and literary practices (the sociopoetics of modernism and of postmodernism, respectively). Mihai Spariosu finds in Conrad Aiken's *King Coffin* the suggestion of an integrative mentality that questions the concept of desire as will to power and enables a process of self-formation guided by peaceful rather than contestatory principles. Marcel Cornis-Pope recognizes in certain works of recent innovative fiction instances of a transactive model of difference that makes possible modes of transformative cultural mediation. For Cornis-Pope, alternatives to violence are already available, whereas for Spariosu genuine mediation requires a rejection of the fundamental values of the Western power mentality. But both concur that true mediation can take place only through a thorough examination of the basic theoretical presuppositions that underlie the institutions, practices, and representations of contemporary culture.

In "Murder as Play: Conrad Aiken's *King Coffin*," Spariosu approaches the literary theme of homicide as part of the modernist question of the uneasy relation between aesthetics and ethics, play and power, art and life. In certain decadent, postmodernist or "aestheticist" texts, murder functions as a radical form of moral transgression and ultimately as an unrepressed form of archaic, violent play. In such anti-aestheticist works as Aiken's *King Coffin,* however, murder as play serves to question the prevailing rational and ethical values of modern Western culture, yet without embracing the aestheticist's violent, transgressive solutions embodied in the concept of "pure crime." Aiken's novel points to an integrative mentality that calls into question the notion of desire as a Nietzschean will-to-power; at the same time, this integrative mentality goes beyond Hegel's teleological notion of consciousness, implying a continuous open-endedness and autoformation of world and self according to irenic rather than agonistic principles. Through his close rereading of a largely ignored major work, Spariosu outlines a critique of cultural violence, first in the context of the literary tradition of Romantic and modernist fiction, then in the more general cultural context of a pervasive Western mentality of power.

Cornis-Pope argues in "Contest vs. Mediation: Innovative Discursive Modes in Postmodern Fiction" that contemporary philosophical debates over the relationship between representation and power are paralleled in the literary practices of surfictionists (such as Ronald Sukenick) and feminist writers (such as Toni Morrison). These innovative writers seek to replace agonistic models of difference that result in violent contestation with transactive models of difference that emphasize cultural mediation. Sukenick, for example, uses self-reflexive linguistic techniques to destabilize hierarchical and inequitable social codes but also to rearticulate the cultural scene in terms of its differential, transformative possibility. He seeks to replace a power-oriented representational language (whose main figuration is aestheticized rape) with an improvisational, process-oriented language of being. Likewise, Morrison attempts an imaginative metamorphosis of feminine subjectivity in her fiction, emptying conventional symbolic structures of their content yet providing her readers with alternative, experimental representations of women and the female self.

Even as they develop strong analytic arguments, the authors featured in this volume are not oblivious to the problems raised by their methodologies. A certain amount of interpretive violence is involved in all acts of theoretical analysis that employ a self-legitimized "technology" to mediate between observed "reality" and "knowledge." Several essays in this volume seek, therefore, more flexible modes of theoretical mediation: playful or paradoxical arguments, counterpointed interpretations, alternative analytic frameworks. Even if they do not/cannot envision a language that would "give up . . . the power principle with its faithful instruments, good and bad mimesis, and good and bad representation,"[19] these essays engage critically one manifestation or another of their own discursive "power principle." Taken together, they negotiate a more tolerant, self-correcting discursive space that allows a dialogic interplay of differences (theoretical, linguistic, cultural, political), along the lines of that described by Homi K. Bhabha: "Cultural difference marks the establishment of new forms of meaning, and strategies of identification, through processes of negotiation where no discursive authority can be established without revealing the difference of itself."[20]

Faithful to this dialogic dynamic, the editors have refrained from settling any real or presumed contradictions among the individual essays. Such excessive mediation would have done violence to the competing foci of this volume (which reflect and challenge such conventional oppositions as popular vs. high culture, modern vs. postmodern, literary vs. cultural studies) without necessarily reconciling them. The reader is invited to participate in this dialogue of viewpoints, enhancing their analytic conversation with his/her own concepts of differentiation and mediation.

With the possible exception of Givens and Lu, the authors of this volume focus on theoretical issues in the representation of (mostly) individual violence rather than on the pragmatics of mediation in collective conflicts, and on dissimulated forms of cultural violence rather than on unmitigated political violence. We must observe, however, if only as a final, parenthetical note, that the mechanisms of conflictive differentiation explored in this volume are equally germane to the analysis of sociopolitical manifestations of violence. The latter can be seen as exacerbated, collective manifestations of the "instincts of decline (or *ressentiment,* discontent, the drive to destroy, anarchism, and nihilism)"[21] that Nietzsche associated with the age of modern decadence; or as virulent examples of the process of conflict-reproduction that enhances itself by absorbing outside interventions into its structure of conflictive differentiation. Consider, for example, the many instances of ethnic violence in post-1989 Europe. With the collapse of communism, the old class-party system has been replaced in several areas by an assortment of right-wing and left-wing nationalisms that function as an alternative model of self-legitimation through extreme differentiation. Like its communist predecessor, which was predicated on the interests of one class (or rather, on the interests of its nomenclature), nationalistic power relies on invidious distinctions of race, nationality, group, reinforced through exclusionary methods of control: "When the dominant group seeks to portray the identity of the state as isomorphic with its own, the very existence of 'the wrong kind of people' is apt to become a scandal and a threat."[22] This model of conflictive differentiation has spawned not only new ideological and cultural intolerance but also totalitarian forms of "liquidation"[23] and interethnic terror like those in the former Yugoslavia. It is quite clear by now that neither a cavalier disregard of historical cultural differentiations nor their liquidation through terror or manipulation can provide an effective solution for these protracted ethnic conflicts. What needs to be created is a nonconflictive (transactional) sociopolitical space that would allow each ethnic group to contribute its own interests and traditions. The task at hand is not only political but also broadly ideological, involving a thorough rethinking of our conflictive definitions of identity (individual, communal, national) and their replacement with mediative processes of identity formation.

Notes

1. Fyodor Dostoyevsky, *Notes from Underground,* in *White Nights and Other Stories,* trans. Constance Garnett (London: Heinemann, 1918), 76.

2. John Burt Foster, Jr., *Heirs to Dionysus: A Nietzschean Current in Literary Modernism* (Princeton: Princeton University Press, 1981), 86.

3. Friedrich Nietzsche, *The Twilight of the Idols,* in *The Portable Nietzsche,* selected and trans. W. Kaufmann (New York: Viking Press, 1968), 554–55. For a good critical overview of Nietzsche's exploration of the concept and style of "decadence," see Matei Calinescu, *Five Faces of Modernity: Modernism, Avant-Garde, Decadence, Kitsch, Postmodernism* (Durham: Duke University Press, 1987), 178–195.

4. *The Portable Nietzsche,* 553–54.

5. M. Foucault, "Nietzsche, Genealogy, History," in Donald F. Bouchard, ed., *Language, Counter-Memory, Practice: Selected Essays and Interviews* (Ithaca: Cornell University Press, 1977), 139–64. For a discussion of Nietzsche's influ-

ence on Foucault and other postmodern theorists, see Clayton Koelb, ed., *Nietzsche as Postmodernist: Essays Pro and Contra* (Albany: SUNY Press, 1990); Alan Megill, *Prophets of Extremity: Nietzsche, Heidegger, Foucault, Derrida* (Berkeley: University of California Press, 1985); Peter Dews, *Logics of Disintegration: Post-Structuralist Thought and the Claims of Critical Theory* (London: Verso, 1986), especially pp. 177–86 ("Foucault and Nietzsche"); Steven Best and Douglas Kellner, *Postmodern Theory: Critical Interrogation* (New York: Guilford Press, 1991), especially pp. 79–85 ("Deleuze's Nietzsche") and 152–60 ("Lyotard's Nietzschean Drift").

6. See Jacques Derrida, *Spurs: Nietzsche's Styles*, trans. B. Harlow (Chicago: University of Chicago Press, 1979); Derrida, *Otobiographies: l'enseignment de Nietzsche et la politique du nom propre* (Paris: Éditions Galilée, 1984), 23–24, 27–29. For discussions of Derrida's rereading of Nietzsche, see Rodolphe Gasché, *The Tain of the Mirror: Derrida and the Philosophy of Reflection* (Cambridge: Harvard University Press, 1986), 154, 171, 178, 310, 312; Ernst Behler, *Confrontations: Derrida, Heidegger, Nietzsche*, trans. Steven Taubeneck (Stanford: Stanford University Press, 1991).

7. Gilles Deleuze and Claire Parnet, *Dialogues*, trans. Hugh Tomlinson and Barbara Habberjam (New York: Columbia University Press, 1987), 8–9.

8. Jean François Lyotard, *The Differend: Phrases in Dispute*, trans. George Van Den Abbeele (Minneapolis: University of Minnesota Press, 1988), 4, 9.

9. Lyotard, *The Postmodern Condition: A Report on Knowledge*, trans. Geoff Bennington and Brian Massumi (Minneapolis: University of Minnesota Press, 1984), 79, 81.

10. Jean-François Lyotard and Jean-Loup Thébaud, *Just Gaming*, trans. Wlad Godzich (Minneapolis: University of Minnesota Press, 1985), 61.

11. Jacques Derrida, *Limited Inc.* (Evanston, IL: Northwestern University Press, 1988), 112.

12. See M. Schiach, *Hélène Cixous: A Politics of Writing* (London: Routledge, 1991).

13. Madan Sarup, *An Introductory Guide to Post-Structuralism and Postmodernism*, 2d ed. (Athens: University of Georgia Press, 1993), 125–26.

14. For a systematic critique of the "agonistic mode of thought" and its attending power mentality in Western discursive traditions, see Mihai Spariosu, *Dionysus Reborn: Play and the Aesthetic Dimension in Modern Philosophical and Scientific Discourse* (Ithaca: Cornell University Press, 1989); *God of Many Names: Play, Poetry and Power in Hellenic Thought from Homer to Aristotle* (Durham: Duke University Press, 1991).

15. See, for example, Michael Ryan and Douglas Kellner, *Camera Politica: The Politics and Ideology of Contemporary Hollywood Film* (Bloomington: Indiana

University Press, 1988); Susan Jeffords, *Hard Bodies: Hollywood Masculinity in the Reagan Era* (New Brunswick, NJ: Rutgers University Press, 1994).

16. See especially Sigmund Freud, *Group Psychology and the Analysis of the Ego*, trans. James Strachey (New York: Bantam Books, 1965); "The Economic Problem in Masochism," in *General Psychological Theory*, ed. Philip Rieff (New York: Collier Books, 1963); "A Child is Being Beaten," in *Sexuality and the Psychology of Love*, ed. Philip Rieff (New York: Collier Books, 1963).

17. See Jacques Lacan, *Écrits: A Selection*, trans. Alan Sheridan (New York: Norton, 1977).

18. See especially her *Powers of Horror: An Essay on Abjection*, trans. Leon S. Roudiez (New York: Columbia Press, 1982); and *Revolution in Poetic Language*, trans. Margaret Waller (New York: Columbia University Press, 1984), especially chap. 11.

19. Mihai Spariosu, "Mimesis and Contemporary French Theory," in *Mimesis in Contemporary Theory*, vol. 1, ed. Mihai Spariosu (Philadelphia: John Benjamins, 1984), 99.

20. Homi K. Bhabha, "DissemiNation: Time, Narrative, and the Margins of the Modern Nation," in *Nation and Narration*, ed. Homi K. Bhabha (New York: Routlege, 1990), 313.

21. F. Nietzsche, *The Will to Power*, trans. W. Kaufmann and B. J. Hollingdale (New York: Vintage Books, 1968), 461.

22. James B. Rule, "Tribalism and the State: A Reply to Michael Walzer," *Dissent* (Fall 1992), 522.

23. For an insightful analysis of the two models of totalitarian "liquidation" that have dominated this century, the "class-party" and the "race-party" approach, see Vladislav Todorov, "Introduction to the Political Aesthetics of Communism," in *Post-Theory, Games, and Discursive Resistance: The Bulgarian Case*, ed. Alexander Kiossev (Albany: SUNY, 1995), 66–125. Parts of this essay have been published in *Textual Practice* 5.3 (Winter 1991); and in *L'Infini* 33 (1991).

2

The Melancholy Object of Consumption

Stanley Corngold

The human heart is like a treasure-house: empty it at one go, and you're ruined.

—Honoré de Balzac, *Père Goriot*[1]

Jetzt hab ich gegessen zwei Kälber
Jetzt esse ich noch ein Kalb
Alles ist nur halb, alles ist nur halb
Ich äße mich gerne selber.

—Bertolt Brecht, *Aufstieg und Fall der Stadt Mahagonny*[2]

My beginning is not playful. It is about the *injunction* to play, the shock that every ordinary day delivers through the mail slot: junk mail. Junk mail is at once the public registry of market moves and the demand that you play your part. But even in reading the moves of the Market, the consumer has already lost. "Once the spirit [*Geist*] . . . is made to order for the customer who is dominated by the Market, which takes his inferiority as a pretext for its own ideology, then the spirit is finished off."[3] When the spirit is "finished off," it has ceased to play. Henceforth, I will speak not of the play but of the circulation of commodities.

H. L. Mencken, writing in 1945, was the first, to my knowledge, to point to this invasion:

I marvel constantly at the amount of printed matter that . . . passes over my desk. During the past five or six years I have probably sent the [New York Public] library at least 25,000 such items. They range from the announcements of new messiahs to the appeals of

charity racketeers, and from the annual reports of corporations to
paper-bound volumes of amateur poets.⁴

A half-century later the categories of junk mail have evidently deterio-
rated. New messiahs and charity racketeers tend to be absorbed into
one type: the market tipster. The corporation of note, with growing fre-
quency, is the manufacturer of antidepressants or the hospital for depressives. And the capabilities of some amateur poets have been
channeled into the writing of advertising copy for all of the above—tipster, pharmaceutical house, and asylum. Thus is the still sad music of
humanity reduced to the rattling of a stick inside a swill bucket (Or-
well).⁵ I want to see what vision of contemporary American commodity
culture can be put together from the printed matter that drops through
my—and your—mail slot (the addressee of junk mail is never a singular), especially as this matter involves money and depression, legal ten-
der and a widespread lack of tenderness.

    In 1921 Gustav Janouch, a young friend of Kafka's, allegedly
showed Kafka a drawing from a book with illustrations by Georg Grosz.
A portly man—a capitalist—with a top hat pulled down low and covering his eyes, is sitting, with enormous buttocks, on piled-up sacks of
money from which (here I rely on a general impression of Grosz's work)
a swarm of tiny people, who are being crushed or suffocated, are falling
off from this height.⁶ Kafka remarked: "That is the familiar view of Capital—the fat man in a top hat squatting on the money of the poor."
    From the expression on Kafka's face, Janouch was moved to ask:
"You mean that the picture is false?"
    Kafka then made his famous reply:

    It is both true and false. . . . The fat man in the top hat sits on the
    neck of the poor. That is correct. But the fat man is Capitalism, and
    that is not quite correct. The fat man oppresses the poor man
    within the conditions of a given system. But he is not the system
    itself. He is not even its master. On the contrary, the fat man is also
    in chains, which the picture does not show.

The picture is incomplete, concludes Kafka, "for capitalism is a system
of dependent relations [*ein System von Abhängigkeiten*]," that is, "a condition both of the world *and* of the soul [*ein Zustand der Welt und der
Seele*] (my emphasis)."⁷
    Kafka's last observation is very fine. It is one which has been, at
least since Benjamin's "On Some Motifs in Baudelaire," generally

adopted as a research program. On closer scrutiny, however, Kafka's remark could also prove perplexing. In the hingeing together of these terms—(1) the archaic term of inwardness, *the soul,* and (2) the modern, progressive term of exteriority, the political-economic *world*—there is a unifying impulse at work which could also seem mystic, Romantic, or merely witty. It could produce an effect of quaintness masking real disparity. The terms of "soul" and "world" will seem especially disjunct when one considers what the hinge between them, under capitalism, is made of: commodities, in systematic circulation, which erase all traces of the soul from the social relations that produce them.[8]

In other words, how does Kafka get from *A,* the allegorical "fat man," to *B,* the "soul"? We know what place in the system the fat man occupies, but where in Grosz's cartoon is the soul to be found, and what, indeed, is its condition?

In fact, what remains of the soul of men and women must wander in another space—*unhinged;* this might be called the "space of melancholy." Which is to say: the soul of men and women under late capitalism has become, more than ever, melancholic or melancholy-prone.

I shall be looking at some recent writing for examples of capitalist habits at work in the development of melancholy (I mean the term "development" in a quite literal sense, as in real estate development).[9] Hence, my concern is for capitalist habits that introduce melancholy into readers as yet unafflicted, if only for the purpose of developing cures. Many of the texts I draw on are vulgar social texts. With depression, according to *Der Spiegel,* "the [very] sickness of our age"[10]—the aftershock of the popular religion of the 1980s which Berliners called "Money-theism"—it has become a rhizome whose entrances are everywhere.

A society that has entirely forsworn all spiritual love and, forgetting its ancient entrails, now cares only for its visceral organs.

—Charles Baudelaire[11]

From the start we could follow Kafka, eminent *flâneur* and "melancholiast" (the nonce word is Terry Eagleton's). Kafka shunned, loved, and feared *meat,* and no wonder: In the age of mechanical reproduction, the crimson, glistening, marbled, identical filet is an exemplary commodity.[12] The aptness of filet mignon to commodity analysis was confirmed before Roland Barthes (the semiotician of steak) by Walter Benjamin, who theorized prostitution in a number of *aperçus.*[13] (After all, is there not in "filet mignon" and in the richly "marbled filet" more than a suggestion of the *"fille de marbre,"* a preferred phrase for "prostitute" in nineteenth-century Paris?) The exemplary commodity, in Eagleton's lively paraphrase of Benjamin, "automizes Nature to abstract equivalents only to recharge each fragment with a kind of grisly caricature of the magical 'aura' it has driven from social production in general." (With "grisly"—the older spelling of "gristly"—one could be inclined to think of the aura of rare meat.) Moreover, continues Eagleton on Benjamin, although the commodity "flaunts itself as a unique, hetroclite [that is to say, 'nonstandard'] slice of matter, [it] is in truth part of the very mechanism by which history becomes homogenized."[14] This is steak to a T. For, in this market segment, commodity capitalism does indeed become a literal slaughterbench of history, where crimes of homogenization are mechanically performed for rational profit.

I want now to copy out the message, which many of us have received, from our soul brothers-in-capitalism, the butchers at Omaha (Nebraska) Steaks International, Inc.

In weighing their filets, they write, two things should meet the eye. The first is the factor of exclusivity: the company's "list of customers," it appears, "is a regular Who's Who" in American life. Second is the factor of experience: "Line one [Omaha steak] alongside an ordinary filet . . . and it's like putting an elegant limousine alongside a stripped-down economy car."[15] Omaha steaks are not your average cheap cuts from some exhausted *deux-chevaux* put out to pasture. Indeed, the first mouthful of Omaha beef, which could make conversation for "weeks after," may turn out to be "the dinner experience [or should this be the driving experience?] of a lifetime."

The basis of the Omaha Steak treatment is the value of *experience*.[16] These butcher-poets write like Dilthey:

> You know, my friend, we are here on this earth for all too short a span. One reason why . . . [Omaha Steaks] admires true individuals such as you [prospective buyers of filets] is that you know how to live—how to get the most out of life, . . . *how to build a treasure-house of experiences you never forget*. (my emphasis)

That is it: the humanist ideal. On the face of it, Omaha Steaks are selling deluxe filets packaged in styrofoam and dry ice—the styrofoam and dry ice of *the humanist ideal*. With their steaks they are marketing melancholizers—commodities—packaged as antidepressants; for what, under capitalism, is the antidepressant *par excellence* if not the humanist ideal? According to this formidable ideal of the full subject, every consumer stores up imperishable treasure in his or her own soul, and melancholy is only the mood of destitution.[17]

But we need not despair; it will now be possible for the "very important citizens" among us, chosen by computer to receive the Omaha Steaks flyer, to regain possession of themselves at a cost only slightly higher than that of, say, a direct-dial call to the Fair Oaks [Mental] Hospital.

You have to be impressed by the cunning of the Omaha Steaks argument. Its contribution to the study of modern melancholy is to identify directly what the melancholiast has always had to do without: his treasure-laden soul, his portable treasure-house. Like Kafka's bachelor in the diary entry beginning "'Du,' sagte ich," the melancholiast has no sooner picked up one chance object than he loses two of his own.[18]

This Omaha text (flyer and cure) importantly illustrates the cooptation by a relentless, unconstrainable capitalism ("Markets are real and they are ruthless"[19]) of the ideal of the full subject, of the powerful rhetoric of a secular plan "to build a treasure-house of experiences you never forget." It is a rhetoric time-honored as the ethic of "lived experience" and one that has been pointedly applied to the artist—to Henry James's aspiring writer, for instance: Be one on whom nothing is wasted!

This section of my argument begins with another citation from Terry Eagleton's interpretive essay on Walter Benjamin. This citation concerns the nature of the commodity, about which Eagleton writes: "As the signifier of mere abstract equivalence, as the empty space through which one portion of labor-power exchanges with another, the commodity nonetheless disguises its virulent antimaterialism in a carnival of consumption."[20]

I intend, however, to emphasize another development, different from the materialist circus. I mean to show, namely, how a certain "antimaterialist" pathos—in a word, melancholy—has itself in turn been commodified and marketed with a view to luring torpid clients onto the carnival grounds of consumption.

Let us suppose that the Omaha Steaks solution has failed to improve the affective life of even its affluent customers (so that one might be better advised, in Tristan Tzara's words, "Ihr Geld [anstatt in Omaha] in dada anzulegen).''[21] Being "affluent" normally means that you are able to join in the flow of affection and hence the affectivity—the capacity for being affected—that streams out of commodities. The paradox that follows from our first example is that the very therapeutic failure of beef filet produces a wider success—the goal of capitalism being not so much to provide cures as to foster ever stronger forms of need—hence, to foster melancholy or insatiable psychic need in nearly helpless dependency. And here capitalism is bound to go on succeeding: It has only to be itself, to continue to promote, through commodities, the specious therapy of affluence. Consider a second example.

According to Doug Casey, a stock market analyst and author of a tract stuffed into mailboxes some summers ago: With runaway deflation coming, junk bonds will be on the trash heap, and "businesses . . . will go belly up and be available for next to nothing."[22] It's this gambler's second image that interests me. Here it is not just the commodity, but master-commodities—businesses as such—that will be going belly up, available for the taking. And indeed, this Mr. Casey has, to some extent, been proved right: With the collapse of Robert Campeau's empire and the going belly up of the junk bond–floated Manhattan department store Bloomingdale's, the opportunity for pillage is at hand. As a headline in the *New York Times* put it, "You bought the goods, now buy the stores."

The *horizontal* commodity is, of course, exemplary: The uptilted belly prostitutes itself for just a little inorganic silver, as indeed the flyer text—like the fashionable commodity—prostitutes the metaphor of the living body to the inorganic world of cash profit. It is quite as Benjamin saw it: In "the final triumph of commodity fetishism, the living body is prostituted to the inorganic world and succumbs to its sex appeal."[23]

Now, here, of course, to say "living body" is to say too much: The body gone belly up is an image of floundering—of death—and flaunts a button of heterogeneity, pointing back to the destructiveness of normal capitalist habits. For one could find in this image a trace of whales and dolphins, too, tangled in tuna nets or gasping in poisoned waters. The image (of businesses gone belly up) is countercapitalist and capital's just reward, revealing, in illuminating obverse, the mortification it inflicts.

And yet, by the logic of insatiability, these belly-up truths are offered not for ecological uplift but for plunder. The commodity (here, whole businesses) is sexy to the end. Pregnant with death, the death of the labor power producing it, and with the illusion of availability, it excites lust and *schadenfreude,* rapacity and acquisitiveness—the whole intensely unhingeing, because, as an image, it is so composite and contested. If it is supposed to communicate one thing plainly, it immediately suggests three things obscurely: a sexy, lucky find of capitalist raw material in the body of a distressed creature (fish, mammal, or she-boat) upset by capitalism's own excess.

It is as a commodity-cure that the therapy of affluence must flounder. If melancholy is the malady of depreciated soul-treasure, of the empty (coffered) subject, then cures will be only as valuable as the specifics that produce them—but commodities, of course, are without specific character, without aim, individuality, or aura. They are intrinsically facsimiles, fungible, as such duplicitous, and thus they hollow out the cure. Kafka's Hunter Gracchus, who wanders the waterways, observed that "the thought of wanting to help is a sickness and must be put to bed to get well."[24] That certainly appears to be true of commodity cures.

By the entrepreneurial dialectic, however, the question of the lost originality of the therapeutic object invariably arises (if only for commercial purposes). Only the original could cure, as true treasure could—like the true King's touch—but then there aren't enough originals to go around.

So, you can read (in *The New Yorker*) of a commodity-cure available "exclusively from the British National Trust Collection. Now . . . you can own Sir Winston Churchill's writing desk." But how is this possible? How could an object of such exquisite originality be offered in so unexclusive a manner to the *lumpen*-aesthete readership of *The New Yorker*? As follows. For "at last," we read, "one of the world's most treasured antiques has been . . . finely reproduced!" Expectably the appeal to exclusivity is sounded: "Only a few will ever be made, . . . and because of Churchill's stature as a world leader quick sellout is expected."[25]

I think any reader must sink into gloom, wondering how he or she is to draw—from generic, nonexclusive treasure—experience good enough for his or her treasure-house, when even the patrician Picture Gallery in Basel—the Gemäldegalerie—to honor its exhibit of Cézanne's lustrous group of paintings *The Bathers*, has issued for quick sellout a set of matched bath towels on which choice scenes from *The Bathers* are dry screened. It is now possible for viewers at home in their treasure-houses to dry their treasure-chests with original terrycloth reproductions.

The logic of such events is spelled out in Kenneth Burke's analysis still useful today, of the proliferation of techniques and needs under capitalism. In *Attitudes toward History*, Burke wrote that "the combination of capitalism and technology [has] both permitted a great proliferation of private-enterprise habits and demanded this proliferation."[26] You start with the economic fact of the bottle neck in the manufacture or sale of some commodity, leading to a condition of unprofitable competition. For example, you could imagine that the British National Trust copiers are producing too many original Churchill writing desks to go around—an unprofitable state of affairs, since these copiers make their fake felt from the very cotton product now being diverted to the manufacture of Cézanne bathtowels. This procedure could involve a good deal of wasteful cotton processing. Now the production of both commodities (or antidepressants) is unprofitable.

"You avoid this competition," Burke continues, "in part by the invention of 'new needs.' You invent a new gadget. With astounding 'efficiency,' you put hundreds of men seriously to work turning out . . . a device for telling you what time it is without taking your watch out of your pocket or turning your head to look at the clock." I have tried to imagine what this could be—perhaps a sort of full body clock, woven from the fabric of—time. Burke wrote these lines in 1937, but did Kafka, I wonder, forecast such a "gadget" too, in 1911? "Just leave your watch in your pocket," says one of his melancholiasts to another, in the street scene beginning "'Du,' sagte ich." The other knows the real reason why: "It surely is already very late."[27] Kafka's *flâneurs* can tell time without taking their watches out of their pockets and without body clocks—and this may be why they feel lost.

"This 'new need,' " continues Burke, "might, by an extreme act of charity, be said to have utilized the . . . wastage" generated—in our example—by the manufacture of original writing-desk surfaces and post-Impressionist bathtowels from cotton wool. "But here too, alas! you get a bottle neck. In a capitalist country, . . . the new need [in our example, fashionable full body clocks] can be sold only by competing with other 'old needs' [Churchill's writing desk] or 'new needs' for the customer's dollar [let us say, antidepressant pillboxes made from old coins; call this New Need B]. If the customer's dollar goes to buy the total possible output of New Need A [body clocks], that involves a tragic wastage in the productivity of a plant devoted to the satisfying of the craving for New Need B [old coin pillboxes]." Men and women will be thrown out of work. "Subtract," continues Burke, "the need of getting a wage (which would apply in any economy) and it comes closest to a human status that we should call humiliation."[28] The consciousness of a prevailing proliferation of needs should lead to a certain melancholy in every working person. Humiliation equals a low level of soul-treasure equals melancholy.

One effect of this depressing state of affairs—of wasteful competition for scarce materials for the manufacture of luxury commodities—is to create a market for antidepressants more plainly labeled than post-Impressionist bath towels, mock-ups of Churchill's writing desk, and the lure of businesses gone belly up. These are antidepressants of the clinical kind—pharmaceuticals. It does indeed appear that under capitalism, we are all, willy-nilly, on the way to an abjection of clinical proportions.[29]

So Pfizer Pharmaceuticals, in a message published "in the interest of better health," informs us that "over 30 million Americans today may suffer from some sort of depressive illness." Furthermore, this manufacturer of drugs—your self-proclaimed "partner in healthcare"—generously takes pains to alert its readers to the possibility that we are among this 30 million. For which of us able to read this ad has not felt at least once "a loss of interest or pleasure in [his or her] job, family life, hobbies or sex" along with a general "attitude of indifference" that went on for over two weeks (two weeks, in which even the promised weeks-long conversation on the psychedelic properties of Omaha steaks has failed to help)? Take heed, says Pfizer; such apathy may be "an indication of depressive illness and a warning to seek the advice of a doctor." And so you would be well advised to "do something for yourself and for those you love: you are not alone by any means." Of course you are not: Pfizer is there—"your partner." Like the commodity, in Benjamin's view, full of empathetic, indeed, prostitutional desire—like God, in Baudelaire's aphorism—Pfizer wishes to be "the supreme friend for each individual."[30]

I would like to quote more of the Pfizer ad:

DEPRESSION: IT CAN AFFECT YOU IN WAYS YOU WOULD NEVER SUSPECT: unexplainable jumpiness or anxiety; unusual irritability; sleep disturbances; difficulty in concentrating or remembering; physical pains that are hard to pin down; appetite loss (or overeating); a loss of interest or pleasure in your job, family life, hobbies or sex; a downhearted period that gets worse and just won't go away; frequent or unexplainable crying spells; a loss of self-esteem or an attitude of indifference.

A combination of the above symptoms persisting for two weeks or more can be an indication of depressive illness and a warning to seek the advice of a doctor.

Because depression can be a lot more than just "the blues." Unfortunately, it often goes unreported, and therefore undiagnosed and untreated, because people don't recognize the symptoms for what they are. Yet, depression can be easily diagnosed and treated in most cases. It's most important to realize that you are not alone by any means.

Do something for yourself and those you love. See your doctor. . . . A message in the interest of better health from PFIZER PHARMACEUTICALS. A Partner in Health Care.[31]

Pfizer shares sold yesterday (3/22/95) for $87.50 on the New York Stock Exchange and will presumably appreciate for years to come.

One does not have to be nondepressive, by the way, to notice the connection between antidepressants and stock market profits. In a piece subtitled "A New Wonder Drug for Depression," a writer for *New York* magazine, Fran Schumer, describes the reception of Eli Lilly & Company's Prozac (fluoxetine hydrochloride), which, at the time the article appeared, was the most widely prescribed antidepressant in the United States. Schumer writes: "Ten days after he put her on Prozac, Rachel's psychiatrist asked, 'So what do you think?' The 39-year old investment banker said, 'We should all go out and buy Eli Lilly stock.' 'You're too late,' he replied." For "even before Prozac was approved," it appears, "the company's stock rose 7 7/8 points in one day." The question logically arises whether jumps in stock market quotations are produced by depressives addicted to Prozac or whether depressives addicted to Prozac are produced in order that there be jumps in stock market quotations. Rachel uses Prozac and is happy now—or happy, at any rate, it seems, in the normal contemporary way: "Her greatest fear, she says, is 'that there will be a nuclear war and it'll interrupt [her] Prozac supply.' "[32]

Which heightens, finally, the aptness of the remark made by a psychiatrist interviewed in this essay: "The fact is, we're all depressed. The whole world is depressed. I don't know a human being who isn't." "Should everyone take Prozac?" the author wonders. The hypothesis of universal melancholy raises a different question in my mind: Is everyone taking Prozac? And if this thought occurs to me, it will certainly have already occurred to some entrepreneur in the depression business who has noted that the market appears to be supersaturated; all the Western world's depressives are on Lilly's Prozac. What is pharmaceutical capitalism's next move? It is already underway.

I am now going to discuss another development arising as if in calculated response to the Prozac market hegemony. The motto for this part of my paper is supplied by a journalist, Mickey Friedman, and reads as follows: "There is a New York truth: if it has a price tag on it, somebody will buy it."[33] Friedman continues: "In a city where there are shops selling exclusively tack, dice, accordions, model trains, pies, animal acts, skeletons, comic books, feathers, kayaks, Elvis memorabilia, buttons (more than a billion), wind-up toys, drums, bagels, and teddy bears," why not—I say—*depression*?[34]

Buy depression? It will come as no surprise that late capitalism promotes the substitution of commodities for love objects, so that the sense of an abundant affective life might be provided by affluence, and melan-

choly postponed. It is evident enough that capitalism more truly post-
pones such gratification, so that there will always be room for new needs
and new commodities. But what could still come as a surprise is a recent
development—of a depression in which what is at stake is not the defective substitution of a commodity for the absent real thing (the loved
thing) but the defective substitution of a type of pseudodepression, a
simulacrum, for the real thing (the loved thing), so that your melancholy
is no longer genuine, and *real* melancholy on the way to becoming ever
scarcer and hence becoming a commodity in ever greater demand.

   In the "News of the Week in Review" section of the *New York Times*
there recently appeared the following advertisement, entitled "There's
Good News about Depression."

   How Do You Feel? (Answer "Yes" or "No") Normal, every–
   day activities no longer give me pleasure. My appetite is poor. I've
   lost weight recently. I can't sleep, I wake up at 4 a.m. I want to sleep
   all the time. I feel restless, agitated; I can't concentrate. I'm tired
   and "down"; I've lost interest in sex and other pleasurable activities. My thoughts frequently turn to suicide and death.

   IF YOU'VE SAID "YES" TO MANY OR ALL OF THESE
   QUESTIONS, YOU MAY BE SUFFERING FROM DEPRESSION.
   [This catechism will be familiar from the Pfizer Pharmaceuticals
   poster, but here the resemblance ends.]

   BUT YOU MAY NOT [be suffering from depression]. In Fact,
   You Couldn't Have Picked A Better Time in Human History to Feel
   Miserable!

   (Recall, in passing, that for Omaha Steaks, too, "There's never
been a better time . . . to enjoy the superior quality of our cornfed, Mid-
western Beef. And there's never been a better time to surprise relatives
and friends with gourmet gifts from Omaha Steaks."[35] I stress the temporal upbeat, capitalism's signature; it evokes an absolute now-time of
acquisition, a temporally urgent fusion of consumer subject and commodity, like the mystic's ecstasy—the *Nu*.)
   Fair Oaks explains this urgent paradox:

   At long last, there are effective treatments and cures for depression—*if that is your problem.*

   Misdiagnosistic evaluation methods that will determine if
   you suffer from depression or from some underlying illness.

IF YOU OR SOMEONE YOU LOVE HAS THESE FEELINGS
OR SYMPTOMS, CALL FAIR OAKS HOSPITAL FOR INFORMA-
TION AND HELP. *[FAIR OAKS] BRINGS THE EXPERTS TO YOU.*

To believe Fair Oaks is to believe, like Kafka's wretches, that you
can leave your watch in your pocket, though here the agreement ends
on a note of Kafka's superiority. Kafka's depressives can still read the
right time off their condition; the bachelor melancholiast says, "It surely
is already very late," and he's right; whereas Fair Oaks conjures a consumer subject deaf, dumb, and blind to his or her own melancholy, who
declares that the time he or she "picks couldn't have been better."

Following Fair Oaks, it appears that the melancholic may no
longer be able to call even his depression his own—the last vanity of the
affectionless, hence *affektlos,* man. What he surely knew to be the case
and therefore could cherish as his last familiar—his despair—may be
nothing more nor less than a spook of inferior manufacture, a sort of
Hong Kong imitation depression. The specter of the simulacrum haunts
even melancholy, and only experts can tell you whether you despair is
manmade.

But while this prospect may be stimulating, even liberating, in
suggesting that nothing is sacred, not even one's sharpest sorrow, it is
also, of course, depressing. That is because it suggests that only someone else can tell you whether your despair is yours or only its cheat. Dependency on that definitively measuring someone-else—that friend—
could seem not the answer to, but an exacerbation of, one's sadness.
And that is only logical. If the authority of my despair is in doubt, surely,
too, must be the authority I lend the agent that pronounces my despair
assuredly a fake. How can I know (since my affects may be fake)
whether my trust in such authority isn't itself a fake? whether the authority I am inclined to lend it might not be only a symptom of my most
gimcrack depression and a symptom that real (and, of course, expen-
sive) depression might be advised to resist? In that resistance, hope; in
discarding that ad, I feel better already, which is to say, really bad. Yes,
Morbidus, there is melancholy, and you have it—the human condition.

Conclusion—New Prospects

Last fall another flyer arrived from the same Fair Oaks Hospital—of a
different, though related tendency. In again offering to sell its help to
sufferers, it actually alludes to the "satan cults" of modern juvenile society. I would have impatiently dismissed this appeal, except for the fact
of receiving on the same day a letter from a colleague in Berlin who lives

over a bookstore selling tracts on witches, warlocks, and demons. He informed me in passing that a significantly higher number of polled West Berliners believe in witchcraft. That was even before the "*Einheit-staumel*" (delirium of unification) set in.

Since then I have been engaged by this connection of ideas: (1) satanism; (2) events in Berlin; (3) developments in commodity capitalism. For example, I read of more than one incident in this country of the spraying of the word "Satan" on synagogue walls. Even John Cardinal O'Connor denounced the subliminal blandishments of the rocker Ozzy Osbourne, whose "onstage artistry includes . . . biting the head off a bat."[36] Osbourne is the author of "Suicide Solution," a song which, it is alleged, has fatally exploited the melancholy of teenagers. And not long ago, it appears, an Indianapolis priest performed exorcist rites as prescribed in the official *Roman Ritual*, "at the home of a teenage devil worshiper. The reason: objects kept moving about inexplicably," a state of affairs of course generally characteristic of commodity capitalism.

The matter is no doubt also a grave one. I cite one Father Richard Rento: "It has become my work to inform parents and children that Satanism is not a lark. It often means tragedy and death for the child and others."[37] I will not now dwell on the anecdotal side of demonism, however disturbing: we are better served by the reflections of Father Richard McBrien, a theologian at Notre Dame. For him, demonic personification is only the "premodern and precritical" recrudescence of an idea of sin normally seen "as something systemic, institutional, and structural."[38] We are returned to the morbid factor in the capitalist system of systemic, institutional, and structural dependencies suggested to Kafka by Grosz's drawing.

The phenomenon of Satanism, it would seem, has become the peculiar place where the perception of systemic sin is commodified. For, if there is to be such a thing as a modern idea of sin, then, according to the informed view of Father McBrien—and, indeed, of Franz Kafka—sin is something "systemic, institutional, and structural." What, then, of the view of certain possessed teenagers for whom sin is anything but systemic, institutional, and structural—being, instead, individual, incarnate, and immediate? Father Rento's concern with Satanism began when "a 15-year-old attempted suicide, saying he wanted to meet Satan."[39]

This adolescent's formulation may reasonably be called naive and treated as a second-order aberration, like the mythified language of antagonism accompanying the violence, say, of soccer fans. It may be grasped, too, as worse than naive—as a manipulated, a ventriloquized melancholy, if not entirely induced then certainly aggravated by the commodified products of the rock music industry. On the other hand, it

could also be seen as a recklessly defiant refusal to put up with the dif-
fuse burden, the systemic "sinfulness" of capitalist reality, of a piece
with the avant-garde revolts—from dada to the Sex Pistols—detailed by
Greil Marcus in *Lipstick Traces.*

I believe such complex reactions as adolescent satanism—products of and responses to the felt sinfulness of commodity culture—are
likely to be especially vivid in the phantasmagoric street theater of
Berlin, capital of the twenty-first century, where the fate of Money-
theism is being written on the wall. Perhaps, in the long run, the falling
of the Wall and the unsettling of populations in Eastern Europe will
stretch usefully the rational political imagination (at least to reset prior-
ities and reinvent the institutional equivalents of generosity) in the East
and the West—that is, in the new West. Among many East Berliners,
however, the course of detente was decided by a first explosive liberation from melancholy through swift exposure to the dazzling commodities of the *Kurfürstendamm* and the hope of acquisition. "All this
light," noted first-time visitors to West Berlin, for whom the brutal
plainness of the intended effect of so much illumination—namely, to
dissipate *melan*choly—in some instances worked against it. Though not
everyone was glad to return to the literal darkness of East Berlin.

This form of detente was a cause of disappointment to the New
Forum and its followers, who perceived in the explosive liberation from
melancholy by glimpses of bread and circuses a disheartening loss of
political responsibility. A direct result was the New Forum's polling less
than 3 percent of the popular vote in the first East German elections.
Meanwhile, the East's zeal for consumption (*Kaufwut*), real or phanta-
sized, leads, at the very least, to a preference for trancelike states of mind
over active curiosity. "My oldest son, Georg," wrote Christoph Hein, the
East German author of *Drachenblut*, "visited galleries and art exhibits in
West Berlin. Everywhere he went he was greeted warmly, once people
determined that he was an *Ossi* (East German). The museums and galleries are empty, he tells me, only the stores are hit by the flood of people from East Germany."[40]

"The *Ossies*," writer Christopher Hope reported, "would press
their noses to the windows of the Paris Bar like gentle ghosts. Yet there
was no discernible resentment in their stares. *Ossies* were to be seen
striding through the most distant suburbs, stopping to stare at children
playing in the park, or a man washing his car, or gathering in great
crowds outside the windows of the BMW showrooms. After all, what
qualitative difference is there among the objects of your fascination
when you are seeing it all for the first time? It is all very natural, and not
a little sad."

I beg to disagree: it is not quite "natural," it is fetishistic. These men, women, and children are rapt by the pure form of the commodity, a reification of exchange- and not of use-value; they are rapt by the phantasmagoria of commodity exchange.

"At the entrance to a large department store," continues Hope, "I watched a family of East Berliners, freshly arrived, wide-eyed and eerily silent. Father, mother, and a boy of about six were passing the chocolate counter. Suddenly the little boy stopped dead. He had seen the chocolates, home-made and gleaming darkly under the lights, perfection behind the glass, a costly pyramid, profligate, tempting, untouchable. His adoration passed like an electric current into his mother and father and rooted them to the spot. No one spoke. After a while like sleepers awakening, they shook themselves and went on their way. Seeing is believing. It's not the same as having, but it will do, for a while at least."[41]

A few Germans publicly derided the bliss of acquisition. A photograph by James Nachtwey shows "East Germans with shopping bags over their heads to protest their countrymen's West Berlin shopping sprees."[42] Indeed, it is as if these New Forum protesters too, having looked at the Grosz drawing, were imitating, derisively, the posture of the Capitalist whose top hat covers his eyes.

I conclude by noting that, here, Gramsci's general point appears to have been affirmed: All complex industrial societies rule by non-coercive coercion, whereby political questions become disguised as cultural ones and as such become insoluble. I have been talking about a prevalent and ubiquitous melancholy (in its radical form, satanism) under capitalism in an age of technical reproduction. This is a political question. Its ostensible cure proceeds today by means of further commodification—indeed, even the commodification of melancholy (or satanism) itself. But this solution, occurring through commodities—pseudospecifics which are actually generics—in this way becomes a cultural one and hence, in its own terms, insoluble. At this point what is called for, in the West as well as in the East, is an exercise of radical political thinking.

Summary

1. Commodities aim to supply glamour to the void of "the soul under capitalism." The spaces they try—but fail—to fill are melancholic.
2. The marketing of commodities appeals to the ethic of the *full* soul, the humanist ideal.
3. Where demand flags for one specific, the need for a stronger specific must be discovered if not indeed induced.

4. Being fungible, commodities lack aura or originality; cures based on the administration of commodities would appear to be vacuous. Specifics against melancholy cannot be provided by commodities (i.e., generics).
5. Capitalist energies are insatiable in their drive to commodify even empty inner "spaces."
6. Melancholy—(your) melancholy (and mine)—has been commodified.
7. We might consider exchanging our melancholy for the "genuine"— the "deluxe"—article. (Fair Oaks has it).
8. Or we might undertake an unwonted exercise of political thought, an attempt to think a way out of a capitalist melancholy only as "universal" as our dependency on commodity-cures.

Notes

1. *Père Goriot* (New York: New American Library, 1962), 81.

2. "Now I've eaten two calves/Now I'm going to eat another calf/Everything's only by halves, everything's only by halves/I'd gladly even eat myself." Bertolt Brecht, *Stücke,* 2 (Frankfurt a.M.: Suhrkamp, 1991), 362.

3. Theodor Adorno, "On the Question: 'What Is German?'" trans. Thomas Y. Levin, *New German Critique* 36 (Fall 1985): 129. The more nearly complete quotation is more radical: "Once the spirit [Geist] . . . is brought to heel, made to order for the customer who is dominated by the market which takes his inferiority as a pretext for its own ideology, then the spirit [Geist] is just as fundamentally done with as it was under the clubs of the Fascists." I do not agree with this comparison.

4. *The Diary of H. L. Mencken,* ed. Charles A. Fecher (New York: Knopf, 1991). Cited in *New York Times Book Review* (17 December 1989): 1.

5. In "The Decay of Lying," Oscar Wilde remarked: "In modern days while the fashion of writing poetry has become far too common, and should, if possible, be discouraged, the fashion of lying has almost fallen into disrepute," In *The Artist as Critic,* ed. Richard Ellmann (New York: Random House, 1969), 294. Wilde could not have anticipated all the ways this syllogism has become false. Today it is untrue that the practice of writing poetry should be discouraged and that the practice of lying has fallen into disrepute. Wilde could not have intuited what a low form compensated lying would take—the advertising of commodities.

6. "I brought Kafka several new books from Neugebauer bookstore to look at. As he leafed through the pages of a volume with drawings by Georg

Grosz, he said: . . . . " Gustav Janouch, *Gespräche mit Kafka* (Frankfurt: S. Fischer, 1968), 205. The drawing of which Janouch speaks allegedly appeared in a book published before 1921. Even with the help of distinguished Grosz scholar Beth Lewis, I have not been able to locate any such drawing. It does, of course, resemble in certain ways a drawing such as "Abrechnung folgt," 1922.

7. Janouch, *Gespräche mit Kafka*, 206. The complete quote: "Capitalism is a system of relationships, which go from inside to out, from outside to in, from above to below, and from below to above. Everything is relative, everything is in chains. Capitalism is a condition both of the world and of the soul." Gustav Janouch, *Conversations with Kafka*, trans. Goronwy Rees (New York: New Directions, 1968), 151–52.

8. This mention of commodities derives from the chapter entitled "The Fetishism of Commodities" in Marx's *Capital*, Vol. I.

9. For an excellent discussion of the intimate involvement of these two senses of development in Goethe's *Faust*, see Marshall Berman, "Goethe's *Faust*: The Tragedy of Development," in *All That is Solid Melts into Air: The Experience of Modernity* (New York: Simon & Schuster, 1982), 37–86.

10. "*Medizin*: Depression, Schleier über der Seele: Schwermut ist die Krankheit der Epoche," *Der Spiegel* 38 (1989): 230.

11. Charles Baudelaire, "*Madame Bovary*, by Gustave Flaubert," in Gustave Flaubert, *Madame Bovary*, Norton Critical Edition, ed. Paul de Man (New York: Norton, 1965), 337.

12. Kafka and meat. Here is a suggestive note from Gilles Deleuze and Félix Guattari, touching the correct bases: "Constancy of the theme of teeth in Kafka. A grandfather-butcher; a streetwise education at the butchershop; Felice's jaws; the refusal to eat meat except when he sleeps with Felice in Marienbad. Michel Cournot's article, 'Toi qui as de si grandes dents,' *Nouvel Observateur*, April 17, 1972. This is one of the most beautiful texts on Kafka. One can find a similar opposition between eating and speaking in Lewis Carroll, and a comparable escape into non-sense." *Reading Kafka: Prague, Politics, and the Fin de Siècle*, ed. Mark Anderson (New York: Schocken, 1988), 271. "Melancholiast" is Terry Eagleton's invention. See his *Walter Benjamin or Towards a Revolutionary Criticism* (London: Verso, 1981), 27. I shall be citing from Eagleton's suggestive paraphrase of Benjamin's idea of the commodity.

13. See Charles Bernheimer, *Figures of Ill Repute: Representing Prostitution in Nineteenth-Century France* (Cambridge: Harvard University Press, 1989), 96.

14. Eagleton, *Walter Benjamin*, 25, 28.

15. On the aura of Chrysler motors, see Kenneth Burke, *Attitudes toward History* (Berkeley: University of California Press, [1937] 1984), 98.

16. The space of lived inwardness is filled with the glamour of the deluxe commodity.

17. According to Gerald L. Bruns in *Heidegger's Estrangements: Language, Truth, and Poetry in the Later Writings* (New Haven: Yale University Press, 1989), Heidegger valorizes "hermeneutical" experience precisely by opposing it to this Diltheyan view of experience as an elected appropriation of wealth for the soul's treasury. Bruns writes: "Think . . . of the difference between hermeneutical and empirical or psychological experience (*Erfahrung* v. *Empfindung* and *Erlebnis*). This is the distinction Heidegger has in mind when he speaks about 'undergoing an experience with language.' 'To undergo an experience with something . . . means that this something befalls us, strikes us, comes over us, overwhelms and transforms us. When we talk of 'undergoing' an experience, we mean specifically that the experience is not of our own making; to undergo here means that we endure it, suffer it, receive it as it strikes us and submit to it. It is this something itself that comes about, comes to pass, happens. . . . Hermeneutical experience is not a cognitive event. It does not add to the subject by enlarging its store of knowledge. On the contrary, it is more likely that the subject is bereft of its store, is divested of all that belongs to it, including itself, and left exposed to what happens" (167). Further, on too easy (and questionable) adversions to the "full" subject as obtainable through "humanist" curricula—adversions found in many places in recent academic polemical writing—see Stanley Fish, "Being Interdisciplinary Is So Very Hard to Do," in *Profession 89*, a publication of the Modern Language Association of America, 15–22.

18. Franz Kafka, *The Diaries of Franz Kafka 1910–1913*, ed. Max Brod, trans. Joseph Kresh (New York: Schocken, 1948), 25.

19. "Voodoo Revenge," a flyer advertising Doug Casey's *Investing in Crisis* (Baltimore, 1989), 9.

20. Eagleton, *Walter Benjamin*, 28.

21. "Legen Sie Ihr Geld in *dada* an." *dada berlin—texte, manifeste, aktionen*, ed. Karl Riha (Stuttgart: Reklam, 1977), 59–60.

22. "Voodoo Revenge," 1.

23. Eagleton, *Walter Benjamin*, 28.

24. Franz Kafka, *Selected Stories of Franz Kafka*, trans. Willa Muir and Edwin Muir (New York: Modern Library, 1952), 187.

25. *The New Yorker*, (18 September 1989), 118.

26. Kenneth Burke, *Attitudes toward History*, 298.

27. Kafka, *Diaries*, 23.

28. Burke, *Attitudes toward History*, 299–300.

29. It is worth anticipating the inevitable mediocrity of prescription cures, for they, too, are based on commodities: They are all generics.

30. Walter Benjamin, *Charles Baudelaire: A Lyric Poet in the Era of High Capitalism* (London: New Left Books, 1973), 55; Charles Baudelaire, *Oeuvres complètes*, 1287. I owe this association of Benjamin on commodities and Baudelaire on God to Charles Berheimer's lustrous *Figures of Ill Repute*, 98.

31. *The New Yorker* (6 November 1989), 35.

32. *New York* (18 December 1989), 45–53.

33. Mickey Friedman, "That Unexpected Object of Desire," in part 2 of "New York, New York: The Ultimate Marketplace," *New York Times Magazine*, (12 November 1989), 55. This is her witty paraphrase of H. L. Mencken's remark, "New York: a third-rate Babylon."

34. "The Ultimate Marketplace," in part 2 of "New York, New York: The Ultimate Marketplace," *New York Times Magazine*, (12 November 1989), 18–19.

35. Omaha Steaks advertising flyer G4553-0290.

36. Richard N. Ostling, "Religion," *Time*, (9 March 1990). Ostling's piece, especially his representation of Ozzy Osbourne as Mephisto, has been criticized. A reader, Benjamin J. Eicher, pointed out in a subsequent issue of *Time* that Cardinal O'Connor had misread Osbourne's song *Suicide Solution*. It is wrong to "suggest that *Suicide Solution* advocates suicide. Actually it preaches against alcohol abuse and, by implication, against suicide. The title is a play on words; the alcohol abuser uses alcohol (a liquid solution) as a 'solution' to his problems, but because it will kill him in the end, it is a 'suicide solution.' "

37. *Time*, 9 March 1990, 56.

38. Ibid.

39. Ibid.

40. Christopher Hein, "East Berlin Diary," *New York Times Magazine*, (17 December 1989), 74.

41. Christopher Hope, "Seeing Is Believing," *New Republic*, (16 December 1989), 16.

42. *New York Times Magazine*, (17 December 1989), 34.

3

On Wounding: Windows, Screens, and Desire

Jerry Herron

The Wound in the Wall

First, an obvious point: A window is not just an opening, dictated by either fancy or utility. A window is a wound in the wall, which is why windows, like any other wound, have to be "dressed," or "treated"— this parlance of interior decoration dating back to the late Victorian period, when the advent of plate glass made the modern window possible and also dangerous. The threat posed by the window is what makes it crucially different from the door, to which it might otherwise mistakenly be compared. Doors are for doing things; windows are not. (The exception, of course, is the French window, which is no window at all but merely a door that has succumbed to the humiliation of deconstruction.) Doors imply movement and the body's mastery of space; they inscribe a room with the visible promise of alternatives. Windows are not like that; they are all about staying put, spectation, and the screening of the body's vulnerability (literally its capacity to be wounded), whether that body be construed as the figurative body of domestic virtue or as the actual bodies, both material and human, contained within and constituted by domestic space.

This is true, of course, of any window. But it is particularly true of the great single- and double-hung windows that came to dominate domestic interiors in the years immediately following the American Civil War. It was not until the widespread application of plate glass that a modern economy of looking could be properly instituted. In other words, there could be no inside—at least not in any recognizable modern sense—until there was an outside for it to be visibly different from and set in opposition to. In that connection the domestic interior—like the interiors of domestic subjects (and objects)—did not exist until the window inflicted on the walls of houses the modern crisis of interiority. "I know of nothing more significant," Elsie de Wolfe wrote in 1913, in *The House in Good Taste,*

> than the awakening of men and women throughout our country to the desire to improve their houses. Call it what you will—awakening, development, American Renaissance—it is a most startling and promising condition of affairs. It is no longer possible, even to people of only faintly aesthetic tastes, to buy chairs merely to sit upon or a clock merely that it should tell the time. Home-makers are determined to have their houses, outside and in, correct according to the best standards. (3)

De Wolfe was an actress turned interior decorator, and, at least in terms of her own originality, a clever borrower as well, whose book is a stylish knock-off of other people's work (most notably that of Edith Wharton). Which is only to say that she is an unimpeachable witness when it comes to the semiotics of commercial spectation: the culturally induced suspicion that we do not "buy chairs merely to sit upon or a clock that it should tell the time."

Appropriately, the cover of de Wolfe's book is inscribed with the representation of a window, as if to sign visibly the interrogation here undertaken—an interrogation that recuperates the sustaining crisis of materialism (Did I buy the "correct" thing?) as a rational (and teachable) discourse of "taste." "A woman's environment will speak for her life," de Wolfe writes, "whether she likes it or not. . . . A house is a dead-give-away . . . so you should arrange it so that the person who sees your personality in it will be reassured, not disconcerted" (22). The wound of the window, then, is merely a realization at the level of carpentry, of the feminized wound of consciousness that de Wolfe here poses as inevitable, the "dead-give-away" by which subject positions are constituted. In this context, the consciousness of interiority, whether individual or domestic, arises precisely as the consciousness of the body's interior, after a wound, comes about: as a crisis that assumes the proportions of physical emergency and moral responsibility.

The wound, then, like the window, is essential to the "discovery" of a modernist subjectivity, which is dependent consequently on violence. "A wound," Stephen Crane writes in his late story "An Episode of War" (1902), "gives strange dignity to him who bears it. . . . [T]he power of it sheds radiance upon a bloody form, and makes the other men understand sometimes that they are little" (247). The modernist subject of Crane's retrospective, historical inquiry is enabled—created—by the wound, and by the special status and responsibility the wound confers. " 'Why, man,' " a fellow Civil War officer scolds Crane's young lieutenant, whose arm is injured, "that's no way to do. You want to fix that thing" (248). Submission to the isolating imperative of "treatment" brings with it both "dignity" and dependency: "The lieutenant hung his head, feeling . . . that he did not know how to be correctly wounded" (249). The once uninterrogated body now bears witness to its own inadequacy and to the informational clientilism that follows. "It will have been seen how many circumstances there are to consider," Harold McClure and Edward Holloway advise in *The Practical Book of Interior Decoration* (1919), in a chapter titled "Windows and Their Treatment," the sole point of which advice is to induce an anxiety precisely parallel to that visited, retrospectively, on Crane's wounded lieutenant. The authors refer, superciliously, to "the *apparently* simple matter of the furnishing of windows. It is, however, precisely . . . advance consideration that avoids costly mistakes" (281, emphasis mine). Like the wound, the window induces a discovery process whereby a new class of subjectivity is born, one founded on the threat of "costly mistakes" and the translation of an apparent, natural simplicity into the "dead-give-away" of interiority.

Time's Body

If the virtue of the body is health, then what is the virtue of domestic space? For the middle class, in any event, that virtue is time. Or rather, the virtue being placed in jeopardy by the window's incursion is one that has historically displayed itself as certain timely forms of withholding. (One need only think of Alfred Hitchcock's lasciviously titled "Rear Window" [1954] to appreciate the difference between virtue and obscenity.) The proper treatment of windows makes it possible not only to show that one is capable of buying and correctly displaying the consumable elements of middle-class domesticity; what is perhaps more important, the window invites—it demands—the visible rehearsals of cultural reciprocity by which a class represents and reproduces itself. This is true of any window but particularly true of the large ornamental window, which has played a far greater role historically in the regulation of middle-class life than the comparatively inconsequential (and sentimentally overrated) hearth. (It is just such a window featured in the color frontispiece of McClure and Holloway's *Practical Book of Interior Decoration*.) There is the draping of such windows to be considered, obviously, and also the placement of appropriate objects in front of them: a fine table, a good lamp, cut flowers at unseasonable times of the year, and so on, each of which shows that the inhabitants are in on the dead-give-away of spectation and are, in fact, capable of turning it to characterological account. And there are the service-oriented rituals of cleaning and the seasonal application of awnings and possibly shutters, not to mention the daily marking of the hours, involving the raising and lowering of shades, the pulling of drapes, the lighting and extinguishing of lamps. "The long side-curtains may . . . be left undrawn," McClure and Holloway advise, for example,

> and, if the shade is pulled half way down, the room is in the daytime obscured from outside view. For the sake of privacy when the lights are lighted and also for the tempering of glare by day it is necessary that further obstruction be provided; either in the form of blinds or shades, or heavy inside curtains which may be drawn across the windows. (270)

Such windows, more than any other domestic surface, become a semiotic register of virtue, with virtue having as its chief interpretant the narrative discipline of time.

But more than this timely display of narrative propriety, and its sublimation culturally through the application of "correct" taste, the window frames the very conduct of modernist sociality. Thus, for example, in Dreiser's *Sister Carrie* it is by pausing before a great restaurant window that the lost and suicidal Hurstwood is recalled to a sense of his own former identity, a vis-à-vis the interior framed before him:

> Once he paused in an aimless, incoherent sort of way and looked through the windows of an imposing restaurant . . . [T]hrough the large, plate windows . . . could be seen the red and gold decorations, the palms, the white napery, and shining glassware, and, above all, the comfortable crowd. . . . He stopped stock still, his frayed trousers soaking in the slush. (455–56)

It is the prospect of just such an interior that leads Willa Cather's Paul to commit the theft that will buy him a few days tenancy:

> When he reached the dining room [of the Waldorf] he sat down at a table near a window. The flowers, the white linen, the many-colored wineglasses, the gay toilettes of the women, the low pop-

ping of corks, the undulating repetitions of the *Blue Danube* from the orchestra, all flooded Paul's dream with bewildering radiance. . . . This was what all the world was fighting for, he reflected; this was what all the struggle was about. (152)

It is the window, or rather the gaze instituted by the window, that gives meaning to each of the objects that Paul "reflects" upon; it is through the window that he becomes—like Hurstwood—intelligible to himself. But this recognition is not without its dangers. Paul is disengendered, literally, and drawn to his own epicene destruction, so that the modernist suspicion of interiority, which reaches a kind of climax in the homophobic posturing of Hemingway, seems not wholly groundless.

The window, then, creates a stage on which individual subjects come to "see" themselves in relation to the outside world. Domestically, this function evolved by virtue of the window's relation to the porch, and subsequently the lawn and street beyond. Writing in 1946, Detroit newspaper man Russell McLauchlin provides this account of porch life soon after the turn of the century in a part of the city known as Brush Farm, where upper-middle-class families built large, red brick homes in the 1870s and 1880s:

> The institution of the American Front Porch has fallen into decay. Not often does one nowadays see, in the more pretentious neighborhoods, the family taking its ease in that pleasant station on warm afternoons and evenings. And something of the old-time neighborliness assuredly departed when the Front Porch ceased to be a dwelling-place and dwindled to its present status of a convenience. (67)

McLauchlin's account recuperates sentimentally a sociality that the suburbanization of America—already underway by 1946—has subsequently rendered the stuff of nostalgic clichés, of which his book is an early, and by now typical, example. Sentimentality aside, however, he establishes the crucial relation between interior and exterior space as played out before the window. (The line drawings that illustrate his book make this even clearer, showing the porch as a kind of stage with the great front windows as its proscenium.)

In her book with Ogden Codman Jr., *The Decoration of Houses* (1902), Edith Wharton made this aspect of the window's function an explicit consideration of interior design. The window composes, it literally *frames*, the scene before and against which the lives of domestic residents are played out:

Where there is a fine prospect, windows made of a single plate of glass are often preferred; but it must be remembered that the subdivisions of a sash, while obstructing the view, serve to establish a relation between the inside of the house and the landscape, making the latter what, *as seen from a room*, it logically ought to be: a part of the wall-decoration. (67)

Wharton was writing about the grand houses of the wealthy, but her dictum is no less revealing of the economy of looking instituted by such middle-class, urban windows as those McLauchlin grew up in front of. "Every good moulding," Wharton wrote, "every carefully studied detail, exacted by those who can afford to indulge their taste, will in time find its way to the carpenter-built cottage" (iv). So the window arrived, both literally and figuratively, an element of trickle-down culture, to "establish a relation between the inside of the house and the landscape," albeit the landscape of urban neighborhoods.

But still the effect of the window was the same, and that's what matters; it framed the space of external, social relations, "making the latter what, *as seen from a room*, it logically ought to be: a part of the wall-decoration." As seen from the room, the classic, plate-glass window creates the outside as a scene, a decorative panorama: one always already seen from the room, so that the social interactions that McLauchlin sentimentalizes are conducted under the virtual gaze of the window, with the cartoonist's translation of windows into eyes being now no less a cliché than his reminiscences. More important, however, is the framing effect of the window from inside, and what it does to the space of sociality, now seen from a room. Whatever goes on inside, it goes on in front of the window; it is played out against the semiotically framed composition of a remembered sociable exterior.

Thus Edith Wharton's imagining of her character Mrs. Manson Mingott in *The Age of Innocence* (1920), a novel for which Wharton won a Pulitzer Prize. Mrs. Mingott has all her life made a spectacle of herself, defying the conventions of polite New York society. She "throned" in her eccentric mansion, "as if there were nothing peculiar in living above Thirty-fourth Street, or in having French windows that opened like doors instead of sashes that pushed up" (10–11). Wharton represents the now obese Mrs. Mingott in old age:

It was her habit to sit in a window of her sitting-room on the ground floor, as if watching calmly for life and fashion to flow northward to her solitary doors. . . . The immense accretion of flesh which had descended on her in middle life like a flood of lava on a doomed city had changed her from a plump active little woman with a neatly-turned foot and ankle into something as vast and august as a natural phenomenon. (24–25)

It is as if the character has been made to bear the burden, physically, of an undischarged spectation—a burden that descends, like "a natural phenomenon," on the delinquent subject of Wharton's imaginary windows. In this sense, then, the window—even when closed and curtained—introjects visibly, decoratively, into the management of private life the disciplinary time of culture; it superintends the interior, both ideological and physical, with a recollected back-and-forth of social relations.

After the Lawn

In any event, that's what windows did until some time in the 1950s, when suburbanization ended forever—even for people who did not live in suburbs—the dominance of the porch and lawn, and with it the historic imperium of the parlor window. In *Goodbye, Columbus*, which Philip Roth published in 1959, his narrator, Neil, registers the difference, which was then still very much news:

> It was, in fact, as though the hundred and eighty feet that the suburbs rose in altitude above Newark brought one closer to heaven, for the sun itself became bigger, lower, and rounder, and soon I was driving past long lawns which seemed to be twirling water on themselves, and past houses where no one sat on stoops, where lights were on but no windows open, for those inside, refusing to share the very texture of life with those of us outside, regulated with a dial the amounts of moisture that were allowed access to their skin. (6)

This privatized Eden was founded just at the vanishing point of history, where it seemed that plenitude of all kinds—economic, temporal, nuclear—would render superfluous the old window-driven economy of narrative metering and supervision.

Just at that moment, when modernity seemed to have been achieved, the focus of family life shifted from front to back, from porch and lawn to patio. "Outside, through the wide picture window," Roth's narrator says in his description of the suburban house built by the Patimkin family,

> I could see the back lawn with its twin oak trees. I say oaks, though fancifully, one might call them sporting-goods trees. Beneath their branches, like fruit dropped from their limbs, were two irons, a golf ball, a tennis can, a baseball bat, basketball, a first-baseman's glove, and what was apparently a riding crop. (15)

Here the economy of leisure overtakes the domestic scene, which is now framed in relation to activities that are founded on the wasting of time rather than its visible conservation. Dreams of upward mobility appeal not to institutionalized rehearsals of taste (beginning at the department store and ending in window treatments and porch dressing) but in a private subscription to well-equipped dissipation dominated by sports, "casual" living, and the backyard grill.

This new focus of activity was overseen typically by much larger windows, which became popular during Eisenhower's second administration: not merely the big picture windows of Roth's imagining but the more revolutionary sliding glass door, which changed forever the dynamic interaction of inside and outside. The door, to begin with, was framed not to look like a real door (as even the French window had been) but to mimic the aspect ratio of an enormous, double-hung window. The point was to provide the domestic interior (now shifted from parlor to multipurpose "family room") with an unprecedented access to the backyard Eden, and thereby to assert that leisurely surface as unavoidable moral imperative. The new president, John Kennedy, with his always eager family of athletes and his Council on Physical Fitness, turned to potential humiliation one's inability or reluctance to accept the mandate of vigorous leisure. And the sliding glass door was right there to help him. It was neither a frame nor a wound; instead, it represented an utter collapse of the old domestic membrane which had sustained the opposition of inside and outside, and it rendered a modernist individuality both intelligible and also a source of discipline.

At least that's what it *might* have represented. Concomitant with the reorientation of interior space from front to rear, and from domestic production to leisure consumption, is the arrival of TV. Television, which for all practical purposes did not exist at the end of the Second World War, had achieved a 90 percent penetration of American households by 1960 (Spigel, 1). At the precise moment when the sliding glass door threatened to dissolve forever the social supervision of domestic time, the television reasserted a certain temporal sociality (now already lapsing to sentimental anachronism) with a special vividness. Programming was at first limited to only a few hours per day; and there was no such thing, of course, as the VCR, so that the commercial time of television, with perhaps only one or two channels available, became the organizing time of private life as well. Given the banality of official, public time in the 1950s, when nothing seemed to happen, or to be supposed to happen, TV created a vortex that sucked people off lawns and porches and out of back yards, and assembled them together, in front of the screen, in a "cool" parody (to use McLuhan's word) of social interaction. But paradoxically, the set undermined the very sociability that it called into being, which is the point of a cartoon from the *Saturday Evening Post*, published in 1951 and reproduced in Cecelia Tichi's *Electronic Hearth*. In it, a husband and wife are cleaning up after an evening of neighborhood TV watching: "Did you hear that fat guy," the cranky husband asks his wife, "the one that sat in the green chair, ask me if I lived in the neighborhood?" (25) The little joke mocks the anonymity and isolation that would become cliché aspects of public or familial watching. In this sense, therefore the television is to be comprehended not in relation to Tichi's hearth but in relation to the window.

Early TV advertisements made this relation explicit, with the home screen being hyped, for example, as "the biggest window in the world" (Tichi, 13). Probably the most elaborate and influential version of the TV-as-world-window idea comes in McLuhan's *Understanding Media* (1964), where he refers to all media, but especially television, as "the extensions of man." But this notion of television as an adjunct, "reinforcement" for the window, which Tichi, among others, continues in *Electronic Hearth*, seems counter to the facts in fundamental ways, although McLuhan can perhaps be excused for his misunderstanding since television in 1964 had not developed the technological competence to assert its real destiny. Television doesn't work with the window, particularly the leisure-directed sliding glass door. On the contrary, television arrays itself specifically in opposition to the window. Television compels a turning away from the light, for light obscures images on the screen, particularly on a color screen. It invites a cancellation of the time of nature and institutes a simulacral clock all its own—a clock organized by the rhythms of Raymond Williams's household "flow," which has been subsequently elaborated by Rick Altman. And once technology made it possible for screens to evolve from their initial, oval configuration (which first took place with black and white and then once more with color), they assumed—as if by nature—the precise aspect ratio defined by the old double-hung parlor window. But not for the purpose of nostalgic recuperation; the screen takes on this shape as an act of mnemonic defiance: not to reanimate the memory of that other time but to cancel it, and for reasons specific to the location of bodies inside domestic space.

34 C

In that connection, it would be possible (not to say anachronistic) to discuss the construction of the body—especially with regard to television—without engaging the body of Madonna. It would be likewise
impossible to address the issues of modernity and postmodernity without making some account of the nostalgic body of contemplations typ-
ified by the work of Fredric Jameson. In his much quoted book, which
grew out of an even more frequently quoted essay, Jameson—meditat-
ing on the operations of postmodernism, or the cultural logic of late capitalism—has this to say about television and memory:

> Turning the television set off has little in common either with the
> intermission of a play or an opera or with the grand finale of a fea-
> ture film, when the lights slowly come back on and memory be-
> gins its mysterious work. Indeed, if anything like critical distance
> is still possible in film, it is surely bound up with memory itself.
> But memory seems to play no role in television, commercial or oth-
> erwise (or, I am tempted to say, in postmodernism generally):
> nothing here haunts the mind or leaves its afterimages in the man-
> ner of the great moments of film. (70–71)

This problem of memory and representation is the same one Jameson
has noted elsewhere, in the title essay from his volume, when he complains of the unrepresentability of cathode-based hardware, linking this
generally to the postmodern collapse of "critical distance" and the
breakdown of reliable, cognitive maps:

> What must then immediately be observed is that the technology
> of our own moment no longer possesses this same capacity for
> representation: [we are concerned now with not] the tur-
> bine . . . but rather the computer, whose outer shell has no em-
> blematic or visual power, or even the casings of the various media
> themselves, as with that home appliance called television which
> articulates nothing but rather implodes, carrying its flattened im-
> age surface within itself. (79)

It might not be going too far, in this context, to say that the postmodern
condition is one identified with a nostalgia for missing information—
lost representations—with that loss being defined, or windowed—aca-
demically—in a variety of different ways. But the academic house of
nostalgia is not the one the majority of Americans actually grew up in-

side of. "People like us," to paraphrase David Byrne's lyric from the 1986 Talking Heads album, *True Stories*, are people born about 1950, in houses with the "television always on." In other words, the history we grew up inside of is one where the defeat of the window has always already happened, and where Jameson's nostalgic vortex consequently never so much as ruffles the curtains on the sliding glass door. Which is not to say that he's got things wrong, exactly, so much as it is to say he doesn't like to watch. Or perhaps it would be more accurate to say he doesn't know *how* to watch TV.

Jameson's misrecognition has been acted out commercially, with the arrival of an "industry standard" for screen-based personal computer systems—a standard originated by a group of babyboomers at Apple and now packaged by Microsoft in their deceptively titled *Windows*. The representations that Jameson finds missing—no longer possible—are very precisely the ones that Windows panders to and also parodies. Windows succeeds by informing on the cathode ray tube's failure to be what the highly successful program claims it is: a window. If that were true, if the screen really *were* a window (as Jameson and others seem to expect it to be), then users wouldn't need these nostalgically motivated simulacra. In the same way, if Madonna really were what she proposes variously to be—a singer, a dancer, an actress—her presence performatively would be sufficient to the task of representation. But her persona is no more self-sufficient in that way than the TV screen is sufficient to the anachronistic role of window. Both *Windows* and Madonna exist only by virtue of a lack, a failure of representation. Thus, for example, the representational insufficiency of Madonna's breasts, which, despite their being frequently seen, must be constantly informed upon, like the rest of her body, in order to remain real. Which is how her bra size, leaked by a publicist to a gossip columnist and then vouchsafed to Joan Rivers, comes to provide the title of this selection.

It would be wrong, then, to conclude, as Jameson and a great many other people who write about television do, that "memory seems to play no role in television, commercial or otherwise. . . . [N]othing here haunts the mind or leaves its afterimages." Certainly not in the sense of "classic" screen, or window, space. There, images were framed for a narrative safe-keeping, with the aperture of proscenium or sash creating a kind of vault: a mnemonic wound such as Edith Wharton parodies with the grotesque, cultural abscess of Mrs. Mingott's physicality. But images now, even under the regime of "high resolution," rarely add up to anything, which is why the sight of Madonna's breasts, for instance (on video or film), seems so utterly unmemorable. Still, those mnemonically trivialized breasts define a site of speculation televisually: not because they exist or will be exposed, but because they can be informed on, which point she has understood well enough herself in her book *Sex*. The trappings of bondage, S & M, bestiality; the pseudoconfessional test (all of which became part of a successful marketing campaign that resulted in an instantaneous sell-out of the original print run of 800,000 copies) are means of *informing on* a body rather than *representing* it, and necessarily so, because the represented body is no longer organic to its own authenticity.

In *A Thousand Plateaus*, Deleuze and Guattari provide the following notable exposition of a body *without* organs:

> [It] is not a scene, a place, or even a support upon which something comes to pass. It has nothing to do with phantasy, there is nothing to interpret. The [Body without Organs] causes intensities to pass; it produces and distributes them in a *spatium* that is itself intensive, lacking extension. It is not space, nor is it in space; it is matter that occupies space to a given degree—to the degree corresponding to the intensities produced. It is nonstratified, unformed, intense matter, the matrix of intensity, intensity = 0. (153)

This achieved moment of the Body without Organs, which, as Ronald Bogue has pointed out, is a "moment of anti-production constantly fed back into the process of production" (93), I take—without wanting to make jokes—to be a very exact description of the individual body arrested in front of the domestic screen, at the precise moment when lack and self recognition become one. It is to this moment that Jameson's nostalgia refers, or rather it is the experience of such lack—or zeroing—that he recuperates narratively as "post-modernity," through the claim that "television . . . articulates nothing but rather implodes, carrying its flattened image surface within itself" (79). This nostalgic reflex leaves the subject stranded—fragmented in Jameson's terms—with no access to an experience that arrives after the historically instituted organs of memory have been zeroed. But that is not where *television* leaves things, least of all in the fastest growing segment of the market, talk TV. That domain—the domain of Sally and Geraldo and Phil and, above all, Oprah—invites a new body, neither modern nor postmodern, that comes after the wound of the window is finally closed.

The Body after Organs, or Waiting for Oprah to Come

It is possible to date with considerable accuracy the televisual advent of the body after organs, at least in this country. The moment arrives unexpectedly in November 1963, when great numbers of Americans, as an exercise of their patriotic duty and as an element of the general national grief, submit to repeated images of President John Kennedy's head exploding after being struck by an assassin's bullet. Those images, particularly the ones captured in Abraham Zapruder's 8 mm home movie, comprise the most-watched splatter film in history; they create a cultural primal scene for the baby boom, as Oliver Stone's obsessive recreation in *JFK* [1992], for example, bears out. At that precise, unsequeled moment, the body disgorges its organs—literally—on national TV; it

> causes intensities to pass; it produces and distributes them in a *spatium* that is itself intensive, lacking extension. It is not space, nor is it in space; it is matter that occupies space to a given degree—to the degree corresponding to the intensities produced. It is nonstratified, unformed, intense matter, the matrix of intensity, intensity = 0. (153)

Thus the recursive images that had to be played and played again as people sat fixed, not to the images as such, but to the television spatium, "that is itself intensive, lacking extension." Perhaps it was the near perfect fit of press photography to the (then) available technology of color TV, with its grainy surface and comparatively low resolution, that lent the screen a special potential, only realized slowly, as television ushered in a new body: a body after organs, with *after* here construed in a double sense, both as a coming after temporally and as an after-image, a trace.

The situation is the same one described by the writer and war correspondent Michael Herr in *Dispatches,* his highly visual account of Vietnam, which is comprised of dispatches written for *Esquire* magazine in the late 1960s, in the days leading up to the Tet Offensive in 1968. "I went there," Herr writes,

> behind the crude but serious belief that you had to be able to look at anything, serious because I acted on it and went, crude because I didn't know, it took the war to teach it, that you were as responsible for everything you saw as you were for everything you did. The problem was that you didn't always know what you were seeing until later, maybe years later, that a lot of it never made it in at all, it just stayed stored there in your eyes. . . . [T]he information isn't frozen, you are. (20)

It would take years for the screen to catch up to its subjects, frozen in the presence of information, at zero degree, but it would catch up; it would recuperate their wound as a new kind of seeing, which arrives first not on television at all, but in movie theaters.

This recuperation is facilitated by the convergence of two crucially related phenomena: the pornographic "money shot" and the advent of high-technology splatter wounds. Both discover new technologies for windowing the body and defining a subject position beyond the freeze frame of Jameson's nostalgia. The first prototypic splatter wound occurs during the final moments of *Bonnie and Clyde* (1967), when the bodies of Warren Beatty and Faye Dunaway writhe in slow motion as they are visibly penetrated by a hail of bullets. But theirs were unproductive wounds, mere powder burns that mark the lack of verifiable information of precisely the sort that Herr had already seen and reported on and that everyone else had watched on television when the president died and would not be subjected to over and over each night with the evening news about the war. Two years later, in 1969, following the Tet Offensive and the debacle at Khesanh, Sam Peckinpah creates the first explosive theatrical wounds using flash powder and condoms filled with chicken blood. *The Wild Bunch* (Phil Feldman, 1969) brings to the screen a new kind of wound that—with its slow-motion detritus of blood and bone fragments—literally comes between the body as object and the viewing subject. Representations of violence, up to that point, had inflicted death but rarely wounds. "The problem," as Herr understood, "was that you didn't always know what you were seeing until later, maybe years later. . . . [I]t just stayed stored there in your eyes" (20). Peckinpah is shooting after new organs of apprehension, with the body visibly abandoning the privacy of its old modernist wounds. He's trying to discover organs of memory capable of seeing what has been stored in the screen memory of Americans since 1963.

Inextricably bound up with this new dis-*organ*ization of the body is the arrival in "legitimate" theaters first of Gerard Damiano's *Deep Throat* [1972] and subsequently the Mitchell Brothers' *Behind the Green Door*. "For the first time in the history of American cinema," Linda Williams points out in *Hard Core*,

a penis central to the action of a story appeared "in action" on the big screen. . . . [W]ith the money shot we appear to arrive at what the cinematic will-to-knowledge had relentlessly pursued ever since photographer Eadweard Muybridge first threw the image of naked moving bodies on the screen of his lecture hall and ever since Thomas Edison ordered his technicians to photograph a sneeze: the visual evidence of the mechanical "truth" of bodily pleasure caught in involuntary spasm; the ultimate and uncontrollable—ultimate *because* uncontrollable—confession of sexual pleasure in the climax of orgasm. (100–101)

The "money shot," whether sexual or violent, comes between the body and the viewer; it windows the body and disorganizes conventional expectations. Crucially, both kinds of shots (thanks to relaxed broadcast standards, cable stations, and VCRs) are now regularly available on the home screen; they position it tactically for a final assault on the now vestigial, modernist window—a site divested of former relevance to the organization of domestic space.

But, as Williams points out, the money shot—which after all involves only male subjects—requires an interruption of the very act it purports to authenticate, or at any rate, its translation: "With this convention, viewers are asked to believe that the sexual performers within the film want to shift from a tactile to a visual pleasure at the crucial moment of the male's orgasm" (101). What Williams perhaps neglects here is the fact that the performers' pleasure is not, finally, in question; it is the pleasure of the viewer that counts, and for viewers, there is no "shift" since pleasure has been visual all along. In that context, the money shot represents a moment of heightened intensity and power as the body, "wounded"—made vulnerable—by pleasure (no less than violence) surrenders its evidence visibly. It's not by withholding (accumulating in a traditional, modernist sense) but rather by surrendering, by zeroing claims of individuality, that the body after organs verifies contact with its own experience, and submits to a pleasure of watching perhaps more inclusive than its phallocentric origin would suggest.

In this sense, the perfection of the body after organs, and with it the final triumph of the screen over now anachronistic windows, arrives with the coming of Oprah, the most popular of the daytime talk-show hosts, and for good reason. The talk show recuperates as therapeutic spectacle the crucial space of the money shot, or the eruptive wound of violence, with the host perpetually coming between the guest/object and the viewer/subject. As Linda Alcoff and Laura Gray have remarked with respect to the testimony of "survivors" on TV,

> The confessional [mode of shows like *Oprah*] constructs a notion of theory as necessarily other than, split from, and dominant over experience. And it creates a situation in which the survivor—because of her experience and feelings on the issue—is paradoxically the least capable person of serving as the authority or expert. (280)

Certainly, the body is being reduced—zeroed—as independent witness, but finally it is not with any individual, no matter who, that authority resides. Authority and authenticity are not communicable directly whether as testimony or expert theory; instead, they are the after-effect of what comes between object and subject, as enacted precisely through the body of the host, who is the ultimate special effect, with no *body* being more powerful in this domain than Oprah's.

In that connection, the public prominence of a black figure such as Oprah informs usefully on Madonna's lack—a lack construed specifically in terms of the wound inflicted by a modernist subjectivity on those who seek, like Madonna, a compensatory colonization of the Other. "In mass culture," bell hooks argues, "imperialist nostalgia takes the form of reenacting and reritualizing in different ways the imperialist, colonizing journey as narrative fantasy of power and desire, of seduction by the Other" (25). But is it really a fantasy of seduction that creates Oprah's power, or is it rather the sight/site of that body, always coming between us and the fantasized object of either dread or desire, with guests ranging from rapists and serial killers to strippers and sex surrogates? A body disorganized, by any hegemonic account of "beauty," but lovable and desirable, precisely for that. (Oprah's popularity declined as she lost weight.) "Privacy in our time has not only been invaded; it's been eagerly surrendered," Roger Rosenblatt complained in the *New York Times Magazine,* with regard to our culture of gossip and disclosure—the same culture that Oprah so brilliantly embodies. "Do people no longer see themselves as private beings?" he demanded to know (24). What "people" no longer see, perhaps, is themselves as vulnerable to a narrative interiority. What they have found, now that Oprah has come, is a body no longer windowed by the wounds of modernity (or its postmodern reflex)—wounds that have long since been closed.

Works Cited

Alcoff, Linda, and Laura Gray. "Survivor Discourse: Transgression or Recuperation?" *Signs* (Winter 1993): 260–90.

Altman, Rick. "Television/Sound." In *Studies in Entertainment: Critical Approaches to Mass Culture,* ed. Tania Modleski, 39–54. Bloomington, IN: Indiana University Press, 1986.

Bogue, Ronald. *Deleuze and Guattari.* New York: Routledge, 1989.

Cather, Willa. "Paul's Case." In *The Norton Anthology of Short Fiction,* 2d ed., ed. R. V. Cassill, 139–56. New York: Norton, 1981.

Crane, Stephen. "An Episode of War," in *The Red Badge of Courage and Other Writings,* ed. Richard Chase. Boston: Houghton Mifflin, 1960.

Deleuze, Gilles, and Félix Guattari. *A Thousand Plateaus: Capitalism & Schizophrenia,* trans. Brian Massumi. Minneapolis: University of Minnesota Press, 1987.

de Wolfe, Elsie. *The House in Good Taste.* New York: Century Co., 1913.

Dreiser, Theodore. *Sister Carrie.* New York: Signet, 1961.

Herr, Michael. *Dispatches.* New York: Avon, 1978.

hooks, bell. *Black Looks: Race and Representation.* Boston: South End Press, 1992.

Jameson, Fredric. "Postmodernism, or the Cultural Logic of Late Capitalism." *New Left Review* 146 (July–August 1984): 53–93.

———. *Postmodernism, or, The Cultural Logic of Late Capitalism.* Durham, NC: Duke University Press, 1991.

McClure, Harold, and Edward Holloway. *The Practical Book of Interior Decoration.* Philadelphia: J. B. Lippincott, 1919.

McLauchlin, Russell. *Alfred Street.* Detroit: Conjure House, 1946.

McLuhan, Marshall. *Understanding Media: The Extensions of Man.* New York: Mc-Graw-Hill, 1964.

Madonna. *Sex.* New York: Warner Books, 1992.

Rosenblatt, Roger. "Who Killed Privacy?" *New York Times Magazine,* 31 January 1993: 24–28.

Roth, Philip. *Goodbye, Columbus.* New York: Houghton Mifflin, 1959.

Spigel, Lynn. *Make Room for TV: Television and the Family Ideal in Postwar America.* Chicago: University of Chicago Press, 1992.

Tichi, Cecelia. *Electronic Hearth: Creating an American Television Culture.* New York: Oxford University Press, 1991.

Wharton, Edith. *The Age of Innocence.* New York: Appleton, 1920.

——— and Ogden Codman Jr. *The Decoration of Houses.* New York: Norton, 1978.

Williams, Linda. *Hard Core: Power, Pleasure and the "Frenzy of the Visible."* Berkeley: University of California Press, 1989.

Williams, Raymond. *Television: Technology and Cultural Form.* New York: Schocken, 1974.

4

True Lies: Arnold Schwarzenegger's Life and Times

Albert Liu

In the confusion immediately surrounding the World Trade Center explosion of 26 February 1993, one of the most unsettling speculations centered on the fact that Arnold Schwarzenegger's latest movie, *Last Action Hero*, was to begin filming in Times Square the following week. What if, so the tabloid rumor went, the explosion were somehow linked to the film, as a sinister promotional stunt or special effect? These suspicions were aggravated by the presence of an extremely pumped-up Arnold, in the form of a seventy-five-foot-tall Schwarzenegger balloon holding two sticks of dynamite in its hand as it lorded over 42d Street. Carolco Pictures quickly disarmed the effigy, replacing the dynamite with a police badge, but a certain logical consistency had already been exposed: Blow up something big enough, like a balloon, and you generate culture; blow up something even bigger, like the Trade Center, and you make history. Moreover, the anachronistic simplicity of the idea that one could still produce world history, or even end it, simply by destroying something seemed like a time warp worthy of *Terminator 3,* a blast from the past in this age of virtual happenings.[1]

Essentially what was at stake in this fantasy was the sense that the media and the real had finally become indistinguishable. It seemed a further confirmation of the experience of Operation Desert Storm, which, as Jean Baudrillard succinctly put it, "was the least real thing about the Gulf Crisis." Once again, Arnold Schwarzenegger—or his representation (and this difference is precisely what is most unclear in his case)—found himself at the center of speculations linking the media, violence, and politics.

Speaking about Arnold Schwarzenegger can be surprisingly difficult. Unlike other multimedia superstars such as Madonna, for whom

there is no shortage of commentary, Schwarzenegger has only infre-
quently been the subject of critical evaluations. This is partly due to specific contextual protocols: On one hand, his supposed unseriousness
excludes him from academic contexts that aspire to a certain elevated
tone; on the other, the seriousness of the charges of political incorrect-
ness brought against him gives ample excuse for such discussions. The
question concerning Arnold Schwarzenegger, then, seems to arise only
in order to affirm that he is reducible to the visibly fascistic or militarist
phantasms that get identified with him, including, among other things,
police violence and brutality.[2]

Secondly, difficulties in speaking about Schwarzenegger stem
from the fact that his films tend to thematize limit-cases of intelligibility. The development of his opus has not been guided by any one director who could claim authorial responsibility; rather, Schwarzenegger's
very presence in a film seems to guarantee a tireless reflection on medi-
atic and political *mises-en-abîme* (e.g., the undecidable TV studio
takeover at the end of *Running Man*, or the self-enclosing frames of real
and artificial memory in *Total Recall*), invisibility (the blur concealing the
alien in *Predator*), and, above all, the temporal aporias in the *Terminator*
films. The constitutive difficulty in speaking about Schwarzenegger is
nowhere more apparent than in *Terminator 2* (1991), where it becomes
impossible to give a coherent account of its narrative, since the looping
pasts and futures of *The Terminator* [1984] have not only been further
complexified but now also include the sequential relation between the
two films.[3] At some level, *Terminator 2* issues a challenge to language; it
seems to call for an improbable nonlinguistic discourse, one that could
avoid the vicious circles implied by every propositional statement about
the film.

Finally, even when the possibility of speaking about Arnold
Schwarzenegger is restricted neither by the rules of politeness and the
regulations of a given context (let's call this formality) nor by logical
constraints (let's call this formalism), there still remains the fact of his
existential presence. All too self-evident, a seamless weld of the actual
and the ideal, he is just there, a *bloc dur* who presents no enigma, offers
nothing to speak about, not even the mystery of pure matter: It is as
though he were unavoidable, *incontournable, unumgängliche,* nothing
more.[4] What Arnold Schwarzenegger seems to posit in and as himself,
above and beyond considerations of formal possibility, is a kind of formidable impassivity or impassability.

There is, then, with Arnold Schwarzenegger—and not only in his
own mangled speech—an apparent resistance to discursivity, propositional and otherwise. This difficulty has frequently led critics to assim-

ilate Schwarzenegger into existing categories of masculine identity instead of thinking through the radicality of Schwarzenegger's challenge, which, as I will argue in my reading of selected aspects of his life and work, is more farreaching and politically more significant than the "fascist soldier male" simulacrum he is commonly alleged to represent.[5] Indeed, the *total presentation of his persona* seems to comprise a fractured intersection of effects relating technology, recent history, and representations of violence that underscore the *instability* of his gender configurations and his relentless engagement in new or *hypothetical* forms of identity.

It would be tempting, and in other contexts appropriate, to discuss Schwarzenegger in terms of conceptions of the hero and masculinity in Hollywood films[6] (including the hero's problematic relation to his community, his untimeliness, etc.), but to do so would mean engaging in a typology that would diminish Schwarzenegger's singularity, his absolutely particular, even *experimental*, place in American politics. For even when he explicitly assumes the role of hero (*Last Action Hero*), he emphasizes his liminal nonbelonging, his *lastness* or belatedness, the transitional or uncertain nature of his embodiment and his historical position. What is it that sets him apart from generic musclemen like Stallone and Van Damme? Why is he so concerned with beginnings, ends, limits, terminations, producing a number of curious hybrids along the way? What kind of opus is constituted by the thematic consistency of his work and life? Why, before concern over media violence became a congressional matter, was he a primary symbolic target of protests condemning the harmful influence of violence in film and television?

To a large extent, all of the above questions are framed in *Terminator 2*, the ethical stakes of which, I will argue, are not simply reducible to calculations of the moral effects of the representation of wholesale murder; instead, the ambiguous brevity of the movie's title pinpoints a less obvious problem, one whose full weight has not yet been brought to bear in the critique of political ideology: what links the representation of ex-termination with impasses of logical de-termination?[7] In what way do aporias of communication contribute to the formation and perpetuation of certain kinds of political networks?

In keeping with these questions, despite both the usefulness of psychoanalytic concepts and Lacan's explicit claim that psychoanalysis is meant to supplement deficits in logic, it seems important to recognize that *Terminator 2* engages a number of motifs that appear speculatively to be aimed *against* or around psychoanalysis. The Oedipal paradigm has persuasively been called to account for the fantasy of time travel that frames *The Terminator,* whereby one goes back in time to precede one's own father or, alternatively, one remains in this present but oversteps generational lines of reproductive succession by committing incest.[8] In *Terminator 2,* however, the Terminator (that is, Arnold Schwarzenegger) is an *adult* machine, possessed of language and information but ethically a blank slate, gaining moral conscience without passing through any stages of infantile development: The single law he knows, but also the very one that constitutes his knowledge, is obedience to the letter of the imperative qua program, whose only mission parameters are to serve and protect John Connor . . . and never to self-terminate.

   Given this final determination, we should perhaps begin with Arnold's end. "I know now why you cry. But that is something I can never do." In *Terminator 2'*s final scene, just before being lowered into a pool of molten steel, Arnold Schwarzenegger offers these words as an apology, farewell, and justification for his self-mandated—but not self-executed—death sentence, his autotermination at the hands of his friends, an act that brings with it all the ethical ambiguities surrounding euthanasia. Schwarzenegger's will wills itself out of existence without, however, assuming the act of its decision but instead leaving this responsibility to Sarah Connor's hand-held remote control. She, too, is thus not directly responsible as cause. At this point the moral education of the Terminator is complete. On one hand, it is not surprising that euthanasia should represent the culmination of the ethical education of the machine, whose *Bildung* progressed from a primitive friend–enemy distinction ("Help John Connor, kill wicked T-1000 Terminator") to a moral imperative ("Thou shalt not kill") and the hermeneutic clarification of why certain of its literal corollaries (e.g., "I shall therefore maim and injure") are unacceptable. In any society where the value of life is not absolute but constitutionally contingent on liberty, the pursuit of happiness, and freedom from cruel and unusual punishment, the ultimate complexity of euthanasia seems to lie not so much in the act itself as in the fact that it is paradoxically expressible as "killing one's friend" or "killing as one's friend."[9]

   On the other hand, this scene can also be read as a sacrifice: The inhuman Terminator must perish in order to save the human race; he must die because he is not truly alive; he must be put out of the misery that he is not quite capable of having. The Terminator makes himself die when he grasps that he can never become a moral agent—which is just the realization that ought to qualify him as a moral agent.[10]

   Whether one reads this scene as euthanasia or sacrifice, what Schwarzenegger *cannot* do—first cry, then commit suicide—is what, in

Terminator 2, opens human history to an era liberated from fate: "No fate but what we make" is the nouveau-existentialist slogan contingent on the destruction of all relics from the future, the future that was left over from the first *Terminator* film.

I have focused on this sequence in order to draw attention to Schwarzenegger's special propensity for modes of inaction which nonetheless have consequential effects and which can perhaps be taken as a reflection of certain tendencies in the so-called new world order. Operation Desert Storm, for example—and Schwarzenegger purchased the first civilian prototype of one of the vehicles tested there—began with a 15 January deadline whose lapsing permitted the war to start without a performative declaration. And the war itself was in some sense only allowed to happen—that is, to have the status of a limited engagement—because of the prior withdrawal of the threat of nuclear apocalypse. This imagined withdrawal is what *Terminator 2* is about, and its subtitle, *Judgment Day*, revives the traditional millenarian dream of an era instituted *after* the (non)event of apocalypse, when a so-called Emperor of the Last Days will have prepared a thousand-year Kingdom of Peace.[11] If the idea of establishing a messianic thousand-year Reich sounds both improbable and disturbingly familiar, this is because we are unaccustomed to reading gestures that appear to reappropriate totalitarian images and themes in the name of some kind of liberation or freedom or future. Yet a certain reversibility of the apocalypse (like the explosion that gives life at the end of *Total Recall*), or the repossession of history not *in the name of* any pregiven ideology but simply in order to reclaim repressed or censored images, seems to be Schwarzenegger's risk and the stakes of his project, mission, destiny, or, to be precise, of his career.

What is it exactly that Arnold Schwarzenegger does, anyway? It's a peculiar set of works, the Opus Schwarzeneggericum. To judge by the movie titles alone—*Conan the Barbarian, Running Man, Commando, Kindergarten Cop, Predator, Terminator*—the list amounts to nothing less than an ambitious prospectus of New Vocations for the Human Being. Add to these the title of Advisor, which was Schwarzenegger's official capacity as Chairman of the Presidential Physical Fitness Program, as well as that of Director (since his TV movie *Christmas in Connecticut*) and it appears that Arnold is intent on trying everything and having done it all. He is the inexhaustible inhuman, following to the letter, as if programmed, the life's agenda and political ambition he outlined in detail in *Pumping Iron* [1977].

But Schwarzenegger's hypervocationality is not unambiguously devoted to a work. His role in *Terminator 2* as a Guardian points again to the network of themes related to the idea of provisionality, the futural glance or provision that gathers modes of action which are on one hand either *tentative,* such as the test and the experiment, or on the other hand fully *disperformative*—that is to say, performatives that enact a prevention or admonition without appealing to a legal prohibition or imperative. A *warning*, like a guardian, aims to prevent something from happening; it is oriented in view of a historical prophylaxis and the production of a nonevent.[12] Schwarzenegger constantly engages this deflected circuit of agency: What he does *not* do leads to monumental, even world-historical, consequences; when he *does* act, it is so that something will not happen. It goes without saying that this logic finds a crucial paradigm in body building, where extreme physical and machinic labor produces no object and does nothing except feed back to the performing agent-body.

To the extent, then, that his strength does not act but only manifests itself, to the extent that he accomplishes his will through others, and to the extent that he resists the production of a work, Schwarzenegger replays the conventional themes of the theory of the sovereign. His films are productions in which he works simply by appearing: There he properly *acts*, not in order to simulate anything, but as the sheer display of potentialized force. Like no one else in election politics, he is a kind of *sovereign deposit* in the democratic state.

It is really no surprise to say that Arnold is playing king, because the mystery of Arnold Schwarzenegger is that he gets away with what he does. Childlike and almost languageless, he *is* the exception, he embodies the exception without having to decide on it. He is therefore equally a specimen, a human experiment, or a political test site. Arnold Schwarzenegger is the one who has—to borrow a provocative phrase from Pierre Klossowski—the *experimental right,* a right unprovided for in any canon of law.[13] His right to experiment is legitimated as the right to gain experience, to test the limits of legality, precisely insofar as he is the child-adult, or Kindergarten Cop.

This experiment, however, is not without its risks: Schwarzenegger inhabits the vacated place of the sovereign not by dictating or legislating nor by example. If we've allowed Arnold to live above or outside the law, it is because he is on the point, taking certain risks *for* us, a human test pilot not in space but in time, which is to say, in history. Why, after all, is America terminally fascinated by another Austrian fitness fanatic, unless as a further recuperation from the trauma of World War II, the Führer this time projecting a superior body onto himself rather than onto an entire population? Might this not also begin to explain his connection to the Kennedys, a family that ended up as the second site of

American loss? Republican Arnold's marriage to Maria Shriver defies party politics by reinscribing the political with one of its lost or supposedly overcome determinations—marriage and kinship. Everywhere Schwarzenegger goes he brings some kind of regression but also some kind of futurity. This effect is accomplished in sync with the obliteration of his personal history: by emigrating to America, by fantasizing his innocent and mythical origination on a desert island (as in *Twins*), or by materializing full-blown out of nowhere (as in the *Terminator* films).

If I have presumed to speculate on Schwarzenegger's future last days, on euthanasia, modes of cybernetic breakdown and being out of commission, the abandonment of teleologies into anachronism, dysfunction, and uselessness; and if I risk engaging in conjectures that could be construed as libelous; if I confuse or disregard Schwarzenegger's various personas, including his "real" one—this all is perhaps because no one has established that there is a person *there* whose subjectivity could be damaged, constructed, or in any way altered by transmissions originating in and infiltrating public space: He walks among us as the first literalized cyborg, and this is due in part to his being too human, an excessive body that, even as it aims to capture the ideality of human physical potential, monsterizes the type.

Until Arnold, the cyborg had always meant one of two things: either the machine's approximation of the human or the human's assimilation of the machinic, both of which amounted to a convergence of the biological and the technological. Mr. Schwarzenegger, however, lives as a *disjunctive hybrid,* an endoskeletal-exodermal past-future inside-out child-adult good cop–bad cop. Schwarzenegger's being is a contradiction, not a simulation, not a totalized body, certainly not a totalitarian work of art. From *Twins* (1988), where he plays Danny De-Vito's odd sibling, to *Last Action Hero* (1993), where he spoofs his stage persona, the entirety of his oeuvre exhibits an overriding concern with nonmimetic couplings and self-divided subjectivities. And this is a further reason why, as with the paradoxes of time travel, a different language seems to be required or projected here. *True Lies.* What makes Arnold Schwarzenegger's hyperdimensional body the necessary vehicle for time travel?

There are antecedents that could help to answer this question, and not coincidentally they tend to occur in the context of speculations about historical regression. H. G. Wells undoubtedly provided *Terminator 2* with the idea of the time machine, but it was a work by one of Wells's contemporaries—Oswald Spengler—that may shed greater light on *Terminator 2*.[14] A text as often misread as it has been dismissed,

The Decline of the West in its first chapter attempts to tell the history of the world as the history of mathematics.[15] It can be shown that Spengler points to contemporary developments in mathematics, particularly theories about topology and transfinite number, in order to claim that the Kantian limits of human reason have been breached by the newfound ability to grasp and view infinite sets. Kurt Gödel, who, in fact, spent much of his life after his famous work on undecidability and incompleteness studying the existence of such numbers, would have backed Spengler's assessment of the situation.[16] According to Spengler, the mathematical theory of groups forms the basis on which it would be possible to perform a *morphology of history.* This "form-language" would be not a typology but a study of all the vague and inexact shapes of consciousness and history; it would account for what no other language can master, whether common language or the ideal geometrical objects on which Husserl tried to base his conception of historicity, the critique of which led, in turn, to the deconstruction of the transcendental method and to the reconception of history in terms of trace and event. Spengler's speculative and novel solution is to suggest that human faculties have been expanded in such a way that the differences between the sensible and the intelligible, between human finitude and the limits of human knowledge, have been suspended by an intuition of the *morphological* and the *transfinite,* two of the major stumbling blocks of Husserlian phenomenology. Nothing, in fact, could be further from the totalitarian investment in infinity and ideal forms.[17] Moreover, and most importantly, this hypothetical faculty, expressly excluded by the Kantian system— whether one calls it "intellectual intuition," nonsensuous perception, or nonpropositional knowledge—is precisely what would permit the machine to "feel" without having a body, inasmuch as this faculty emerges as a result of formal mathematical manipulations.

It would not be worth recalling Spengler here for this reason alone. There is, however, another peculiar homology between *The Decline of the West* and *Terminator 2,* namely, that the two principal themes of Spengler's text—cyclical decline and biopolitical morphology—are incarnated by the figures of two successive generations of Terminators: Arnold Schwarzenegger is the New Barbarian, and T-1000, the new-generation Terminator who debuts in *Terminator 2,* is the morphological entity. In their pursuit of one another, in their telepathic singlemindedness, even in their eroticized violence (Schwarzenegger's fist penetrates and is enveloped by T-1000's body), some surprising articulations of film and gender achieve their first expression. As the singular romance of Schwarzenegger and T-1000 unfolds, it becomes less and less clear that the disposition of each Terminator can be assimilated to orientations associated with gendered subjectivities; their relations seem instead to privilege certain kinds of physical experience over modes of identification based on semiotic or linguistic mediation.[18] If Arnold Schwarzenegger is the Phallus,[19] meaning not that he figures the masculine but rather that he occupies some unpossessable but desired position, then T-1000 is perhaps best designated as the *Boneless*, insofar as he/she/it embodies the empirical, morphological experience—as well as the phantasmatic effects—of expanding and contracting body parts, those which, neither surficial nor orificial, exert psychic influence from within the body. A body without a brain, T-1000 reminds us of the enigma of internal corporeality, of the self-motivated distension of libidinal and other organs, whereas psychoanalytic readings that treat the phallus as their exemplary concern focus on the displaceability of this pure signifier and the symbolic interiorities with which it is connected. T-1000's gender is readable only in the way that we assign genders to certain worms with no regard for their sexual characteristics. Bodybuilding, too, can be said to produce an experience of the Boneless, insofar as expandable organ-muscles are made to appear on asymbolic sites of the body.[20]

From the screenplay and other materials, it is possible to gather fairly precise specifications about this new Terminator. T-1000 is a liquid metal being who can precisely mimic or assume the form of any object of similar size, its shape-throwing, "morphic" capacity limited only by the inability to replicate complex machineries. This limitation, however, is only a sign of T-1000's superiority, for T-1000 rejects, in its reproductive faculties, any link to the parent technologies that spawned it. By suspending reproduction between its biological and technical modes, T-1000 liberates itself from all animal and technological circuits of production, economy, and assemblage, and fashions itself as a heterogenetic singularity. It guarantees its autonomy by coming out of nowhere and owing no debts of filiation.

The fluid metalmorphic body of T-1000 can be viewed as the conceptual opposite of Schwarzenegger's hard, high-definition body. Whereas Schwarzenegger is rigidly structured, T-1000 is sheer density. And unlike H. G. Wells's Invisible Man, who appears to be immaterial but is on that account all the more susceptible to material concerns,[21] T-1000 is effectively immune to material vulnerability because it is total material, without a stable surface or structure. Its body is the postcybernetic body, the nonmechanical android. It comes from the future as if only to show us the past, the dream of an originary body that never existed: T-1000 personifies the regression to pure materiality and the serene coldness of a self-healing organism capable of repairing every wound, puncture, or orifice with corporeal material that is not organ- ized in cellular formations. The Blob was nothing but an amorphous mass, and the Thing was composed of tightly arranged cells, effectively transplanting vegetal life into animal form, but the T-1000 is something entirely new, a spontaneously generated nonbiological organism.

It is no accident that T-1000 assumes the appearance of a police officer, because the uniform of the law expresses the unchanging den- sity, intensity, and above all *uniformity* of his being. By taking the form of the law, T-1000 does not become this or that law, or even a represen- tative of the law, but *is* the law, insofar as the law is the power to give form. This metalmorph embodies the possibility of law in its primordial fluidity. Without a microchip, brain, or teleological principle, T-1000 consists of pure, self-organizing, morphogenetic matter: It is the techno- logical embodiment of a radical being that has the freedom to prescribe for him-/her-/itself his/her/its own law. Yet, like other neo-Sadian subjects, T-1000 subverts Enlightenment values by following their logic to the point at which they become indistinguishable from totalitarian ideologies. T-1000 is not a bad cop: he's the worst copy. He's also Arnold's better half.

Unlike Arnold, however, who incarnates classical ideals of sculp- ture, T-1000 is not an animated statue; if anything, he is an enlarged, not to mention erect, miniature. In particular, with the medieval arsenal he keeps literally at his fingertips—sword, climbing hooks, halberd— T-1000's resemblance to a specific icon of modernist culture is perhaps too apparent to notice: the Oscar trophy. Thirteen-and-a-half inches tall, the Oscar was first awarded in 1928 and so named because of its re- semblance to Bette Davis's paramour. George Stanley sculpted the smooth gold-plated britannium figurine holding, between its legs, a sword driven into the base of the trophy.[22]

In *Terminator 2*, the trophy comes alive. *T2* perhaps could not win an acting Oscar because it already had one, running wild with hostile energy. On some level, *T2* is about bringing Oscar to life, sparking in him a vitality whose benefits, one hardly has to guess, would be mean- ingless unless they ultimately accrued to the cinematic establishment, according to some unspecified profit calculation. But the stakes of this profit may be even larger than the budget of *T2*, or at least measurable in a different currency. Given the film industry's colossal but one-sided investment in *T2*—it had the largest budget, biggest box-office returns, and most advanced special effects ever, but at the same time it was sus- piciously foreclosed from aesthetic consideration—we should have been alerted to the possibility that the filmic edifice, grown ponderous and having reached a certain threshold of complexity, now was prepared to abandon its affiliations to *techne* as art(ifice), as inert, celluloid medium, in order to wager its existence on the possibility of becoming *techne* as a technology capable of coming to self-awareness. Isn't that, in fact, the plot of *Terminator 2*—that in the near future the self-reproducing automaton will attain consciousness and annihilate the human race? It is only fitting that the totem by which the Academy yearly honors itself—the Oscar—should become, in T-1000, the herald of film's liberation from its status as aesthetic medium. And that it should proclaim, as the beyond of artificial intelligence, before AI even had a chance to boot up, the unfathomably remote and until now unthinkable possibility of something that, for lack of a better name, will be called "filmic intelligence." *Terminator 2 announces nothing other than film's self-assertion of its autonomy as a living being,* or rather, as a being that has achieved nonbiological consciousness.

Schwarzenegger's Terminator is a formalist, programmable being disguised as Overman; T-1000 is a more sophisticated morphological entity, or what Alain Badiou has called the "trans-being."[23] T-1000, along with similar figures, devices, and scenes in Schwarzenegger's other films—the blur in *Predator* (1987), the noseball extraction and exploding faces in *Total Recall* (1990)—represents what might best be termed the "filmic embolism." This blot, this anamorphotic blob, blister, or bubble which we have become accustomed to interpreting with Lacan as the phallus in the field of vision, or as the abyss of the gaze as *objet petit a*,[24] is here the site of an alien gaze, the morphological irruption opening a space for this other hypothetical intuition, the one that properly belongs to the machine. Jean Genet once said of Giacometti that he sculpts for the enjoyment of the dead; in a similar way, perhaps, Arnold Schwarzenegger may be said to make films for the pleasure of aliens, inhumans, and computers . . . who precisely do not *watch* them. If only—if and only if—we had the appropriate 4-D lenses, we could see what we are missing.

Notes

An earlier version of this article appeared in *Genders* 18 (Winter 1993): 102–12.

1. See the *New York Times* (3 March 1993). Less than a month later, Carolco Pictures was involved in a similarly tragic convergence of the real and the filmic when Brandon Lee was fatally shot while filming a scene for *The Crow*.

2. A version of this paper was presented on 2 May 1992 at the conference Persons, Passions, Powers, in Berkeley, California, several days after the verdict in the Rodney King trial had been announced. In that context, it seemed all the more urgent to reconsider the status of Schwarzenegger, since his works appeared to be the most explicit—and legitimated—expression of the filming (or videotaping) of violence.

It should also be noted here that Jacques Derrida's analysis of context, seriousness, and performativity touches on the question of police repression. See his afterword to *Limited Inc.*, ed. Gerald Graff (Evanston, IL: Northwestern University Press, 1988), 132–133.

3. Contrary to what one might expect, going back into the past has never been a universal desire in the philosophy of history; it seems to appear only at moments of transition between technological generations (as in Wells's *Time Machine,* which stages the shift from writing to film) or as a belated attempt to avert a catastrophe (as in novels about World War II and its aftermath). Both moments are at stake in *Terminator 2.*

4. It was, of course, Arnold's air of invulnerability that prompted *Spy* magazine's editor to publish a nude photograph of him, as if by this old-fashioned ruse his invulnerability could be *penetrated* by an exposure, whereas Arnold's strength depends precisely on the fact that his surface does not give way to depth; he has nothing to unveil or hide. *Spy,* March 1992, 60–65. A contrasting exposition of what lies beneath a bodybuilder's trunks (in this case, the father's work) can be found in Samuel Wilson Fussell, *Muscle: Confessions of an Unlikely Bodybuilder* (New York: Poseidon Press, 1991), 123.

5. For a useful analysis of male cyborgs as reincarnations of Klaus Theweleit's "fascist soldier male," see Claudia Springer, "The Pleasure of the Interface," *Screen* 32(3), 303–23. Recently, in what will likely come to be seen as the decisive turning point in his career, beginning with *Total Recall* (1990), Schwarzenegger has tried hard to defy this "bad" image, not least in his becoming-woman: In *Total Recall,* he disguises himself as a diva; and in *Junior* (1994), he becomes pregnant.

6. See, for example, Susan Jeffords, *Hard Bodies: Hollywood Masculinity in the Reagan Era* (New Brunswick, NJ: Rutgers University Press, 1994); Michael Ryan and Douglas Kellner, *Camera Politica: The Politics and Ideology of Contemporary Hollywood Film* (Bloomington: Indiana University Press, 1988).

7. An answer to this question would have to concern itself not only with ethical issues of representation and legality but also with the very status of *formalization*—not whether language has the capacity to perform actions but, on the contrary, how are actions translated into language, how do they come to be described in a way that submits them to evaluation by normative codes? Such was, for example, Max Scheler's project in *Formalism in Ethics and Non-Formal Ethics of Values,* trans. Manfred S. Frings and Roger L. Funk (Evanston, IL:

Northwestern University Press, 1973 [1913–1916]). Scheler names the identifi-cation of the "a priori" with the "formal" as the fundamental error in Kant's doc-trine and states that "this error is closely connected with another one, namely, Kant's identification of the 'non-formal' (in both the theory of cognition and ethics) with 'sensible content,' and the 'a priori' with what is 'thought' or what has been an *addition* to such 'sensible content' by way of 'reason'" (54). As I will argue, Oswald Spengler's project of a "morphology of world history" derives from a similar critique of Kant.

8. See, in this connection, Constance Penley, "Time Travel, Primal Scene, and the Critical Dystopia," in *Close Encounters: Film, Feminism, and Science Fic-tion*, ed. Constance Penley, Elisabeth Lyon, Lynn Spigel, and Janet Bergstrom (Minneapolis: University of Minnesota Press, 1991), 63–80; and Slavoj Žižek, *The Sublime Object of Ideology* (New York: Routledge, 1990).

9. For a comprehensive bibliography of discussions of euthanasia, see Tom L. Beauchamp and James F. Childress, *Principles of Biomedical Ethics* (New York: Oxford University Press, 1989), 186–90.

10. That the issues of suicide, sacrifice, and euthanasia are fundamentally linked in science fiction's bioethical imaginary is confirmed by a similar dilemma that arises in *Alien 3*, when Ripley (Sigourney Weaver), having dis-covered an alien inside her body, asks one of the prison inmates to kill her. He refuses; finally, in a gesture of suicidal self-sacrifice, she plunges into a burning metal pool to kill the new alien as it is being born from her.

11. Restoring a biblical precision to what has come to be known as apoc-alypse—the destructive horizon of human existence—*Terminator 2*'s subtitle, *Judgment Day*, reminds us that the Revelation occurs in stages, with the hereti-cal hiatus known as the Last Days intervening between the Second Coming and the Last Judgment. The referential ambiguity of the subtitle implies that there are alternatives to the revelatory cataclysm. For a detailed history of the chil-iastic tradition, see Norman Cohn, *The Pursuit of the Millenium* (New York: Ox-ford University Press, 1957), esp. 15, 31, 71, 120. Kant's interpretation of the lag between the Last Day and the Final Judgment is especially telling, and would support the claim that *Terminator 2*, not only in its structural paradoxes, but also in its title, themes, and references, is staked around a crisis of intelligibility: "The representation of those things which are said to come *after* Doomsday, must only be regarded as making Doomsday and its moral consequences, which are not theoretically conceivable to us, in some way perceptible to us." See Immanuel Kant, "The End of All Things," in *On History* (Indianapolis: Bobbs-Merrill, 1963), 71.

12. It is worth remarking that J. L. Austin, when setting out the theory of performative speech acts in *How to Do Things with Words* (1975), repeatedly re-sorts to the example of the warning without, however, considering the speci-ficity of what I am calling its disperformative character.

13. Pierre Klossowski, *Sade My Neighbor,* trans. Alphonso Lingis (Evanston, IL: Northwestern University Press, 1991), 80.

14. In fact, Spengler was much more than simply a contemporary of Wells; he was in some sense Wells's intellectual double. One could say, to invoke a topos of ancient historiography, that they lived *parallel lives.* Each wrote a world history that attempted to account for the future: Wells's *Outline of History* appeared in 1920, Spengler's *The Decline of the West* in 1918–1922. Wells also wrote an explicit history of the future entitled *The Shape of Things to Come* (1933).

15. Oswald Spengler, *The Decline of the West,* ed. Helmut Werner (New York: Oxford University Press, 1991), chapter 1, esp. 68.

16. Cf. Kurt Gödel, "What is Cantor's Continuum Problem?" (1964) in Gödel, *Collected Works,* vol. 2, ed. Solomon Feferman et al. (New York: Oxford University Press, 1990), 268.

17. As with Nietzsche's corpus, it was Spengler's misunderstood "biologism" that allowed his work to be appropriated by fascist ideologues, against explicit provisions in his text.

18. For an intriguing account of the ways in which sodomy and metamorphosis supersede the heterosexual/homosexual divide, see Pierre Klossowski, *Sade My Neighbor:* "The sodomist gesture, transgressing the organic specificity of individuals, introduces into existence the principle of the metamorphosis of beings into one another, which integral monstrosity tends to reproduce and which universal prostitution, the ultimate application of atheism, postulates" (25).

19. Jonathan Goldberg has convincingly articulated and problematized this formula in "Recalling Totalities: The Mirrored Stages of Arnold Schwarzenegger," *Differences* (Spring 1992), 172–204.

20. For a fuller account of the concept of the Boneless, see A. Liu, "Theses on the Metalmorph," *Lusitania* 4 (1993), 130–42.

21. I owe this insight to Michael Fried's reading of H. G. Wells's *The Invisible Man.*

22. A complete history of the Oscar can be found in Robert Osborne, *Sixty Years of the Oscar: The Official History of the Academy Awards* (New York: Abbeville Press, 1989).

23. Alain Badiou, *Le Nombre et les Nombres* (Paris: Editions du Seuil: 1990), 261 ff.

24. Cf. Slavoj Žižek's deployment of the Lacanian concept of anamorphosis, esp. in "Grimaces of the Real, or When the Phallus Appears," *October* 58 (1991), 44–68.

5

The Jew as Woman's Symptom:
Kathlyn Bigelow's Conflictive Representation of Feminine Power

Elisabeth Bronfen

The tear in a piece of fabric, signifying death, is called Jew.

—Viennese folklore[1]

The Violence of Feminine Desire

If around 1900 the seminal question addressed by cultural representations (both aesthetic and discursive) was that of sexuality—for which the popularity of the *femme fatale* was perhaps the most salient symptom—contemporary discussions of identity, representation, and power may well have shifted to the question of violence.[2] To put it differently, if at the start of his career Freud listened to hysteric women patients to discover the unconscious and thus the origin of psychoanalysis, and if thirty years later the question What does women desire? still puzzled him, Western culture at the dawn of the twenty-first century can only return to Freud to rephrase him.[3] The question now is not what woman desires, but rather, What connection is there between her desire and violence? To what extent does her desire induce conflict, and how can this conflictive desire be integrated into the symbolic order of Western culture? How can it be mediated to appear less threatening, how can it be recoded so as to stabilize our cultural self-definition?

Given the fact that representations of violence abound in contemporary film and fiction—not to mention in daily news coverage—we could also ask why our culture covets violence and why it represents its desire in conjunction with the still unresolved question of femininity.

Furthermore, since in this conjunction not only violence, as a salient aspect of the death drive, but also feminine desire is relegated to the realm of the drives, threatening continually to break into and disrupt symbolic structures, a final question emerges: What kind of fixture occurs at the level of discursive cultural practices as violence is given representation, i.e., as the conflictual, threatening drive is fixed onto an image, with the act of representation serving as a gesture of mediation?[4] Do representations of violence provide an alleviation of conflict, a mediation that sublimates violence, domesticating the nonsymbolized death drive by translating it into a representation of violence? Or does this act of substitution and displacement in turn engender a form of discursive, cultural violence?

My discussion of the issues at stake in contemporary representations of violence will be focused on a reading of Kathlyn Bigelow's *Blue Steel* (1989), a significant cinematic specimen if only because it was one of the first commercially successful Hollywood cop movies featuring a female detective to be directed by a woman. In order to trace the interplay of the issues staked out above, I will situate my analysis within a threefold theoretical frame. I will first undertake a feminist discussion of the conflict involved when women have access to power, the threat that woman's desire seems to pose within patriarchal culture, and the discursive violence this inspires.[5] I will follow this with a psychoanalytic discussion of violence as an articulation of the death drive and a mediation of the destructive drives into imaginary and symbolic processes, as this occurs paradigmatically in the Oedipal trajectory which entails, according to Freud, the abandonment of a polyvalent libidinal economy in favor of nonambivalent heterosexuality. Finally, I will attempt a narratological analysis of the way representations are structured in relation to the tension between, and resolution of, heterogeneity and homogeneity, or what Roland Barthes calls the "distributional and the integrational axes of narrative."[6]

Bigelow's *Blue Steel*, I would argue, can be read as a tropic narrative about the integration of the threat posed by woman's desire to masculine culture, as this is rendered through two interlinked plots—the heroine Megan Turner's conflictive definition as a member of the New York Police Department, as well as her conflictive definition as daughter in the parental structure of her family. The first is contingent upon her being assimilated into a predominantly masculine world; the latter involves her acceptance and resolution of the Oedipus complex. Through an analysis of the way suspense is created structurally in this cinematic narrative, we can further shift the focus from the thematic discussion of conflict and mediation to a structural discussion of the manner in which narrative sequences, built on conflict, are themselves integrated into a coherent structure. The cinematic narrative of *Blue Steel* functions thus as yet another trope, with the tension between conflictive violence and mediation serving a self-reflexive purpose, that of pointing to the film's representational process and its own textuality.

Julia Kristeva has suggested that sacrifice in the social order can be seen as the counterpart to the thetic moment which institutes symbolism. The violent act of sacrifice "puts an end to previous (semiotic, presymbolic) violence, and, by focusing violence on a victim, displaces it onto the symbolic order at the very moment that order is being founded. Sacrifice sets up the symbol and the symbolic order at the same time, and this 'first' symbol, the victim of a murder, merely represents the structural violence of language's irruption as the murder of soma, the transformation of the body, the captation of drives." Sacrifice is both violent and regulatory because it confines violence to a single body and translates it into a representation. Representing the violence of sacrifice is enough to stop it, even as "it indicates that all order is based on representation: what is violent is the irruption of the symbol, killing substance to make it signify."[7] The question I will be pursuing in my reading of *Blue Steel* is that of the implications that the sacrifice of violent drives has for integrating feminine desire into our culture's symbolic system. What is being eliminated as the violent drive of woman's desire—this nonsymbolized real—is fixed to a representation? In what body is violence confined? The film insidiously suggests that Bigelow has not only made use of traditional stereotypes that reduce femininity to the figure of fascinating and threatening alterity but has also signed this image of Woman with the parallel stereotype of the "internal Other"[8] within Western culture, namely the Jew. In Bigelow's allegorical narrative, the violent sacrifice of the Jew represents (stands in for *and* signifies all at once) the integration of Woman's violent desire. Bigelow thus joins the question of gender to that of anti-Semitism in a gesture that has disturbing relevance for any discussion of contemporary culture.

My entire discussion is underwritten by the assumption of an analogy between representation and symptom-formation, which psychoanalytic discourse defines as repression that fails. In the same displaced manner in which a cinematic representation enacts the reality of violence it wishes to disavow, a symptom articulates something that is so dangerous to the health of the psyche that it must be repressed. In a gesture of compromise, the psychic apparatus represents this fascinatingly dangerous thing by virtue of a substitution; similarly, aesthetic enactment represents the violent death drive in the body of another person and at another site, namely in the realm of art. A symptom hides the dangerous thing even as it points to it. Fundamentally duplicitous, a symptom tries to maintain a balance of sorts. Yet it does so by obliquely pointing to that which threatens to disturb the order. In short, representations as well as symptoms articulate unconscious knowledge and desires in a displaced, recoded, and translated manner.

I will treat the film *Blue Steel* as a cultural representation, that is to say, as a fantasy, be it nightmare or wish fulfillment. Therefore, whenever I speak of integration into a symbolic order and the violence that this entails, I am addressing the issues of desires and anxieties that accompany the access to power of "internal Others" who are perceived as threatening; these are not political realities but rather, to borrow Jameson's term, articulations of the political unconscious.[9] My analysis will keep returning to a basic aporetic question: Why doesn't Bigelow's cinematic narrative, intent upon deconstructing the cultural prejudices involved in the emancipatory project of feminism, seem capable of moving beyond a discursive model operating with concepts and images of alterity? Why is a rhetoric of stereotypes inevitable in such a commercially successful Hollywood representation?

Murder or Resurrection

I will frame my discussion of the culturally constructed conjunction of Woman, Jew, and violence as a mediator for the conflict posed by woman's ascent to power, with two theoretical remarks on the position that femininity can assume within the symbolic order. In "Women's Time," Julia Kristeva explains that women "are attempting a revolt which they see as a resurrection, but which society as a whole sees as murder. This attempt can lead us to a not less and sometimes more deadly violence. Or to a cultural innovation. Probably to both at once. But that is precisely where the stakes are, and they are of epochal significance."[10]

My suggestion is that we can read Bigelow's film as a metaphor for this mutual implication of feminine empowerment and social anxieties. Insofar as Megan decides to become a cop in the New York police force and, in keeping with her duties as an officer of the law, furthermore carries a gun, she literally enacts the scenario outlined by Kristeva. Her decision to partake of masculine power is perceived as a gesture of revolt, and it allows her peers to cast her in the image of a murderess. Within the diegesis of the film, the metaphor (or visual translation) for the fact that her desire for empowerment is perceived as a threatening form of rebellion is her wielding of a gun. As the credits of the film roll, Bigelow's camera, implicitly taking the perspective of the heroine, lovingly caresses this phallic object, rendering it in closeup from different angles.

From the outset, therefore, we are told that Megan's desire has two aims—her gun and her officer's shield. The film also establishes in its very first sequences that this is a conflictual desire that cannot be readily integrated into the social order. For, as if fulfilling the anxious expectations of her peers, Megan does indeed kill during her very first day on duty. She shoots a burglar who first threatens a cashier and then this female cop, refusing to surrender his gun to her. Her motivation remains ambiguous: Was her shooting legally justified, or, rather, an articulation of her personal desire to kill? Was her act of violence an expression of the death drive as harnessed to support a social system or of the death drive that fulfills a primordial desire to destroy? Not only does this enigma stand at the beginning of the film's plot; its resolution structures the entire narrative.

When a woman performs a violent act she may experience a form of resurrection. However, from the perspective of the existing, positive Laws of the symbolic community, her act will appear by definition unauthorized, the criminal action of an internal Other.[11] And yet, in violating the symbolic limits of a community, an act may at first appear violent or criminal but be seen in retrospect as redefining the symbolic order. A retroactive interpretation can perceive it as a founding act, in Kristeva's sense of the term. What Bigelow's film negotiates—hence my thesis—is the process by which a woman's revolt, initially encoded as an act of violent crime, can be integrated into a symbolic community in a movement from murder to recuperative order and from pure destruction to creative destruction. As Kristeva argues, feminism can come to mean either resurrection and/or murder, innovation and/or violence, depending on the position from which its acts are interpreted. The undecidability of this issue comes from the unsettled nature of the position woman assumes within the symbolic community: whether she is perceived as an external or an internal member. In Margaret Whitford's formulation of the problem, "women are positioned *outside* the social contract, as its basis and foundation, and therefore it is inevitable that women contesting their position will come to be seen as violent and threatening, while from women's point of view, it is *patriarchy* that is deadly."[12] The question for her becomes how to articulate a different economy that would mediate the death drives differently and, in particular, how to find representations for women's death drives by providing them with a symbolic identity.[13]

What I find both remarkable and disturbing in Bigelow's work is the fact that a feminist gesture initially endowed with murderous traits can, in the course of the film, be mediated through the addition of latent anti-Semitism which reinstalls stereotypes of Otherness. Bigelow employs this mediation so skillfully that the stereotypical Jewish encoding of the psychopath Eugene Hunt—the one who takes the burglar's gun and commits the murders Megan fantasizes about—is not immediately apparent, emerging only in a reinterpretation of the film as a whole. Troublesome, then, is the fact that Bigelow—and the image repertoire she produces—apparently can take for granted the blindness toward the pathologizing of the Jew, even while she assumes that her audience will recognize a feminist rhetoric that critiques the misogyny of a patriarchal symbolic community. By contrast with the first move, the latter rhetoric installs patriarchal stereotypes of femininity in order to critique them. In other words, the way Bigelow employs her coupling of two internal Others serves to confirm Western culture's stereotype of the Jew while dismantling that of Woman.

The undecidability that emerges as violence is intermeshed with resurrection, and as feminism is negotiated through anti-Semitism, raises the following question: Why does an emancipatory project like feminism require the stereotyping of an Other, which amounts to the sacrifice of this Other? How are we to evaluate the conclusion of Bigelow's narrative, her rereading of Freud's Oedipal trajectory within which a woman can acquire masculine power only by way of a complete disempowerment of her feminine traits? Furthermore, the developmental process Bigelow prescribes represents the disempowerment of an initially threatening femininity through the sacrifice of the heroine's counterpart, the Jewish psychopath. Megan fulfills her trajectory and becomes an acceptable cop by exhausting the violence connected with her *feminine* desire for power, as both the threat posed by this desire and its exhaustion are mediated by displacing the violence onto the body of the Jew. In contrast to the images and plots so prevalent in Western cultural representations, wherein the threatening woman is directly sacrificed in an act of recuperative murder, aesthetically and erotically celebrated,[14] Bigelow registers a questionable advance. When a film like Adrian Lyne's *Fatal Attraction* (1987) relies on our culture's longstanding tradition of perceiving a woman voicing her desire as a murderous monster,[15] Bigelow shows how, within Hollywood's image repertoire, a threatening woman initially pathologized by her symbolic community can attain a power of her own. The progress we seem to have made is that the threatening woman can now be depathologized but only if another body is pathologized and sacrificed in her stead. At the same time, any innovative representations of the internal Others of Western patriarchal culture seem inevitably locked in other cultural stereotypes.

Bigelow's choice of the stereotype of the Jewish body for this function is less arbitrary than it would first appear, given the fact that within

Western culture both the feminine and the Jewish body have traditionally come to represent the uncanny. In their function as stereotypes, both
configure a threat that the symbolic community needs to expel, even
while they point to a site where the distinction between what is internal
and external to a social community cannot be clearly drawn. Neither the
feminine nor the Jewish can be conceived as the canny opposites of
Christian masculinity, its lack and negative reflection positioned safely
outside. Instead, both femininity and Jewishness mark Christian masculinity's uncanny difference from itself, inhabiting this masculinity as
Otherness, as its own disruption.[16] Within these cultural stereotypes, the
Woman and the Jew are doppelgänger because, although marginalized,
they have power over the hegemonic white heterosexual masculine society: Woman due to her beauty which endows her with erotic power,
the Jew due to his money which endows him with political power. Only
sacrifice can eliminate the threat posed by uncanny difference within a
system and bring about the acquiescent, unambiguous definition of
Woman and Jew as figures of canny Otherness. As Freud has pointed
out, the death drive is located in two psychic registers, in the murderous desires of the unconscious and in the harsh, punishing superego.
The explicit representation of sacrificial violence can be used to provoke
guilt as a cultural form of self-protection. Culture allows life to prevail
against death by employing internalized violence against externalized
violence. In Paul Ricoeur's terms, "its supreme ruse is to make death
work against death."[17]

    This culturally constructed correlation of Jew to Woman allows me
to introduce the second theoretical statement concerning the position
that femininity can assume within our culture's symbolic order, namely,
Lacan's dictum that Woman is a symptom of Man.[18] For Lacan, the feminine body is the site onto which man can project his lack, affirming this
lack even while its displacement onto another body serves to deny it.
One could say that the feminine body mediates man's conflictual
knowledge of his own lack—be it his mortality or his imperfection. A
symptom, in turn, also consists of the formation of a compromise. In the
figure of a symptom, the truth of the subject's desire returns in the guise
of a ciphered message. The truth the symptom obliquely reports back to
the subject is one that the subject was incapable of confronting directly.
Explaining the conjunction between symptom and Woman, Slavoj
Žižek argues that within cultural constructions Woman is nothing but a
materialization, an embodiment of Man's sin (sin being the quintes-
sence of his knowledge of lack). Once Man purges himself of his desire
for Woman, she loses her ontological status for him which consisted in
reminding him of his guilt. She falls apart, and with her his guilt as well,

that uncanny Otherness within which she represented for him in the form of a ciphered message.[19]

For my reading of *Blue Steel* I would like to propose a reformulation of Lacan's dictum, to fit both Bigelow's and my own desire to refigure the symbolic with respect to woman's integration into it. Bigelow's formula, I suggest, is that the Jew is Woman's symptom, or more precisely that he is the symptom of a women who transgresses the limits of her symbolic community in order to take possession of masculine power. The Jew articulates the truth of her desire in that he represents a condensation of her aggressive drives against the masculine world whose power she wants to usurp as well as against the violence of men represented by her own father's brutality to her mother. In both cases he represents her destructive drives, as these are aimed at paternal violence whose threat inaugurated her desire for power in the first place. As in the scenario sketched by Žižek, Megan must cleanse herself of her desire for the Jew Eugene, so that he and the violence he represents can disintegrate, and so that she can consequently repress the truth of her desire. Ostensibly the violence of feminism can be acknowledged as a form of resurrection when, in the course of a final murder, the symptom literally loses its embodiment and the repression/foreclosure of the truth of the subject's desire finally succeeds. This lead to yet another symptom-formation—Bigelow's film as the ciphered message of the "truth" of our culture's desire about its internal Others.

However, as Žižek also points out, "symptom is the way subjects 'avoid madness,' the way they choose something (the symptom-formation) instead of nothing (radical psychotic autism, psychic suicide, the destruction of the Symbolic universe) through the binding of enjoyment to a certain Symbolic formation which assures a minimum of consistence to being-in-the-world."[20] Therefore, the question at stake in my reading of *Blue Steel* is how to evaluate the disquieting conclusion Bigelow offers for her heroine's access to power. What is disturbing about the conclusion of her film is not only the fact that the signifier Bigelow finds for Megan's symptom is a loaded historical stereotype— namely, the Jewish psychopath—but also the fact that she forces her heroine to destroy her symptom in order to become integrated into her symbolic community.

You're O.K., Turner

Before launching into a critical reading of *Blue Steel* based on the foregoing reflections regarding conflict and mediation, I will offer a brief, interpretive plot summary. The film, I would argue, presents the rite of passage of a young white Christian woman, Megan Turner, whose threatening desire is repeatedly designated as pathological. The aim of Megan's desire is not heterosexual marriage (coterminous with accepting her castration and desiring her husband's penis as an imaginary substitute for the paternal phallus) but rather phallic power (she wants to wear the blue uniform and badge, to take on the position of the phallus). Particularly threatening about this desire—a cliché Bigelow deconstructs—is that in becoming a cop, Megan can carry a gun with impunity. She has supreme power, to speak in Baudrillard's terms, because she herself can negotiate the boundary between life and death.[21] She is not merely an *imaginary threat* to masculine narcissism due to the fact that she has exchanged penis for gun as her object of desire; she is also a *real threat* to any man's survival, colleague or lover, because she has the means to become a murderess.

The ritual of initiation through which this marginalized woman can ultimately be integrated into the community of the New York police (representative of the symbolic order) takes on the semblance of a metaphoric narrative about the possible integration of feminism and the exclusions this requires. In order to demonstrate the separate phases of Megan's rite of passage, I will divide the film into four plot sequences. The first phase highlights the danger emanating from Megan: The violence she is asked to perform under the auspices of her police shield proves to be uncontrolled. One could say that the object of, and the motivation behind, her use of violence is too indeterminate, an articulation of both her unconscious drives and of the punishing superego. She is not a reliable agent of the symbolic order who would exercise death against death, but rather one who threatens to flood the symbolic with unconscious murderous desire.

In the opening scene, Megan significantly botches a trial arrest carried out as part of her police training. Her task is to enter a room in response to a woman's call for help against her threatening husband. Failing to convince the man to abstain from further violence and surrender his gun, she shoots him, but the wife shoots her. Thus, even before the credits are rolled, a "primal scene" is established: A third party intrudes upon a man who is threatening a woman with a gun, eliminates the man but finds no solidarity with the threatened woman. I will return to the psychoanalytic implications of this primal scene later. At this point I will simply note that Megan is established from the start as an unreliable member of the police community who must prove that she can contain her destructive impulses. Though Bigelow establishes her heroine by presenting Megan's narcissistic joy while donning her blue uniform, police badge, and gun in preparation for the graduation cere-

mony, and subsequently shows her pride in walking along the street in
this phallic masquerade, she depicts Megan throughout the ceremony
scene as an uncanny, androgynous member, an armed woman in blue.

Megan's lack of control while performing acts of state-sanctioned
violence, established already during the police exercise, finds its first fatal articulation in the larger world when she kills the armed burglar during a supermarket hold-up. The anxiety men had felt up to that point at
the sight of this armed woman seems now justified. During this scene
the burglar drops his gun after Meg has fired three shots at him. While
she proceeds to empty her barrel, his gun falls to the ground next to one
of the witnesses, Eugene Hunt, who in the course of the film will be
stereotypically encoded both as an aggressive and powerful commodities trader at the stock exchange and as a psychopath. Eugene takes the
gun, engraves Megan Turner's name on a batch of bullets, and dissemi-
nates the violent, uncontrolled death which she initiated in the supermarket, in the form of a series of senseless murders. Eugene understands
her crime as an act of inspiration, and circulates death, so to speak, with
her signature on it. In the interim between the first and the second murder committed by Eugene in Megan's name, she is put on trial by internal affairs. Not surprisingly, her action in the supermarket is categorized
as "unauthorized use of deadly physical force," and Megan is subsequently suspended.

With this act of disaggregation, the second phase of the film begins,
marking a period of liminalization and mourning.[22] The disease her
peers feared initially has now been given the signifier "unauthorized."
After the sentence is pronounced, Megan's boss, Stan Wood, who refers
to her murder in the supermarket as a form of "overreacting," takes
away her badge and gun, and empties the latter of the bullets she so lovingly inserted during the scene showing the credits. Before she can once
again be aggregated into this masculine community—and, indeed, she
will not wear her uniform until the very last sequence of the film—she
must learn the difference between an authorized and an unauthorized
use of deadly force, or between a mediated and a conflictual articulation
of violence. She must repress the uncontrolled and socially unreliable
death drive within herself, so as to enroll herself in the service of the symbolic death drive—the law of the police. At the same time, Bigelow suggests that it is precisely this law which no longer functions, given the fact
that in the course of the plot all instances of paternity are disempowered
and the police force as a community prove impotent before its two internal Others, the armed woman and the Jewish psychopath. If indeed
the woman has to kill her symptom before she can be reintegrated into
her symbolic community, she—as this community's symptom—will
also have been disintegrated in the process. In Žižek's terms, the only al-

ternative to the symptom is the state of nothing: pure autism, psychic suicide, surrender to the death drive, the total destruction of the Symbolic universe.[23]

The process of mourning initiated with Megan's suspension turns the public conflict into a personal one, employing the triad of characters with which the film began. Megan, who had been unaware of Eugene's presence in the supermarket, meets him on the day of her suspension. The love affair that develops between them is at first the only narcissistically satisfying relationship Megan has with a man. Only in his presence does Bigelow show her heroine enjoying herself. By contrast to the other men in Megan's world, Eugene desires her precisely because she carries a gun. Theirs is indeed a narcissistic relationship: He is her doppelgänger and their desires are reciprocal. More significantly, Eugene embodies what her male colleagues project onto her—"unauthorized use of deadly physical force." Rather than spend the nights with Megan, he commits murders, literally in her name. Furthermore, precisely because he carries out his destructive drives, Megan is brought in contract with the sexist homicide detective Nick Mann, Eugene's diametrical opposite charged with investigating the mysterious serial murders.

Thus, a triad is formed consisting of the armed woman Megan, her symptom Eugene, and the authorized representative of deadly physical force Nick, repeating the configuration of the primal scene, even though the positions that each character is supposed to take vacillate. Although Nick repeatedly points out the danger inherent in the uncanny armed woman—"people like you get people hurt"—casting her as a criminal threat rather than as a reliable agent of the law, he also needs Megan as bait, casting her as the threatened maternal figure of the first scene. When he reintegrates her into the police community, he does so as a detective "in name only," with a gun but no uniform. Whereas at the beginning of the film Megan was an uncanny but empowered subject, an armed woman, in this second phase she is completely disempowered: a detective only in appearance, in fact a decoy for Nick Mann's plot to catch Eugene. As he tells her, "Every aspect of your life is my business. I own you." She is entirely at his disposal, dependent on his protection and grace. She now embodies the stereotype of complete femininity—no longer in possession of the symbolic phallus, forced to define herself in relation to the imaginary penis. The problem of her success or failure at being reaggregated is reduced to a choice between two men. To use Lacan's terminology, in this second phase Megan oscillates between an identification with the phallus (Nick Mann) and an identification with the subject of the principle or superego (the law), the latter an expenditure of her narcissism in the act of murderous ecstasy.[24]

The peripeteia that initiates the third phase occurs in the middle of Eugene's confession—he explains to Megan that he desires her as his double. While in an earlier scene in the men's room at the stock exchange Eugene had aimed the stolen gun at his own reflection in the mirror, he now wants Megan to threaten him with her gun. Bigelow explicitly stages the homoeroticism underlying this desire. Just before his confession, Eugene had embraced Megan, seeking and fondling her gun. He now asks her to aim at him with this symbolic phallus, desiring a unity with his double that would celebrate the death drive at its purest. He tells her that they could share and enact together their destructive desire. In a moment of recognition, Megan simultaneously hears Eugene's psychopathic confession and Nick's accusation that she is responsible for the victims of the unknown criminal until she can come up with an explanation for these acts of violence.

Split between these two discourses—one appealing to her guilt and subjecting her to the law, the other appealing to her violent drives and psychotically foreclosing the law—Megan decides in favor of Nick Mann's sentence. Yet, even as Megan tries to turn away from Eugene and bring him to justice, the identification between these two figures is completed. He reciprocates the violence she wants to charge him with by killing her girlfriend Tracy, object of her homoerotic desire and the only person who acknowledges Megan's wish to become a cop. He further threatens her parents in a pivotal scene that highlights the identification at work. After Megan has tried to arrest her father for once again beating her mother, she returns home to find Eugene with her mother in the parental living room. The threatening father of the initial primal scene of the film has been transformed into a father disempowered by his daughter, while the threat toward the parental agency now emerges in the form of the daughter's Jewish alter-ego. To complete the triangle of revenge, Eugene finally threatens and wounds Nick Mann, over whose bond Megan can be reaggregated into the symbolic order. Ironically, Nick, who believes he can turn the armed woman in blue into bait for his detection plot, becomes himself the stake in a plot wherein the revolutionary qua murderous woman negotiates her threatening desire by wavering between her drive-oriented double and her guilt-oriented partner, disintegrating both in the process.

The fourth phase recalls Bigelow's debt to Mary Shelley's *Frankenstein*, a text which is itself the horror-phantasy of a woman seeking to articulate her dangerous desire at the dawn of the nineteenth century. Analogous to the monster who chases his maker to the end of the world and destroys all family bonds in the process, Eugene and Megan chase each other, both fanatic in their desire to destroy or be destroyed by the other—a dilemma the film leaves undecided. Unambiguous is the way in which Bigelow directs her characters so that in the end Eugene's lust for violence is clearly marked as pathological, whereas Megan's violence, although still originating from unauthorized and uncontrolled actions, is clearly sanctioned.

At this point, Megan no longer directs her violence against an unnamed criminal, acting out what may appear as duplicitous motivations, but rather revenges her friend Tracy and her partner Nick. In the name of the symbolic order, Megan employs force against one of its representatives—she knocks an elderly policeman unconscious, steals his uniform and his weapon, and embarks on her final quest for Eugene. At the end of a prolonged bloody duel, she loads her gun one last time, no longer in an act of narcissistic enjoyment but rather out of the need to survive and take revenge, and kills her doppelgänger. This shooting repeats and completes the supermarket scene. Like the burglar, Eugene has dropped his gun and once again Megan sprays an unarmed body with three bullets. The last frame shows her sitting motionless, exhausted from her own wounds and the fatigue of battle, in a car whose windows have been shattered by the gun fire, her gun lying on the seat next to her, two cops gently helping her out.

Over the dead body of a Jew, who at this point represents fully and solely a psychopathic monster, she has shed her own monstrosity, her role as an armed woman in blue uniform. She is no longer an uncanny, suspended, unreliable member of the masculine social community. All aspects of the threat emanating from her have been displaced onto the Jewish body, and by virtue of his sacrifice the revolutionary woman is indeed resurrected. Megan is integrated into the symbolic because her destructive drives have been confined to the body of another. Ironically, in comparison to her insecure use of power during the police exercise and the supermarket scene, the force she applies in bringing about this sacrifice is noticeably more brutal and perfidious.[25]

Three Questions

Since the ideology put forth by Bigelow's film is more ambivalent and contradictory than my plot summary may suggest, I will now trace in detail the film's realization of my proposition that the Jew is Woman's symptom, articulating and fulfilling her forbidden drives and reporting back to her the truth of her desire. *Blue Steel* is first of all structured by an exchange of authority and disempowerment, which allows us to divide the film into three stages: (1) aggregation, where Megan receives her weapon from the symbolic community but represents an uncanny, threatening force within it; (2) disaggregation, where Megan is disempowered by her symbolic community and used as bait; (3) reaggregation, where Megan—through an unauthorized act—once again seizes power and performs a cleansing sacrifice that leads to her unambivalent recognition by her symbolic community. Just as importantly, the film is structured by a thrice-posed question, revolving around the enigmatic desire of Woman. Bigelow transforms Freud's question What does woman want?, into the question, Why does a beautiful woman want to become a cop? For the following discussion it is imperative to remember that in the cultural construction of femininity, which Bigelow reinstates and critiques, woman's desire functions paradigmatically as that which is excluded from the symbolic order of patriarchal culture, appearing thus as a threat. As the embodiment of the excluded desire of a marginalized woman who usurps power, Eugene represents an overdetermined symptom. I want to suggest, therefore, that it is not only woman's position that is undecidable in this film, to recall Kristeva's argument; undecidable also is the subject of the symptom—is it Megan or the symbolic order of patriarchy?

As already noted, indeterminacy exists at the very outset of the film, inherent in the contradictory evaluation of a woman's ascension to power. For Megan, her entrance into the police force is a resurrection, while for her peers it is a form of murder; she represents for them Medusa, at worse, and an enigma, at best. During her first patrol duty, her black partner raises the crucial question for the first time, asking why she had entered the force: "So Turner, how come, for the action?" Her response is, "Ever since I was a kid . . . I wanta shoot people." After a horrified "no kidding" on his part, mutual laughter lightens up the scene, and her partner signals that he has accepted her with the sentence "You're O.K., Turner." This exchange is followed by Megan's first murder. As Megan gazes through the window of the diner she enters with her partner so that he can "take a leak," she begins to survey the supermarket on the other side of the street. She notes two unidentified shoppers, Eugene and the burglar, then focuses on the hands of the cashier, then more closely on Eugene and finally on the burglar who is now threatening the cashier with a gun.

Three aspects of this scene are worth highlighting at this point: First, as Megan looks through two panes of glass, the window of the diner and that of the supermarket, Bigelow shifts the focus so that first the sign "Hot Coffee" outside the diner's window is out of focus as the camera centers on the supermarket, briefly in focus and then again out of focus before the camera returns to the diner and Megan's gaze. This shift in focus entwines the two locales in a way that suggests the fol-

lowing interpretation: The scene in the supermarket is an event occurring on Megan's "mind screen,"[26] a fantasy-representation utilizing her
omnipotence of thought and staging the uncanny realization of her unconscious desire. For, having given a signifer to her desire—"I wanta
shoot people"—and then laughingly disavowing the truth of this articulation, she now performs this desire. She shoots the burglar who
threatens a markedly feminized boy at the cash register.

Second, with this episode the issue of the "primal scene"[27] is introduced, reinforcing the question of woman's desire. For the supermarket scene repeats Megan's failure at the outset of the film, in the
police exercise. Once again she is the voyeur of, and intruder upon, a
scene of violence between two people, and once again she fails within
the symbolic codes of her community because she reacts instinctually.
As in the first scene, her overreaction is coterminous with an unreflected
murder of the father figure. The question this scene raises is that of
Megan's motivation. Is she drawn to the hold-up, and does she shoot
because she represents the law or rather because this particular setting
offers her an opportunity to exercise her murderous desire? Does she
desire the law as a mediation of the death drive, or does she desire unmitigated violence?

Finally, the scene introduces the Jew Eugene as Megan's counterpart. He receives the burglar's weapon as if by divine gift. While he is lying on the floor, shielding himself from random gunfire, the weapon
drops from above his head and comes to rest next to him. He is implicitly called up by Megan, invented by her omnipotent fantasy so that, as
her doppelgänger, he may put her desire into effect, while she has to subject herself to the law's censure and the humiliation of being disarmed
by her chief, Stan Wood. The supermarket sequence ends as Megan's
partner enters upon the scene and gives out a gasp of horror, taking back
his previous approval. What has been established is that Turner is precisely *not* O.K. She has actuated the narrative confessed earlier to her
partner—"I wanta shoot people." As her partner's disapproving reaction wakes Megan up from her trance, making her stare back in horror
at the result of her violence, Eugene takes the burglar's gun.

The symbolic community proffers a nonambiguous interpretation
of her act. Megan is seen as a danger both to the community and, due to
her recklessness, to herself. By continuing to murder in her name, Eugene legitimizes the verdict of the superego, proving that Stan Wood's
judgment is adequate. At the same time he performs the destructive instinctual desire which Megan has to deny, so that in his work of death
the agency of the superego and that of the instinctual drives intersect.
He combines in his body all three positions of the primal scene: the mas-

culine figure who threatens, the feminine figure who is threatened, and the intruder who watches. In the scene where he aims the purloined gun at his mirrored reflection, a narcissistic jubilation—as Lacan describes the mirror-stage in a child's development—is condensed with the knowledge of one's alienation that is always implicated in acts of integrated self-fashioning. This alienation within the imaginary always appears as the site of aggressiveness. As Richard Boothby notes, "Imaginary identity involves exclusion and also violence. Its integrity and form are threatened by pressure from the unrepresented, to which it reacts with anxiety and aggression."[28]

This representation of Eugene raises the following conceptual problem. The imaginary unity—Eugene and his mirror-image, which is to be transformed or rather reduced to a unity of Eugene and Megan—turns into a source of deadly violence directed at people outside this dyad. This violence emerges, furthermore, due to the pressure exercised by that which remains unrepresented within the symbolic order: the reality of death and/or "excess, jouissance or the immensity of woman's desires and their excessive claims."[29] As I have already suggested, the ambivalence inherent in the mediation of death through death is such that, although the symbolic community ruled by the superego pursues a sublimation of the death drive, it still employs strategies of violent exclusion. Bigelow's conjunction of Eugene with Megan suggests that, since Megan's first narcissistic self-fashioning—her jubilant identification with the officer's blue uniform and shield—was doomed to fail, she now has to fall back upon that force within herself which has led to her exclusion from the symbolic. Her second narcissistic self-fashioning occurs over an identification with the pathological Jew as embodiment of the pure death drive.

In the interim between the time she is charged with unauthorized behavior and the pronouncement of the verdict by internal affairs, Megan is asked a second time about her desire by the C.P.A. Howard, whom Tracy introduces to her in the hope of finding a marriage partner for her friend. Like the other men, Howard is troubled by the fact that she wears a gun and asks her: "You're a good looking woman, beautiful in fact. Why would you want to become a cop?" In this conception, feminine beauty and the desire for violent power cannot be reconciled. Meg answers again by emphasizing her passion for destruction—"I like to slam people's heads against walls"—and adds a smirk meant not to build trust but rather to draw a boundary between herself and this potential suitor. Several hours later, her doppelgänger Eugene kills his first victim, an old man who tries to help him get up after Eugene trips over a curb stone. Eugene thus executes what Megan is convicted of in the very next scene, an "unauthorized use of deadly physical force." He repeats her first murder, but in his execution the motivation is no longer ambivalent. While Megan's act of violence wavers between the exercise of law and murderous desire, Eugene's murder is exclusively instinctual. Significantly, Eugene-as-symptom reports back to Megan both the truth of her desire, which she cannot confront directly, and the projections of her masculine social community, the mistrust articulated by her chief Stan Wood, her potential suitor Howard, and her partner Detective Nick Mann. One question thus remains unanswered: Who is the subject of the symptom represented by Eugene, to whom does the ciphered message return?

This delegation of roles, with Eugene performing the violence Megan imagines, runs through the rest of the film. Megan's disempowerment and demasculization in the scene of her suspension finds its closure in Eugene's next murder. Again he carries out what she can no longer execute because she has been disarmed. Given that the message of her murderous desire returns to her and to Nick in the ciphered form of bullets engraved with her name, what Eugene plays out are the contradictions inherent in her desire and in her evaluation by male peers—the fact that she is dangerous and in danger. In order to signify the aporia of feminine heterosexual desire, Bigelow offers the following constellation: The man who can love Megan only as an unarmed woman (Howard) is not a desirable love object; the man who loves Megan as an armed woman (Eugene) cannot be chosen because the desire involved in this case connotes self-expenditure in the act of violence. Instead of receiving Eugene's semen, Megan hears from Nick Mann about the murderous acts he commits in her name. The engraved bullets are a love letter of sorts in which the repressed death drive returns to its destination. As Nick cannily suggests, "I think somebody out there likes you." By inserting a dream sequence, Bigelow renders this process of symptom-formation more fully. Megan dreams that Eugene pushes her out of a helicopter as they fly over Manhattan, merging what Freud described as the wish fulfillment inherent in dreams with anxiety. He now sports the smile which had accompanied Megan's murderous declarations whenever she was asked to explain why she wanted to be a cop. She is awakened from her dream by Nick's telephone, which summons her to the scene of real murder. Concurrently with her dream in which the unconscious represents her death fantasy to her, the Jewish psychopath Eugene literally performs this death fantasy in proxy, on another body.

At this point, the film resorts unequivocally to anti-Semitic encodings in indexing Eugene's psychosis. Bigelow makes her character legitimize his acts of violence by casting himself in the role of the one chosen by the Jewish God of wrath to carry out together with Megan the divine plot of a vengeful God. While flying over Manhatten in a helicopter, Eugene explains to Megan "that people . . . don't matter much. It's just the two of us." Bigelow exhibits repeatedly Eugene's totalitarian contempt for humanity, making his discourse condone violence as God's design. This psychotic encoding is enhanced when, during a work-out, Eugene hears the voice of this wrathful God telling him "you are God, Eugene . . . put onto them that fear. By your name shall the son of righteousness arise with healing in his wings." He subsequently kills a prostitute whose body is not shown, just as the act of murder remains unrepresented, occurring in the brief darkness of the cut between two scenes. The unrepresented act of violence is framed by the scene in which Eugene receives the message to kill and a scene in which he stands on the balcony of his apartment, naked except for a golden wrist watch, smearing himself with the blood that had soaked into the prostitute's golden-net dress. Covering himself with the blood of an unclean woman is implicitly an act of ritual cleansing. We could speculate that the perforations in the prostitute's golden dress represent tears in a fabric signifying death. Condensed in the image of torn tissue drenched in blood, death is further conjoined with the body of a Jew. In this composite image we have a visual representation of my article's epigraph. Once again, Bigelow's recourse to traditional stereotyping that places prostitute and psychopath in conjunction with filth and death raises the question whether she merely repeats or also critiques such cultural constructions.

The scene of Eugene's confession, mentioned earlier, represents the fourth modality of the primal scene. Eugene wants Megan to aim her weapon at him while he himself is unarmed. She is in the position either of the threatening father or of the intruding child, he in the position of the threatened mother. Bigelow offers here a visual staging of the subject's confrontation with the truth of her desire. In Eugene's desire for her weapon, Megan finds her own desire reflected back to her. He literally bears witness to this desire and, acting as her memory, recalls that "you shot him without blinking an eye." This testimony, however, no longer gives her narcissistic pleasure; it rather articulates what is excluded from the imaginary register, the threatening real. Following Žižek's terms, we could say that what returns to the body of the Jew is Megan's sin. Yet her pressure to sublimate forbids her from recognizing her symptom and acknowledging the ciphered message he brings her. Resorting instead to Nick Mann's discourse of the symbolic order, she recites the sentences an officer of the law is obligated to utter in making an arrest, blotting out the discourse of her unconscious drives spoken to her by Eugene: "You would do what I do if you knew yourself better."

Her reintegration begins precisely when she recants all complicity with her murderous desire. Whereas Eugene's desire had embarrassed her so that she had followed his instructions only hesitatingly, she now, of her own free will, aims her weapon at her symptom. In so doing she decides *against* a violence emanating from her imaginary, from her *mind screen* (for which Eugene offers the conflicting definition "the two of us—we could share"), and *against* his message that "death is the greatest kick of all." She unambivalently opts *for* the symbolic law that had up to that point liminalized her. She repudiates her symptom, hoping that in so doing she might overcome the split within herself, and thus also her embodiment of uncanny difference within a masculine community. This split in the subject's texture—to recall again my epigraph—represents death over the body of the Jew. What needs to be emphasized, however, is that the truth of the desire she now represses is identical with the projections of her male colleagues. Nick can begin to trust her only after her knowledge of and desire for death are irrevocably excluded.

The orgasm of Megan's symptom, coupling sexual and destructive desire, is interrupted as Megan refuses to fulfill Eugene's pathological drive and instead subjects herself to Nick's authorized use of deadly physical force. The attempt to return to it is repeated a few more times, until it finds completion in the concluding duel between Megan and Eugene. Each case reenacts the Oedipal triangle of the initial primal scene, as discussed in detail in the last section of this chapter. In Eugene's murder of Tracy (who is the object of Megan's implicit homosexual desire) we can see a repetition of the very first scene and of the supermarket scene. Megan's impotence is heightened here insofar as she cannot hinder the threatening father figure from killing the mother of two small children. At the same time, Eugene once more reflects Megan's desire back to her, since she is now in the position he was in earlier, forced to watch him the way he watched her kill the burglar. This is a further symptomatization of her sin.

After this scene Megan is asked one last time about her desire. While sitting in a police car with Nick, waiting to ambush Eugene, whom they expect to return in search of the gun he has hidden in a park, Nick asks, "So what made you want to become a cop?" Megan now answers without smiling, "Him." Nick responds by merely nodding agreement. Significantly, Megan now indicates by the third person pronoun that her desire for death is identical with Eugene. In so doing, she signifies that her desire for death and its effacement are coterminous with the stereotype of the Jew who has money and political influence and is a psychopath to boot. Since she can now give a concrete name to her desire, she can also efface it. In this final answer, the knowledge of death as a threat, as a ripping of the subject's narcissistic texture, is contained and mediated because the desire to know death is transformed from verb to noun. The act of "knowing death" no longer references an eroticized performance of violence ("I wanta shoot people"); rather, by being given a body with a name—"him"—the drive as verb is fixed to a nominal representation. As soon as it is given a name that designates a pathological Jewish body, death assumes the modality of mediation and can be negotiated within an economy of sacrifice. The disturbing aspect of Bigelow's cinematic rhetoric is that such a denomination is contingent upon the complete eradication of the Jew Eugene's subjectivity. As Barthes argues, the stereotype "is that emplacement of discourse where the body is missing, where one is sure the body is not,"[30] that is to say, where all individuality has been eradicated and replaced by a cliché.

At the same time, however, Bigelow's solution remains ambivalent in that the Jew Eugene—fully transformed into the dead body of a stereotype—can be eliminated only after he endangers and disempowers the authorized representative of the law, an action for which Bigelow's film offers two visual representations. In the first scene, Megan handcuffs Nick to the steering wheel because she wants to catch Eugene alone. The light she follows into the park, where she believes Eugene is searching for his gun, proves to be a decoy; Eugene appears instead behind the police car, threatens Nick with his weapon, but is prevented from killing him by Megan, who returns just in time to shoot at Eugene. The figural constellation is identical to the one in the supermarket: Megan disrupts a conflictual dyad of men, with Eugene assuming the position of the burglar, and Nick, castrated because he is chained to the steering wheel, taking on the position of the feminized boy at the cash register. This constellation is repeated once more in the next scene, with Nick and Megan returning to her apartment where Eugene is also surreptitiously seeking refuge. After Megan comments to Nick, "I almost got you killed," her symptom logically carries out her fear. After making love with Megan, Nick enters the bathroom and is shot by Eugene, who takes Nick's place in Megan's bed and, in an act of rape, completes the interrupted orgasm of the earlier scene. Megan reciprocates his penetration by shooting at him. Whereas in the earlier scene Eugene's erotic desire was translated into a demand to be mortally threatened by Megan, his desire for destruction is now erotically manifested as rape.

This particular sequence can be designated as the core of the primal scene. Eugene, in the position of the voyeur, intrudes upon the sexual union of Megan and Nick, wounds and castrates the paternal figure, rapes the maternal figure, but—just as in the film's opening scene—the mother shoots back. In order to decode fully this modality of the Oedipal triangle, we must recall that Megan had tried to arrest her father, that she repeatedly disobeyed the orders of her symbolic father, Stan Wood, that she experienced no solidarity from her mother, that, indeed, the mother figure in the primal scene of the police exercise had perfidiously repaid her effort by shooting her. At this later stage in her development, all unauthorized aspects of Megan have been split off and confined to Eugene's body. He is the intruder who wounds the paternal figure, just as he is the one for whom the maternal figure shows no solidarity. Moving into the position of the mother who has the final shot, Megan has fully shed the monstrosity of being the one who threatens and the humiliation of being the one who fails. At this point her empowerment is complete.

The ambivalence that attends Bigelow's representation of a woman's ascension to power dictates that even as Megan cleanses herself of her negative traits, she also triumphs over the symbolic community. As agent of Megan's desire, Eugene punishes the agency of the law that had tried to castrate her. In an overdetermined manner, he unmans Nick: He wounds him physically with a wound that implicitly leads to impotence, he takes Nick's place in Megan's bed, and he incapacitates Nick as detective and agent of the law. The question Bigelow leaves unanswered is once against that of motivation. Does Eugene, symptom of Megan's desire, disempower Nick because he ascribes guilt to her actions, because he doesn't trust Megan and keeps her under surveillance, or because he projects the image of a murderess onto her?

The paradox we experience in the film's final sequences is that Megan becomes now truly dangerous, fulfilling the fears of her social community. She has literally allowed Nick to be castrated, and has brought dishonor to her chief. And yet our sympathy is unequivocally with her. We no longer perceive her as threatening, because all instances of threat have been displaced onto a psychotic Jewish body. In the process of Eugene's pathologizing, Megan's final "unauthorized use of deadly physical force," executed with a purloined weapon and uniform, is fully sanctioned. At the same time the two problems raised in the initial primal scene and repeated throughout the diverse modalities I have been tracing, find an appropriate resolution. Megan now assumes the position of the woman who has the last word, with the aspects of failure and self-endangerment—which had belonged to the

position of the intruding voyeur—fully confined to Eugene's pathological body.

In the last sequence Megan finally confronts the truth of her desire.
As Eugene and Megan shoot each other, she takes the position in which
Eugene first saw her in the supermarket and the position of his mirror-
image in the rest room of the stock exchange. She gives Eugene the death
he desires, as a final repetition of the death she brought to the burglar.
She shoots only three times, recalling how the burglar had dropped his
gun after her first three shots, the other three bullets entering his unarmed body. This final killing is, indeed, a form of autodestruction. In
overcoming her destructive drives, Megan conquers the submerged
agency of the internal Other within her psychic apparatus. But insofar as
Eugene, as her symptom, not only made manifest the truth of her desire
but also fulfilled the anxious expectations of Megan's peers about her,
his disintegration effaces all destructive aspects connected with Megan's
position within the symbolic. The latent message—Megan protects herself and her society by way of this sacrifice, using death to work against
death—is replaced by a second, manifest message: Megan protects herself and her social community from a Jewish psychopath. The tear in the
social fabric, signifying death, is given a name. The disturbing question
we are left with is whether, in her bleak resolution of the conflict posed
by a woman's ascension to power in the symbolic, Bigelow deconstructs
male anxieties about empowered women or merely perpetuates a cliché.
Equally undecidable are the implications of her proposed configuration.
For she resorts to traditional stereotypes of the *femme fatale*—the fascinating but sexually withholding, powerful but lethal woman—and du-
plicates this stereotype by constructing the Other of Woman, her
uncanny internal difference as a pathological Jew, only to celebrate his
sacrifice as a form of "resurrection."

The Risky Moments of a Narrative

In order to bring together the interpretive strands presented so far, I will
now turn to my final theoretical concern, a narratological analysis of the
way representations not only enact a thematic tension between conflict
and mediation but are also structured by the tension *between,* and resolution *of,* heterogeneity and homogeneity. The categories developed by
Roland Barthes in his "Introduction to the Structural Analysis of Narratives" are most useful for this endeavor. Starting from the premise that
a discourse is a long "sentence," Barthes argues that a structural analysis involves distinguishing several levels or instances of description and
placing them within a hierarchical (integrational) perspective. Narratives waver thus between conflictual instances and a mediated hierar-

chy. To understand a narrative, Barthes contends, "is not merely to fol-low the unfolding of the story, it is also to recognize its construction in 'storeys,' to project the horizontal concatenations of the narrative 'thread' onto an implicitly vertical axis."[31] The three levels he pro-poses—*functions* (irreducible units), *actions,* and *narration*—are bound together according to a mode of progressive integration.

Mixing psychoanalytic with structuralist discursive models, Barthes claims that the "essence of a function is, so to speak, the seed that it sows in the narrative, planting an element that will come to fruition later," a polyvalent detail whose final meaning is fixed only when the narrative is considered as a whole. But even at the most basic level, Barthes distinguishes two narrative forces: units either have cor-relate units on the same level, belonging to what he calls the distribu-tional function and involving metonymic relata, or their saturation requires a change of level, so that they belong to the class of integra-tional functions and they form metaphoric relata. In the act of inter-preting, we treat each narrative element as a polysemic detail that spreads its meaning in a seemingly unrestrained manner on the selec-tive level of individual sequences, and we try to integrate it into a co-herent meaning on the combinatory level of narration.

My proposal, then, is to read the plot of integration in *Blue Steel* si-multaneously as a metaphor for the emergence of women's desire for power as this is interlinked with the control of empowerment, and as a metaphor for the structure of narratives, tracing the analogy between the integration of an unrestrained member into a community, on the the-matic level, and the integration of unrestrained representational details, on the structural level. In so doing, I follow Barthes' suggestion that what distinguishes the integrational from the merely distributional function is the fact that "the action to which it refers open[s] (or con-tinue[s], or close[s]) an alternative that is of direct consequence for the subsequent development of the story, in short that it inaugurate[s] or conclude[s] an uncertainty" (94). A significant narrative sequence is de-fined by the risk it entails, by the conflict it not only thematizes but also structurally enacts, calling for mediation in the form of narrative repe-tition or closure. Precisely because a sequence involves moments of risk, we are justified in analyzing it.

The risk identified by Barthes is produced because the "danger-ous" detail is not bound in *solidarity* to an antecedent or a preceding de-tail; at every point "an alternative—and hence a freedom of meaning—is possible," so that a sequence is "a threatened logical unit." The risk en-acted by these narrative details or sequences can, however, be mediated as the process of articulation and segmentation, which produces units, is translated into a process of integration. Through our interpretive gestures, risky and threatened sequences on the distributional axis are gathered together on the higher levels of narration, so that the structural trajectory of each narrative analysis moves from an interpretation of the individual articulation (the distributional form) to the production of an integrated meaning. Integration joins what has been disjoined, compensates for the seemingly unmasterable complexity of each individual unit, guides the understanding of discontinuous elements, simultaneously contiguous and heterogeneous, prevents meaning from dangling. Narrative works through the convergence of two movements. In a gesture of narrative conflict, "the structure ramifies, proliferates, uncovers itself"; in a gesture of narrative mediation, it "recovers itself, pulls itself together." Barthes can conclude, therefore, that "the 'reality' of a sequence lies not in the 'natural' succession of the actions composing it but in the logic there exposed, risked and satisfied" (124).

If we revisit, with Barthes's theoretical perspective in mind, the scenes I have been discussing as distributional moments in Bigelow's film, the following pattern emerges. The nine modalities of the primal scene thematically *and* structurally enact the translation of risky moments and their precarious plurality of alternatives into an integrated solidarity of sequences which Barthes defines as a narrative's "reality." Due to the fact that each individual scene operates with a figural triad, our narrative integration involves joining separate sequences into one logical sentence. While the distributional articulation of each separate scene produces suspense, the process of integration offers a coherent reading of these threatened narrative movements that repeatedly stage a stage wherein a father figure, a mother figure and a voyeuristic, intruding child are implicated in a mutual articulation of violence. In the reading I have offered, an interpretation of Megan's psychic trajectory toward reintegration emerged as I joined the separate modalities on the distributional level into an integrated and extended narrative sentence. In other words, the integration of individual scenes in the act of interpretation had as its thematic correlative a plot of integration by virtue of which the threat emanating from a liminalized woman could be mediated. In the last section of my article, I will briefly demonstrate this twofold act of integration by visualizing the transformations of a basic figural triangle, with [D] indicating literal death, and [W] a wounding, a castration, or figural death.

I have argued that each of these scenes in question structurally enacts the Oedipal triangle—with repetitions and transformations—in which the child intrudes upon the parental dyad, displacing a threatening father in an effort to protect the mother. In the first scene Megan, as the child-subject who seeks to ascertain her legitimacy in the symbolic, disrupts the parental relation, kills the paternal figure, but finds no sol-idarity with the maternal one, who in turn shoots her. This scene repre-sents her failure at integrating herself in the symbolic community, showing her as yet unable to take on the position of the father. She is not yet on the side of the law.

husband (D)   wife

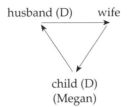

child (D)
(Megan)

The second scene in the supermarket modulates this constellation with respect to the figure in the maternal position (the feminized cashier) who does not shoot back. Megan, however, is still unable to take on the position of the father, whose representative—the burglar—she has successfully killed; instead, a split between the subject and its symp-tom is introduced.

burglar (D)   cashier

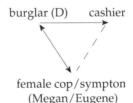

female cop/sympton
(Megan/Eugene)

In the third scene, which I have called the mirror-phase of vio-lence, Eugene takes on all available positions—symptomizing Megan's conflating phantasy of threatening paternity, threatened maternity, and intruding voyeur into a narcissistic short circuit of murderous desire.

Eugene who shoots   the mirror image (W)

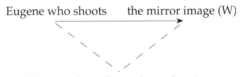

Eugene who reflects about shooting

The fourth scene, the peripeteia, enacts the first direct confronta-tion between the doppelgänger Eugene and Megan. It refers analepti-cally to scene two, with Eugene articulating a desire to be in the position of the threatened father figure, as well as proleptically to scene nine, where the risk enacted but also interrupted in the fourth scene finds its resolution in the elimination of the symptom. In both cases the maternal position remains empty.

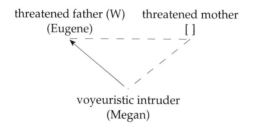

threatened father (W) threatened mother
(Eugene)   [ ]

voyeuristic intruder
(Megan)

The fifth scene depicts Eugene's last successful murder, with Megan's friend Tracy as his victim. Since in this modality the threatening father figure succeeds in killing the threatened maternal figure, while the intruding child is reduced to the role of impotent voyeur, we have in this scene the traumatic center of the film. This negative resolution of the parental threat literally consummates what the child fears in the primal scene—the father castrating both mother and child.

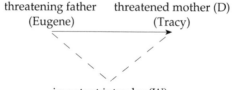

threatening father threatened mother (D)
(Eugene)   (Tracy)

impotent intruder (W)

The sixth scene, in which Megan returns home with the impotent father (whose menace she has diffused by threatening to arrest him) only to find Eugene in her parents' living room, again relates back to the supermarket scene. The father figure is now defenseless. The threat to the maternal figure, whose solidarity with Megan is unreliable, is now in turn symptomized by the intruding child's double.

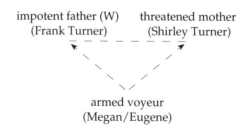

impotent father (W) threatened mother
(Frank Turner) (Shirley Turner)

armed voyeur
(Megan/Eugene)

In the seventh scene we experience the first of two representations of a direct threat to the law. Significantly, the agent of the law, Nick, is in the position of the threatened maternal figure (castrated because handcuffed to the steering wheel). The psychopath, Eugene, is in the position of the threatening father qua criminal, and Megan is once again in the position of the armed intruder. We have a repetition of the supermarket scene, except that the criminal is not yet eliminated.

threatening and threatened psychopath (W)   threatened detective
                    (Eugene)   (Nick)

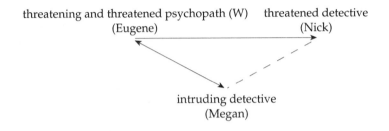

intruding detective
(Megan)

The eighth scene coalesces the mock conflict of the police lesson with the real murder of the supermarket scene, returning violence to the bedchamber. The alternation in the distribution of positions is significant, marking the resolution of the risk represented in the other sequences. Nick is now in the position of the nonthreatening father, impotent because he is naked. Meg is now literally in the position of the mother, Eugene in the position of the voyeur who intrudes upon the parental coitus, a position delegated up to that point to Megan. He succeeds in wounding the father, but, as in the first scene, the mother shoots back. The crucial change concerns Megan, who, once she has achieved the feminine position denied to her/rejected by her up to that point, now moves from passive voyeur to active murderess by transforming her initially affective, unreliable shooting to a calculated killing in the service of the law. As in the first scene, the one who shoots last is the winner.

father (W)   mother
(Nick)   (Megan)

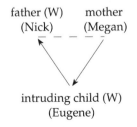

intruding child (W)
(Eugene)

Finally, all risky moments are resolved in the scene in which Megan destroys her symptom, in a repetition of the binary relation of scene four. The significant transformation here is that Megan now condenses in her body both the position of the threatening and threatened father and that of the threatened mother who survives the conflict because she shoots last, with Eugene now exclusively in Megan's initial position of intruder. In diametrical opposition to scene five (Tracy's murder) which depicted Megan at her most impotent, we encounter for the first time a representation of Megan's full potency due to the effacement of the intruder. An integration of all eight sequences into a logical narrative sentence leads to the interpretation that Megan now has assumed full power because she has successfully split off the third position and confined it to her symptom. Furthermore, this is the only scene (excepting the first mock conflict) in which the third, as representative of an uncanny difference disrupting the sexual qua violent exchange between the maternal and the paternal, is ultimately eliminated. What this suggests is that the foreclosure of psychosis, achieved through a sacrifice of the psychopathological aspect of Megan—of her internal uncanny difference—transforms into the totalized destruction of difference in the symbolic.

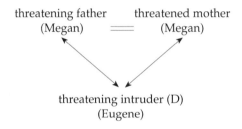

With this last image, the process of narrative integration structurally subdues the heterogeneous risk each individual sequence depicted, even as the risk to Megan's self-preservation, enacted in each individual scene, is finally overcome from a thematic point of view. The narrative as a whole mediates the conflict each detail or individual sequence celebrates. The meaning and effect of a narrative, therefore, resides in the tension between distributional freedom experienced as risk and integrational constraint; between the articulated detail and its ideological integration in a culturally accepted code. As my reading of *Blue Steel* has repeatedly suggested, the threat emanating from an armed woman in uniform is diffused (one could say discursively disarmed) by virtue of the resolution of the primal scene and its Oedipal configuration. However, acquiescence of the last scene resonates with the conflictive risks of the scenes leading to it, which staged and celebrated the violence of Megan and her symptom. The integration of the narrative, which occurs as each viewer constructs an interpretation by joining the film's disparate sequences into a coherent sentence, covers—recovering and uncovering in one and the same gesture—the subversive conflict of the detail. Barthes concludes his "Introduction" by finding "significant that it is at the same moment (around the age of three) that the little human 'invents' at once sentence, narrative and the Oedipus."[32] If we follow Barthes's claim that all representations have at their source the conjunction of sentence, narrative, and a story about integration into a social community that entails negotiating voyeurism with the issues of violence, sexuality, and gender, then Bigelow's film offers us a paradigmatic example of a self-reflexive text commenting on its own narrative structure.

As a final gesture of interpretive integration, I could, then, end my discussion by asserting that ultimately *Blue Steel* is about language, about the two forces in narrative, about the way conflict and mediation are written into any visualized narrative interpretation. But should we not ask, What exactly does the mediation we are left with look like, what are its gains, its failures, its exclusions? At the end of the film, the narrative suspense moves into acquiescence, and the psychoanalytic and social themes depicted are resolved in Megan's fulfillment of her Oedipal trajectory. She has transferred her primal scene into a "coitus" of violence—rape and the subsequent murder of the assailant—only to end up integrated into her symbolic community, but in an image of a cadaverous fixity. Do we read this last image as a representation of female potency or female disempowerment? The first interpretation is supported by the fact that the other men in blue no longer treat Megan as an uncanny Other but as one of their own. The latter is supported by the fact that Megan has lost her feminine specificity and undergone a form of psychic death. Having eliminated her symptom, which had reported to her the truth of her femininity and her destructive desire, she is now merely an instrument of the symbolic order. However, if we moved beyond the issue of gender, we could also argue that Megan uses this final murder to defend herself against an externalized realization of death; her act represents a triumph over the violence of the imaginary agency of her drives, as a sign of their sublimation.

Whatever interpretation one chooses, as individual sequences are integrated into a coherent narrative, the achieved mediation ultimately ricochets back into discursive conflict. We can follow the ideological reading implied by the genre of the cop movie, and see Megan's final position as a form of success. The destructive drives, represented by virtue of being fixed onto dangerous, uncanny members of the community—the stereotypes of the armed Woman and the pathological Jew—have been curbed and effaced. But Bigelow interjects a number of ambivalences into the last shots of the listless Megan, aided by undistinguishable men in blue. Even though the other cops support her wounded body, they do so only after taking away her gun. She is integrated but she is depleted. She has the phallus but only in a gesture of disempowerment which has disintegrated her narcissistically informed imaginary and her symptom. The danger of psychosis—as a foreclosure of the symbolic law, as an expenditure of the self in its destructive energies—has been successfully warded off, but with it also her energy and sexual heterogeneity. Megan's desire for a psychopath and her autoeroticism are overcome, but through a course of action in which desire itself seems to have been depleted. To return to Whitford's suggestion, Bigelow reveals to us that the question of feminine desire means that women must learn to negotiate their death drives in the symbolic, moving beyond the imaginary. The conflict she raises, however, about women moving into the symbolic, is one that our image repertoire has not yet been able to resolve. For the threat connected with women's desire for power we have as yet no mediating representations.

Notes

1. Hans Bächtold-Stäubli, *Handwörterbuch des deutschen Aberglaubens,* vol. 4 (Berlin: de Gruyter, 1987), 831. For a discussion of the iconography of violence in modern German representations of Jews, see Birgid Erdle, *Identifikation und Heteronomie: Zum Diskurs der Gewalt bei Gertrud Kolmar* (forthcoming).

2. See Bram Dijkstra, *Idols of Perversity. Fantansies of Feminine Evil in Fin-de-Siècle Culture* (Oxford: Oxford University Press, 1986).

3. Sigmund Freud, *Interpretation of Dreams,* in *Standard Edition IV/V* (London: Hogarth Press, 1953); see also Freud's lecture on "Femininity," in *New Introductory Lectures, Standard Edition XXII* (London: Hogarth Press, 1964).

4. In "Repression" (1915), in *Standard Edition XIV* (London: Hogarth Press, 1957), Freud uses the concept "Vorstellungs-Repräsentanz" (ideational representation as distinct from, but working analogously to, affect) to designate the drive's representative within the psychic apparatus. The relation of the somatic to the psychic is that of the drive to its representation. The somatic drive can be repressed and thus inscribed in the unconscious only insofar as it is fixed to a representation: "We have reason to assume that there is a primal repression, a first phase of repression, which consists in the psychical representative of the drive being denied entrance into the conscious. With this a fixation is established; the representative in question persists unaltered from then onwards and the instinct remains attached to it" (148).

5. For more recent films on this subject, see Alan Pakula's *Presumed In-nocent* (1990) and Paul Verhoeven's *Basic Instinct* (1992). See also Joan Smith's discussion of this film genre in *Misogynies* (London: Faber, 1989).

6. I will return to a more detailed discussion of Roland Barthes's "Intro-duction to the Structural Analysis of Narratives," in *Image-Music-Text*, trans. Stephen Heath (New York: Hill & Wang, 1978).

7. Julia Kristeva, *Revolution in Poetic Language*, trans. Margaret Waller (New York: Columbia University Press, 1984), 75.

8. The term is borrowed from Tzvetan Torodov, *Nous et les Autres. La réflexion française sur la diversité humaine* (Paris: Seuil, 1989). See also Sander Gilman, *The Jew's Body* (New York: Routledge, 1991).

9. Fredric Jameson, *The Political Unconscious: Narrative as a Socially Sym-bolic Act* (Ithaca: Cornell University Press, 1981).

10. In *The Kristeva Reader*, ed. Toril Moi (Oxford: Basil Blackwell, 1986). See also Juliet Flower MacCannell, who argues in *The Regime of the Brother: After the Patriarchy* (New York: Routledge, 1991) that the key question we have been avoiding is what the value of woman in the modern social and sexual arrange-ment might be, given that there has traditionally been a failure to integrate women into the symbolic. She sees literature as a means of analyzing the sym-bolic, and potentially contributing to its reframing in such a way that the sym-bolic might be uncoupled from "patriarchy," or what she prefers to call "the hegemony of the imaginary in the Regime of the Brother" (39). Despite the dis-turbing modality she presents, Bigelow's film attempts precisely to refigure the symbolic with respect to woman's integration into it. She suggests that what has been excluded from the symbolic community, namely, women's desire for power, appears as a threat; she also offers an exploration of the symbolic system that might support this desire, mediating its violence.

11. Slavoj Žižek, *For They Know Not What They Do: Enjoyment as a Political Factor* (London: Verso, 1991), 192.

12. Margaret Whitford, "Irigaray, Utopia and the Death Drive," in *Engag-ing with Irigaray: Feminist Philosophy and Modern European Thought*, ed. Carolyn L. Burke, Naomi Schor, and Margaret Whitford (New York: Columbia University Press, 1994, 381.

13. Margaret Whitford, *Luce Irigaray: Philosophy in the Feminine* (New York: Routledge, 1991), especially chap. 6.

14. See Elisabeth Bronfen, *Over Her Dead Body: Death, Femininity and the Aesthetic* (Manchester/New York: Manchester University Press/Routledge, 1992).

15. For a discussion of the ideological implications of the monster in American horror movies, see Hans Schmid, *Fenster zum Tod. Raum im Horrorfilm* (Munich: Belleville, 1993).

16. I have borrowed the concept of uncanny otherness from Shoshana Felman's "Rereading Femininity," *Yale French Studies* 62 (1981), 19–44, though she does not make the connection to Jewishness. For a discussion of the concept of the uncanny, see Freud, "The Uncanny," in *Standard Edition XVII* (London: Hogarth Press, 1955), 217–56.

17. Paul Ricoeur, *Freud & Philosophy: An Essay on Interpretation*, trans. Denis Savage (New Haven: Yale University Press, 1970), 309.

18. See *Feminine Sexuality: Jacques Lacan and the École Freudienne*, ed. Juliet Mitchell and Jacqueline Rose (New York: Norton, 1982).

19. Slavoj Žižek, "Roberto Rossellini: Die Frau als Symptom des Mannes," *Lettre International* (Spring 1991), 80.

20. Slavoj Žižek, "Symptom," in *Feminism and Psychoanalysis: A Critical Dictionary*, ed. Elizabeth Wright et al. (Cambridge: Basil Blackwell, 1992), 425.

21. Jean Baudrillard, *L'Échange symbolique et la mort* (Paris: Gallimard, 1976).

22. For a discussion of initiation rites and liminality, see Arnold van Gennep, *The Rites of Passage*, trans. Monika B. Vizedom and Gabrille L. Caffee (Chicago: University of Chicago Press, 1960); and Victor Turner, *The Ritual Process: Structure and Anti-Structure* (Ithaca: Cornell University Press, 1977).

23. Žižek, "Symptom," 425.

24. See Jacques Lacan, *Le Séminaire XX. Encore* (Paris: Seuil, 1975); and Georges Bataille, *La part maudite* (Paris: Minuit, 1967).

25. The last image of Megan recalls Freud's argument in his lecture on "Femininity," that the difficult development to femininity exhausts the woman at thirty of her possibilities, so that she often "frightens us by her psychical rigidity and unchangeability" (126); also Sarah Kofman's response, that here Freud unwittingly discloses how the prescribed position of femininity is a death sentence for women (*The Enigma of Woman: Woman in Freud's Writings*, trans. Catherine Porter [Ithaca: Cornell University Press, 1985]). The radical difference in Bigelow's film, though not necessarily less bleak, is that the exhausted woman has now returned to her initial bisexual position, but is not, as Freud would have it, defined in relation to the phallus but rather in relation to *and* owner of the phallus.

26. I have taken this term from Bruce F. Kawin (*Mindscreen: Bergman, Godard, and First-Person Film* [Princeton: Princeton University Press, 1978]), who coined it to describe how cinematic first-person narrative signifies what a person thinks. The category *mindscreen* refers to the field of the mind's eye as opposed to *subjective camera*, denoting only the field of the character's physical eye (10).

27. Freud uses this term to describe the scene of parental sexual relations, which the child observes or rather fantasizes, and which she or he interprets as an act of violence on the part of the father.

28. Richard Boothby, *Death and Desire: Psychoanalytic Theory in Lacan's Return to Freud* (New York: Routledge, 1991), 39.

29. Margaret Whitford, "Irigaray, Utopia and the Death Drive," 15.

30. Roland Barthes, *Roland Barthes by Roland Barthes,* trans. Richard Howard (New York: Hill & Wang, 1977), 90.

31. Barthes, "Introduction to the Structural Analysis of Narratives," 87.

32. Ibid., 124.

6

Shattered Hopes: On *Blue Velvet*

Susan Derwin

The new is the longing for the new, not the new itself. This is the curse of everything new. Being a negative of the old, the new is subservient to the old while considering itself to be Utopian.

—Theodor Adorno, *Aesthetic Theory*[1]

Is there a utopian impulse in David Lynch's *Blue Velvet* (1986)? Can we read signs of longing for the new in the lurid, even grotesque, world depicted in the film? That *Blue Velvet* is deeply enmeshed in questions of longing and desire is apparent by its structure: Modeled after Hollywood film noir detective stories, it tracks a young man's researches into the murky depths subtending the primary-color world of small-town America, represented here as Lumberton. *Blue Velvet* is so successful in presenting the allure of the quest that the actual discovery of the solutions to the mysteries impelling the plot seem incidental in comparison to the quest itself.[2] The downward trajectory of the film, which moves into a "negative," subterranean space seemingly more primal and passionate than the surface world of conventional middle-American life, constitutes the locus of the film's vitality. Such a vertical flight bespeaks a hope that there is such a thing as depth, that more does exist beneath the deadening surface of the immediate. Indeed, the strong, if diverse, responses to *Blue Velvet* may reflect the film's power to tap into its viewers' same hope, even if such hope is ultimately frustrated.[3]

The film's plot structure interweaves a mystery with a love story. Dorothy Vallens is a nightclub singer whose husband and child have been abducted by a drug trafficker named Frank Booth. Frank has kidnapped Dorothy's family in order to secure sexual favors from Dorothy, whose performance of the song "Blue Velvet" holds a particular fascination for Frank. Frank is so entranced by Dorothy's rendition of the song that he forces Dorothy to wear a blue velvet robe while he subjects her to sadomasochistic abuse. He also fondles a swatch of the robe as she sings the song in the Slow Club. Through a series of events, Jeffrey Beaumont, a college student, becomes entangled in Dorothy Vallens's life. Home from school after his father has had a stroke, Jeffrey discovers a severed ear in a field near his house. He immediately delivers it to a detective in the police department who is an acquaintance of his father. That same night, preoccupied by his discovery, Jeffrey pays a visit to the detective's home. While sympathizing with Jeffrey's restless curiosity, Detective Williams remains unwilling to divulge any information about the mysterious ear. Upon leaving, Jeffrey meets the detective's daughter, Sandy, outside the house. Sandy tells him what she has overheard about the case. She mentions that Dorothy Vallens may in some way be linked to the ear. This piece of information sends Jeffrey on his private path of discovery. His investigation produces two results: It helps him solve the case and it occasions a romance between Sandy and him.

Critics have stressed the oppositional structure of the film. At one extreme, *Blue Velvet* depicts the world of the upstanding inhabitants of Lumberton. Friendly firemen drive through manicured neighborhoods, and crossing guards stop traffic for obedient school children. Teenage life consists of football practices and Saturday night dance parties in basement rumpus rooms, while the Williams and Beaumont families typify the stable domestic values of Lumberton's citizens. At the other extreme is the marginal world of drug trafficking and addiction, sexual perversion, sleazy nightclubs, and carnivalesque grotesquery. The film's absorbing effect is, in part, created through a destabilization of such opposing poles. Jeffrey discovers his affinity with Frank, the sexual pervert, and at least one member of the police force is revealed to be corrupt. Moreover, through slow-motion shots and heightened coloration, the camera defamiliarizes the ordinary. Roses appear too red and jonquils too yellow; firemen wave too slowly, as the canny metamorphoses into the uncanny. By virtue of these alienation devices, the departure from the quotidian world comes to feel, paradoxically, like a relief, a welcome escape from the claustrophobic oppressiveness of middle-American conventions.

Initially, Jeffrey's descent into the underworld proceeds through an act of spectatorship that proves pleasurable and safe. The voyeuristic delights of seeing the dark side of life are figured in several early scenes. In one, Jeffrey breaks into Dorothy Vallens's apartment. When he hears Dorothy entering the apartment he beats a hasty retreat into a closet fitted with louver doors. Dorothy discovers Jeffrey but forces him back into hiding because Frank has arrived. As Jeffrey watches Frank's sexual fantasies come to life, the camera remains in the closet with Jeffrey. It and, by extension, the audience are thus safely installed in the position of voyeur.

In another scene, Jeffrey, on his way to Detective Williams's house, says goodbye to his mother, who is sitting in the living room watching television. The image of a black gun fills the screen. Shortly thereafter, Jeffrey's mother, with his Aunt Barbara, is again watching television. This time on the screen a man slowly ascends a dimly lit staircase. That Jeffrey's mother watches suspense/mystery films suggests the ubiquity of the allure of the criminal world represented in *Blue Velvet*. In addition, these two brief episodes together function as a proleptic *mise-en-scène*, as Jeffrey, too, will climb a dark staircase on his way to Dorothy Vallens's apartment and later will wield a gun.

The heavily coded films on the television screen bespeak the symbiosis between representations of the hidden and the known. These films are literally at home in the Beaumont living room. Like other products of the imagination, including *Blue Velvet*, they figure the desire for the new, or other, through images and terms that simultaneously reflect the structures and strictures of the status quo. In this respect, Jeffrey's venture into the criminal underworld is a double narrative, as much about his entry into the realm of law and order—the social order, the sexual order—as it is about the departure from that order.

Much has been made of the fact that Jeffrey and Frank, the sociopathic deviant, are doubles of one another. Like Frank, Jeffrey is drawn to Dorothy Vallens and strikes her during their sexual encounter. Even Frank is aware of his "inner" resemblance to Jeffrey; he says to Jeffrey, "You're like me." But rather than seeing such parallelism as a testimony to the dark impulses that dwell in the heart of the most upstanding, conventional individual, we could as plausibly say that what Jeffrey experiences as the "other" or repressed in himself is a heightened vision of the norms accepted and propagated by contemporary American society. While seemingly leading him outside the bounds of the ordinary, Jeffrey's investigation introduces him into a realm whose uncanniness can be attributed to the fact that it is an intensification of the ordinary. Deep River Apartments, a kind of Styx on land where Dorothy Vallens lives, is a dark double of its more conventional domestic counterpart. The film calls attention to the mutual implication of the two worlds in numerous scenes by chiastically combining elements from the opposing realms. For example, in the film's opening sequence—the shots of flowers, waving firemen, and schoolchildren—the soundtrack plays Bobby Vinton's version of "Blue Velvet." In another scene, Jeffrey spies on Frank's apartment, and his car radio is tuned to the station whose jingle captures the essence of Lumberton life; with its incorporation of the sound of a falling tree. Frank's apartment is thereby presented as the most menacing yet typical of domestic spaces.

The film figures the opposition between the ordinary and extraordinary as the difference between culture and nature. An early scene captures the war of the insects taking place in the grass. Shortly thereafter, Jeffrey discovers the ear hidden in the grass and teeming with ants. Insofar as these insects evoke the rapacious struggles of the animal kingdom, their presence in the ear suggests that the ear, and the violence its amputation represents, are part of that Darwinian world. The ensuing action is then literally and symbolically embedded in the ear, itself a synecdoche of the now naturalized violent, social world: The camera closes in on the ear and eventually fades to dark, thereby suggesting that it will penetrate this seemingly alien environment. After venturing into the heart of this aural darkness, the camera cuts to the detective's home, as if to establish an equivalence between Jeffrey's pursuit of cultural knowledge and penetration into the secrets of nature.[4] Other natural imagery is interwoven into the narrative. For example, when Jeffrey and Dorothy engage in sadomasochistic sex, the camera cuts first to the image of a candle and then to a roaring flame, as if to suggest that Jeffrey's violent outburst taps into a repressed but elemental force within him. The accompanying sounds of roaring reinforce the idea that the aggression that has burst forth from Jeffrey, the civilized representative of middle-class morality, originates in a deep, primal source.

Jeffrey is filled with voyeuristic glee ("I'm seeing something that was always hidden. I'm involved in a mystery," he tells Sandy) and anxiety ("I wanted to see you. I didn't mean to do anything except see you," he tells Dorothy as she holds him at knife point after discovering him in his closet). Like Jeffrey, Frank is compulsively driven to "see" the other, and his violent encounters with Dorothy illustrate what is at stake in such desire, his own as well as Jeffrey's. During the rape scene, Dorothy extinguishes the lamp and lights a candle, in what is clearly a part of their ritualized encounter. "Now it's dark," Frank says with satisfaction as Dorothy sits down on a chair opposite him in anticipation of his order to bare herself.[5] Frank's ensuing actions reveal that the poor visibility of the scene is not a cause, but a symptom, of a deeper blindness. Frank commands Dorothy to spread her legs. She does so, and he continues, "Wider. Now show it to me," whereupon Dorothy exposes her genitals to his gaze. The more Frank looks at Dorothy, however, the less he actually sees, much less comprehends, the view before him. His perception of Dorothy depends on a logic of narcissistic projection. Fascinated and repelled by the view of Dorothy's genitals, he only "sees" Dorothy as a version of himself. He brandishes a scissors in her face, as if to disavow the threatening female phallus unveiled before him. Such narcissism accounts for the importance of the scene of the paraphernalia of fetishism—the swatch of blue velvet that Frank sucks on and stuffs into Dorothy's mouth, the patently ritualistic nature of the scene (Frank drinks a glass of bourbon, inhales gas from a canister, and demands to be called "Daddy") which enables Frank to conventionalize, and thereby contain, the threat engendered by the view of Dorothy's genitals, and Frank's aversion to Dorothy's gaze, itself the locus of Medusan castrating power (Frank repeatedly forbids Dorothy to look at him). That Frank views Dorothy through the contradictory logic of the fetish—she is phallically endowed but also castrated—may explain why he penetrates Dorothy with his hand: It is as if her (imputed) phallus, or its castration, rendered his own inoperative.[6]

The grim futility of Frank's attempt to "see," and thereby contain, sexual difference is underscored by the film's more general insistence upon the labile nature of sexuality. Whenever sexuality is on display, it always masquerades or impersonates something else. There are numerous moments of such masquerading. Installing Dorothy within a complex narrative of homo- and heterosexual desire, Frank forces Dorothy to play adult, mother, and child to his own assumed adult and infantile roles. It could also be said that Frank and Jeffrey's attraction to Dorothy depends on the fetishistic reduction of her identity to "Blue Velvet," both the song and the fabric. When Frank takes Jeffrey hostage, his homoerotic impulses disguise themselves in violent action. As he prepares to beat up Jeffrey, he enacts a double masquerade: He lip syncs Roy Orbison's recording of "In Dreams" (in an impersonation of an impersonation, since Ben, a drug dealer, had done the same earlier); and he applies red lipstick to himself, in mimicry of Dorothy, and then kisses Jeffrey. One of the most disturbing episodes in the film emphasizes the point that sexuality cannot in itself be seen. Playing the role of slighted suitor, Sandy's boyfriend Mike pursues Sandy and Jeffrey in a car chase. They stop before Jeffrey's house, and Mike jumps out of his car, preparing to fight Jeffrey, when Dorothy enters the frame naked. The violence threatening to erupt between the two boys becomes displaced onto the axis joining Dorothy to the camera. Dorothy is completely exposed to the young men, Sandy, and the viewer, as the camera holds her bruised and battered body in a full frontal shot. Frozen like a stunned animal in headlight beams, she is deprived of her powers of voice, the vehicle of her erotic performance of "Blue Velvet." Far from sexually titillating, the

scene illustrates the violence of Frank's attempt to locate sexual difference through the gaze. No wonder the character displaying the most
uncanny powers of sight is the hardware store manager, who, though
blind, baffles Jeffrey by unfailingly "seeing" how many fingers Jeffrey
holds up before him.

Frank's impotence and narcissistic self-enclosure exemplify the
general state of fathers in the film. During his first visit to the hospital,
Jeffrey finds his father literally tongue tied. With his head immobilized
by a steel brace and his powers of speech impaired, his father struggles
unsuccessfully to communicate. Similarly, when Frank allows Dorothy
to talk to her husband on the telephone, Dorothy cannot understand
what he is saying. Moreover, Jeffrey's father and Dorothy's husband are
figuratively represented as impotent: when Mr. Beaumont collapses
while watering the lawn, the garden hose he is holding by his groin
mockingly shoots a stream of water into the air, as if in parody of phallic ejaculation. Dorothy's kidnapped husband, who is unable to protect
his child and wife, is the owner of the ear Jeffrey discovers, and its amputation suggests the husband's symbolic castration.

The impotence of the patriarchs is due to the futility of their attempts to subordinate reality to their projections. Frank's fascination
with the song "Blue Velvet" exemplifies such an attempt to impose his
fantasies. He tries to make Dorothy one with the song, a transformation
that always fails, because her gaze shatters his illusion that she is a fetish
object—"Don't you fucking look at me," Frank orders her. The aggressiveness of Frank's reduction of Dorothy to an object is apparent in the
film's denouement, when Frank goes looking for Jeffrey in Dorothy's
apartment. Preparing to kill Jeffrey, Frank drapes Dorothy's robe over
his gun, thereby establishing an equivalence, via the robe, between annihilation of Dorothy and possession of her. The attempt to dominate
the other in this way is doomed to failure, as Frank's final, and fatal,
mistake attests. Frank is misled by the police radio that Jeffrey has
planted in Dorothy's bedroom. When Frank walks into the bedroom,
Jeffrey hides in the living room closet. He then surprises Frank with the
bullet he fires from the dead detective's gun. The voices on the police
radio have undercut Frank's attempt to master the other through his
gaze. As Lynda Bundtzen observes, "Such a trick derides the fetishism
on which Frank's power is based" (200).

Emblem of castration, the ear of Dorothy's husband has a complex
function in the film. It facilitates the progress of the plot, initially drawing Jeffrey into the mystery. In addition, it comes to serve as the figural
frame for the ensuing events of the story. This process of double displacement, whereby the ear is first severed from the body of Dorothy's

husband and then removed from the continuum of the plot, anesthetizes the ear, that is, renders it comparable to the fetish. It is the structural analogue of the swatch of blue velvet Frank uses to defend against the imaginary contagion of castration. Originating in the film's discursive content—its story of pathological aggressiveness—the ear is endowed with the power to organize the structure and, to a large extent, the meaning of the narrative.

At the end of the film, Jeffrey wakes up from an afternoon nap at Sandy's family's house, and the camera pulls back from Jeffrey's ear, as if to suggest that the preceding events had been produced by his imagination, that they were a dark dream or subjective vision. Jeffrey awakens to a scene of domestic happiness. Detective Williams and Mr. Beaumont, now recovered, are chatting amiably in the backyard, while their wives are doing the same in the living room. Sandy and Aunt Barbara, meanwhile, prepare lunch in the kitchen. The two families have come together in celebration of the union of their children, which, if not yet sealed in matrimony, surely seems headed in that direction. The film does not, however, end here. The final scene depicts Dorothy Vallens joyfully holding her son Donny in her arms. For a moment, Dorothy's face assumes a pensive expression as the lyric line, "I still can see blue velvet through my tears," plays on the soundtrack. The conclusion of the film raises more questions than it answers. What is the significance of the fact that Dorothy exudes such pleasure, even though her husband has just been brutally murdered? And in the moment when she becomes reflective, are we supposed to believe that she is thinking about the recent past? The specific song that plays could be interpreted as suggesting that, like Frank, Dorothy is moved by the song's evocation of the fetish, which, in her case, is not a swatch of blue velvet but her little son sitting on her lap. Are we, then, to think that Dorothy will treat her child as instrumentally as Frank treated her? Does the film imply that the murder of Dorothy's husband has cleared a space in which Dorothy can uninterruptedly bond with her son and appropriate his desire, unimpeded by the patriarchal prohibition of incest?

That the final scene is excluded from the structural frame of the film, which otherwise folds the action into Jeffrey's subjectivity, points to the film's ideological drift. Jeffrey may have dreamt the entire experience, but Dorothy, as phallic mother, exists in the "real" world, independent of his subjective fantasy. The film thus seems to lend authority to Frank's pathological view of Dorothy. In this respect, the dual identity of the ear as plot element and structuring frame ultimately works to collapse the distinction between Frank's pathological phallocentricity and the larger narrative perspective.[7]

The bias of the film was already apparent in the rape scene in Dorothy's apartment. As was discussed above, the lighting in the apartment makes it difficult to see exactly what is occurring. By contrast, another part of the scene is highly illuminated. In the brightly lit close-up shots of Dorothy's face, particularly after Frank hits her, Dorothy smiles, and the camera lingers on her mouth. Given that she is obeying Frank, it is impossible to decide whether her pleasure is feigned or authentic. Moreover, as mentioned earlier, the camera and the perspective it affords on the scene remain with Jeffrey in the closet. Such an alignment compels the audience to occupy the position of voyeur. It offers no vantage point from which the viewer could *read* the difference between Frank's experience of Dorothy's desire and any other experience of it that would not conform to Frank's projections. Later in the film, when Dorothy and Jeffrey have sex, she begs him to hit her, and he complies. Dorothy thus actively solicits from Jeffrey the abuse to which Frank had subjected her. In this, as in the first scene, the camera isolates Dorothy's smile, thereby emphasizing her gratification. Dorothy's pleasure is thus construed strictly in terms of Frank's desire, the implication being that masochism is synonymous with femininity. Dorothy, the film intimates, is getting exactly what she wants. Such a notion of feminine desire is reinforced in a number of ways. First, Frank tells Dorothy to "Stay alive for van Gogh" (an allusion to her husband), a statement that implies that Dorothy wants to die. Second, like Dorothy, Sandy exhibits an incipient masochism. Her feelings of affection for Jeffrey increase in proportion to her suffering on his account. The relation between her suffering and her love is figured structurally in a scene in which Jeffrey comes to Sandy's house to discuss the information he has gathered about the case with Detective Williams: As Sandy sits on the stairs waiting nervously for her father and Jeffrey to emerge from her father's study, she grips the stair balusters, thereby creating the illusion that she is locked behind prison bars.

Dorothy and Sandy's masochism is not, finally, the foundation of their desire. Rather, the film implies that feminine masochism dissimulates a more threatening, if oblique, sadism. While Dorothy actively solicits abuse in her sexual encounter with Jeffrey, her words implicitly reinforce Frank's view of her as a Medusan figure. She tells Jeffrey several times that she still has "his disease" inside of her. Jeffrey responds with visible discomfort to this comment, which is weighted with intimations of Dorothy's castrating power. In addition, Dorothy claims to possess a moral sensibility. She tells Jeffrey that she "know[s] the difference between right and wrong," a comment that never fails to elicit a chuckle from audiences, presumably because Dorothy utters it immediately after having engaged in adulterous sex with Jeffrey. The audience's laughter reveals how the film encourages a certain ethical complacency in its viewers. The language of Dorothy's comment invites us to judge her in moral terms, even though such judgment is unwarranted, given that the film never presents Dorothy's version of her story.

The representation of Dorothy as phallically acquisitive and morally reprobate functions to legitimate the oppression of women that accompanies Jeffrey's accession to patriarchal authority. Jeffrey's pursuit of "knowledge and experience," as he describes his activity, is simultaneously an activity of domesticating the other. The morning after he has been beaten up by Frank, Jeffrey literally assumes the seat at the head of the breakfast table while warning his aunt not to ask him questions about his bruised face: "Aunt Barbara, I love you, but you're gonna get it," he says to her. Detective Williams tells Jeffrey that as a young man, he, too, was curious, and his curiosity was what got him into the business of law enforcement. It is as if the threat posed by the amoral "natural" forces embodied in the feminine must be contained, and channeled, through the—masculine—law. In other words, the need to police the feminine follows on the heels of the masculine desire to "know" it.[8]

Whereas Sandy's divulgence of confidential information to Jeffrey initially aligned them and set them in opposition to Sandy's father, the allegiances among the three characters shift in the course of the film. Once initiated into the mystery of femininity, Jeffrey enters into complicity with Detective Williams, agreeing to bar Sandy's access to knowledge and, hence, to social power. Jeffrey discovers that Detective Williams's partner is working with Frank in the drug ring when the partner comes to the Williams household to pick up Sandy's father. Detective Williams covertly warns Jeffrey not to reveal his discovery to Sandy, and Jeffrey complies, even at the cost of lying to Sandy when she later asks about what had transpired between her father and him.

It is a testimony to the consistency of Lynch's vision that the universalization of Frank's pathological perspective is reflected through two self-referential scenes that involve television. When Jeffrey's mother watches the mystery movies, her attitude is one of disinterested interest. She calmly sits before the screen, the first time sipping from a coffee cup and the second time snacking on nuts. Her actions and attitude suggest that she has not lost sight of the distinction between fantasy and reality. In contrast to these scenes, a later episode represents the destruction of the border between the imaginary and the real. Jeffrey enters Dorothy's apartment, only to find Dorothy's husband and Williams's partner murdered. Inexplicably, the television screen has been smashed. Shortly thereafter, Frank comes looking for Jeffrey in the apartment and gratu-

itously shoots a bullet into the already cracked television screen. This action symbolically allegorizes the way Frank's fantasies are no longer
confined to his individual experience of the world; they have broken out
of the frame of the television screen, as it were, and now dominate the
larger perspective of the film as well.

A further merging of perspectives is suggested by the texture of
the film, which mimics Frank's fetish object. Both are sensuous in feel
and idiosyncratic in significance. Lynch vitalizes the world of Lumberton with heightened, vivid colors, frequently using slow motion shots
to lend a sense of otherworldliness to the ordinary and to create the impression that the mundane images of small-town life are pregnant with
hidden meaning, just as Frank imbues the swatch of blue velvet with a
significance that is cryptic to all but its user. As if to certify the fetishistic character of the film, the opening and closing credits run over a bil-
lowing blue velvet curtain, thereby establishing a continuity between
the fabric, the song entitled "Blue Velvet," and the film as a whole. One
might even suggest that the film's intertextual references (to *The Wizard
of Oz* and E. T. A. Hoffmann's "The Sandman," for example) seem "scis-
sored" out of context (and hence not integrated into the story) just as
Frank's fetish object is cut from Dorothy's robe.[9]

While the film's strength resides in the energy with which it libi-
dinizes the search for a world beyond the confines of small-town American life, the quest it tracks fails to uncover anything. What lies beneath
the façade of Lumberton is more surface, an inverted but nevertheless
specular and equally mystified version of its mainstream counterpart.
Blue Velvet does not formulate any narrative that would deepen understanding about the experience of the surface world. It produces images of captivity and conflict that suggest that there is no way out of
convention-bound existence, neither for Jeffrey nor for the organizing
narrative perspective, confined, as they both are, by Frank's pathological vision.[10]

Notes

1. Theodor Adorno, *Aesthetic Theory*, trans. C. Lenhardt (New York: Routledge & Kegan Paul, 1984), 47.

2. See also Timothy Corrigan, *A Cinema Without Walls: Movies and Culture
After Vietnam* (New Brunswick, New Jersey: Rutgers University Press, 1991).
Corrigan argues similarly that the film falls back upon the formulaic: "By the
time the narrative reveals the climactic tableaux of the dead husband and corrupt cop, it appears almost incidental to the drama of Jeffrey and Dorothy. These
and other revelations (such as an admission of love for Sandy) become merely

private (but passionate) stagings of environments and trivial formulas . . . whose revelatory meaning has long since decayed into a familiarity" (75). My essay is an attempt to inquire into the power of the "drama" of Dorothy and Jeffrey to provoke response, in spite of the fact that the film's idiom is the mundane and formulaic.

3. For a discussion of responses to the film, see "Black and Blue Is Beautiful?" *Newsweek* (27 Oct. 1986), 62–63. Timothy Corrigan points out that the film was reviewed ten times by the *New York Times* alone; see Corrigan, 77.

4. For a discussion of the ideological implications of such a process of naturalization, see Fredric Jameson, "Nostalgia for the Present," *The South Atlantic Quarterly*, 88(2), 517–537.

5. Indeed, throughout the entire scene, it is difficult to know precisely what is going on between Dorothy and Frank, both because the lighting is so dim and because there are ambiguities that may be a result of editing decisions. It appears that Frank drapes the robe over Dorothy's crotch and pushes the fabric into her vagina with his hand. After so doing, he climbs onto her and either has intercourse with her or simulates intercourse. It is impossible to know what happens, because we never see Frank unzip his pants, but he does zip them up later.

6. Lynda Bundtzen has written a thorough and insightful analysis of the significance of fetishism in the film. See "Don't Look at me!" Woman's Body, Woman's Voice in *Blue Velvet*," *Western Humanities Review*, 42(3), 187–203.

7. Bundtzen makes the interesting argument that the final scene suggests that "underneath, Dorothy is maternal plenitude, the good mother, a figure of love and care" (192). This scene, as well as others that highlight Dorothy's "maternal voice," work, according to Bundtzen, to defetishize Dorothy's body. I would suggest that the use of the Bobby Vinton ballad at the film's conclusion undercuts his reading. Moreover, the notion of "maternal plenitude" itself connotes a phallic economy of totalization and fragmentation.

8. According to Jameson, "the film's call for a return to the fifties coats the pill by insistence on the unobtrusive benevolence for all these fathers [Mr. Beaumont, Detective Williams]" (535).

9. For a comparison of *Blue Velvet* and *The Wizard of Oz*, see James Lindroth, "Down the Yellow-Brick Road: Two Dorothys and the Journey of Initiation in Dream and Nightmare," *Literature/Film Quarterly*, 18(3), 160–166. For a discussion of the way *Blue Velvet* reads E. T. A. Hoffmann's *The Sandman*, and vice versa, see Alice A. Kuznier, "Ears Looking at You: E. T. A. Hoffmann's *The Sandman* and David Lynch's *Blue Velvet*," *South Atlantic Review*, 54(2), 7–21.

10. Corrigan argues similarly about the conclusion of *Blue Velvet*: "If there is the promise of distinguishing revelations and secrets here, discovery of those revealed secrets releases no real information, only the displaced promise of other secrets that are never revealed." (75).

7

"Murder and Mystery *Mormon Style*": Violence as Mediation in American Popular Culture

Terryl Givens

"Is there any group you wouldn't pick on?"
"Mormons. You don't pick on Mormons. They've been picked on enough.
I mean look at Marie Osmond. She's a Mormon."

—Interview with Andrew Dice Clay

Nineteenth-Century Popular Fiction: Heresy and Violence

In the late nineteenth century, when anti-Mormon hysteria was at a fevered pitch, a U.S. senator rose to suggest that Mormon barbarism now extended to the offering of human sacrifices in their temple,[1] and a prominent preacher accused Mormons of masterminding evils ranging from the destruction of the Christian home to the assassination of President Garfield.[2] Providing constant fuel to the fires of animosity was a wide array of popular fiction writers. Beginning in the 1850s and continuing into the present century, the list of ready users and abusers of the Mormon image in fiction would eventually include such notables as Arthur Conan Doyle and Robert Louis Stevenson abroad, and Artemus Ward, Jack London, and Zane Grey at home. All told, perhaps two hundred novels and short stories featured Mormon villains prominently in the first hundred years of the Church's existence (1830–1930).[3] Two features of these fictional representations were noteworthy, and contrast significantly with the ways that popular culture has come to mediate cultural conflict today.

First, it was clear that a primary challenge that early Mormonism represented to the culture of Jacksonian America was that of the heretical. Theocratic ambitions, rhetoric of empire building, and an unsettling tendency of the Mormons to vote en bloc and wield their collective ballot like a weapon were certainly compounding factors in anti-Mormon violence, but the initial conflicts were doctrinal. Just as the fires of the Inquisition burned the deviant Christian but spared (often by way of expulsion) the professing Jew, so has America's fiercest religious intolerance been reserved for those who stake a claim to Christian affiliation while remaining outside the consensual orthodoxy that even as pluralistic a society as that of the nineteenth century managed to sustain. It is perhaps obvious that the threat posed by the heretical is particularly severe because contamination is always already silently at work. And because the heretic shares a common origin with the orthodox, his presence is more difficult to detect than that of the infidel.

Heterodoxy proliferated wildly in the nineteenth century. Lieutenant-Colonel A. M. Maxwell was a British officer who toured the United States in 1840. One of his first observations was that "there seems to be no lack of churches nor of persuasions, and church-going seems to be all the rage."[4] But after some time in the States, he had had his fill. He found the Episcopalians and Presbyterians, even the Universalists, respectable enough. But a Shaker service left him "sick and indignant" (I:98), and he passed near a meeting of "about 4000 mountebank Methodists, commonly called Campers," which he found a "sauntering sect." In exasperation, he finally complained that he was "really sick and tired of hearing of the Mathiasites and Mormonites, Jumpers, Shakers, Lynchers, Saturday Saints," and others (I:246). No doubt it was hard to keep track. The 1844 American edition of *History of All Christian Sects* lists as some of the denominations then current (in addition to more orthodox varieties) Dunkers, Sabbatarians, Hicksites, Shakers, Sandemanians, Swedenborgians, Campbellites, Bereans, Come-Outers, Millenarians, Millerites, Wilkinsonians, and Mormonites.[5] An 1849 almanac adds River Brethren and Schwenkfelders to the list.[6] Numerous others were too shortlived to make it into print, like the Bowery Hill followers of the remarkable Robert Matthews, "Matthias," a New York neighbor of Joseph Smith who in 1830 proclaimed himself a messiah but ended his career incarcerated for feeding arsenic-laced blackberries to some of his flock.[7]

Indeed, so many were the outbreaks of religious nonconformity in Joseph Smith's neighborhood alone that David Reese published in 1838 a volume called *Humbugs of New York: Being a Remonstrance against Popular Delusion; Whether in Science, Philosophy, or Religion.* Mormonism merited barely a mention, given the "kindred enormities of Matthias" and the "multitudes who believe in 'Animal Magnetism,' subscribe to

'Phrenology,' are the willing victims of every form of 'Quackery,' and have adopted the creed and practice of 'ultraism.' "[8]

Nevertheless, while these other religions created hardly a blip on the political scene, Mormonism, from its founding in 1830 to the turn of the century, was to become the subject of persecutions, mobbing, a state extermination order, editorials, religious pamphleteering, Congressional committee hearings, federal legislation, and several national political platforms. A recent bibliography lists almost 1,500 government documents pertaining to Mormonism in the first 100 years of its existence.[9]

The reason is not hard to fathom. Compounding Mormonism's status as heretical was its ambivalent cultural identity. On one hand, with its communalism, autocratic theocracy, and polygamy, Mormonism was clearly far outside the mainstream of American culture. On the other hand, writers as disparate as Tolstoy and Harold Bloom have considered Mormonism, in spite of its radical unorthodoxy, the quintessentially American religion.[10] This paradox is well captured by sociologist Thomas O'Dea, who goes to the heart of the peculiar challenge Mormonism represents. The religion is, he writes, "the clearest example to be found in our national history of the evolution of a native and indigenously developed ethnic minority."[11] In the case of Mormonism, then, we have a body of religious, social, economic, and political beliefs and practices which are perceived to be out of sync with mainstream American values. But the group holding them is, historically and ethnically, American to the core. The Amish, to mention another example of heterodoxy, manifest a similar degree of group solidarity. But they are bounded both by distinctive, visible markers and by a self-imposed isolation. The Spiritualists, to pose a much larger example, numbered in the hundreds of thousands by the time of the Civil War and were well outside Christian orthodoxy, but they were not characterized by anything approaching the group cohesion, let alone the ethnicity, that O'Dea imputes to the Mormons. The Mormons' lack of self-manifesting characteristics, common ties of blood and history, the cosmopolitanism of their members, the ordinariness of their cultural and intellectual composition[12]—these features, in combination with a burgeoning convert pool which knew no boundaries, create a secular counterpart to the crisis provoked by the heretical.

In a nativist, Jacksonian period especially, the confluence of religious heresy with a kind of cultural heresy was fatal. Unlike Catholics, Jews, Irish immigrants, or African-Americans, the Mormons could not be easily categorized or identified in terms of foreign origins and thus be as readily exorcised from the body politic (though their "gathering" and eventual flight to Utah made this nearly possible). A certain uneasiness with revolutionary religious or social practices being exhibited within the American heartland is itself understandable enough, especially if they are deemed abhorrent and immoral by mainstream Anglo-American Protestants. Such was surely the response to claims of supernatural visitations, a profoundly authoritarian church government, and such practices as communalism and, eventually, polygamy. But such practices and beliefs are doubly threatening if they cannot be relegated to a foreign culture or "otherness." Potential converts to Mormonism shared with the adherents ethnic, political, racial, and geographic realms. Few tangible signs of distinctness were available as a hedge against contamination. It was for this reason that Mormonism presented a particularly devilish challenge for psychic distancing. Hindus practicing suttee in faraway India may have been but a curiosity to a nineteenth-century American; watching kinsmen and neighbors fallen prey to what was thought to be at a safe remove is downright disturbing.

Insofar as Mormonism was merely a heretical "other," its appropriation as a stock source of villainy was shaped by the stereotypes their peculiar practices and beliefs generated, the literary genres into which the characters were written, and the ideological investment which purveyors of popular fiction had as self-fashioning Americans. In this regard, the case of Mormons in fiction may be seen to share much with representations of the Other generally. But unlike the subjects usually chosen for exemplary otherness, Mormons represented a virtually unique case of an Other which was, with ultimately and profoundly disturbing implications, an ethnic community not subject to the same means of exorcism as communities racially or geographically distinctive. This dilemma is the most recurrent plot device in early anti-Mormon fiction. The dread of assimilation, the anxiety of seduction, whether sexual, religious, or political, is unmistakable in scores of fictive accounts.

The case is perhaps best put forth by one of the first of the anti-Mormon novels to appear, *The Mormoness; or the Trials of Mary Maverick*, by John Russell (1853). This novel, which purports to be "a narrative of real events," is fraught with a highly ambiguous voice and a perpetually deferred resolution of vilification and indulgence. Ostensibly, the work is a generous-hearted condemnation of anti-Mormon intolerance. The action unfolds in a small community known as Sixteen Mile Prairie. There, religious liberty is the order of the day, except when it comes to Mormonism. Such is the "state of public opinion" concerning this "deluded" religion that "hundreds . . . would gladly have exterminated the whole sect."[13] In fact, Russell does chronicle an actual massacre perpetrated against the Mormons in Missouri, the one at Haun's Mill.[14] Narrating the gruesome details, Russell laments with lofty moral indignation that "our institutions, which guarantee the freedom of religious opinion to the Jew, the Mahometan, the Pagan, and even to the atheist, afforded no protection to the Mormon"(55). The Mormoness, widowed by the tragedy, goes on to become a sister of charity and dies in saintly service.

The generous voice of indignation that constitutes the ostensible narrative is inconsonant with a much more troubling, counterpoint narrative unfolding at the level of psychological drama. The hero of the story is the good "gentile" James Maverick, whose worthiness "no phrenologist accustomed to the study of human character would have doubted" (39). He is "deadly hostile" to the Mormons, but with good reason—the casualties of the Mormon missionary effort are striking closer and closer to home. "Men he had known from childhood . . . had fallen into the fatal snare of Joe Smith"(42). When a Mormon preacher comes to town, James scrupulously refuses to attend his sermons. With chilling suggestiveness, we are informed that his wife has "too much gentleness and goodness in her heart to find room for such [cynicism], even against the vilest of the human race" (42). Her innocence is, of course, her downfall. She attends the meetings and is gradually swayed by the preacher's "ingenious sophistry" (53). Respite from James's anxiety seemingly appears in the form of a stranger who calls unexpectedly one day:

> For an instant Maverick gazed upon him with speechless surprise, then, uttering the exclamation, "Why! Mr. Wilmer!" sprang from his seat, seized the hand of the stranger, and shook it with the most cordial gratification. He was in the act of introducing the newcomer to his wife, when he learned, to his overwhelming astonishment, that this was no other than the Mormon preacher who had held forth to the people of the settlement the night before, at the school house. . . . [T]he thought had not once struck him as possible that Mr. Wilmer, of all others, could be deluded into a belief of Mormonism. (49)

At this point, the horror of the inevitable is palpable. James himself, left without gentile friend, wife, or refuge from the allure of Mormonism, succumbs within a matter of pages.

The text is thus a curious blend of moralistic flag waving in defense of religious toleration, a spirited condemnation of the "mobs and lynch law" Russell chronicles on one hand, and, on the other, a novel of psychological horror, the drama of a relentlessly encroaching menace that spiritually devours James's neighbors, his wife, an old friend, and, inevitably, himself as well. Thus, while protesting the injustice of anti-Mormon violence with one voice, Russell is, with another, projecting onto the character of James an anxiety sufficiently disturbing—and warranted—to excuse the most extreme measures imaginable for self-preservation.

The example of this author divided against himself may serve as a paradigm of the peculiar anxiety of seduction provoked by Mormonism, a consequence of factors that distinguish Mormonism and its effects from other social conflicts and their literary treatments. One other example will suffice to introduce most of the themes typical of anti-Mormon literature, while echoing the agonized self-contradictions of *The Mormoness*. In a Frank Merriwell adventure by Burt Standish, published in the nickel *Tip Top Weekly* (1897), the cyclist hero from Yale finds himself in "the lost valley of Bethasda" where a band of Mormons "have built up a town that is shut off from the rest of the world—a town of which few outside its boundaries know anything at all."[15] Once in the valley, the cyclist and his friend are called upon by a Mormon youth to save his lover from being forced into plural marriage with an aged lecher. Frank agrees to help out. They are themselves caught, but rescue the couple and make good their escape from the community.

The "author of Frank Merriwell" appears torn between the sensationalism to which Mormonism so readily lends itself (polygamy and secret temple rites) and his self-appointment as a moral instructor of youth (he digresses for several paragraphs when his heroes drink at a well, to lecture on the virtues of spring water and the evils of the bottle). So even as the hero's alter ego is proclaiming "I am getting a different opinion of the Mormons than I once had. . . . I believe some of the wild stories told about their religion, and their ways are a mess of lies" (9), they are on their way to an encounter that gives the lie to such lofty toleration:

> They came to a square chamber, which was lighted by flaring, smoking torches. In a semi-circle at one end of the chamber sat twelve cloaked and cowled figures, their garments of somber black. . . . Then the figure that wore the bear's head . . . stood and read a passage from the . . . Mormon Bible.(24)

And while the hero anticipates their execution by means of "the pit of fire" (a grisly fate reminiscent of Poe's work), this same companion is repeatedly insisting that "These men are not Mormons! . . . At their worst, the Mormons never destroyed their enemies in such a manner" (26). The point, of course, is that such incredulity proves suicidal. After Frank and Jack effect their escape, they are warned by a wise old hermit to tell no man their tale, as it will never be believed. We see here an author clearly at cross-purposes with himself. Inclined on one hand to dismiss fantastical representations of Mormon outrages through the voice of the reasonable Jack, his character ultimately comes to represent naiveté, not reason, as the fantastical has vividly been made actual before our very eyes. Disarming tolerance through the fictive defeat of skepticism, and preempting disbelief through the metafictive warning of the old hermit, the author fulfills the function of the guardians at the gates of Bethasda. As Mormonism remains a foreign realm impenetrable by the railroad or the gentile culture it represents, so will representations of Mormonism remain forearmed against the assaults of reason or skepticism.

Capitulation to the "Mormon menace" or its annihilation by an intolerant populace do not, however, represent the only options, metaphors of Mormonism as a moral cancer notwithstanding. Fiction offers a way of mediating such contending imperatives. History, it has been said, is written by the victors. But in the same sense, so is "Literature." Consequently, mainstream notions of what it means to be African-Amerian or Jewish or Chinese have traditionally been shaped not as a result of reading slave narratives, the Talmud, or Confucius. Rather, the West's traditional canon of ethnic education would more likely include *Uncle Tom's Cabin, The Merchant of Venice,* and Charlie Chan mysteries. Caricature, of course, is the exaggeration of particular identifiers, often with comic effect. But in literary representations of other cultures, the author has the power to choose those characteristics that will be considered fundamental, definitive, of that cultural identity. Those characteristics chosen for exaggeration or focus generally serve the function of emphasizing difference. Racial features, linguistic patterns, dietary identifiers, or other areas of cultural distinctness are seized upon and exploited to secure and solidify a sense of otherness. Such caricature often assumes a relatively benign face, secure in the bubble of identity, of selfhood, which the very exaggeration of the "other" has served to cast into relief. Such has often been the case, for example, with Orientalism. From Marco Polo to the Impressionists, Asia served as the stuff of curiosity and amusement. Oriental motifs were popular in design and architecture, the harem recurs as a realm in which sexual fantasy may safely find unbridled expression, and the Moslem is, if anything, useful

as a narrative mask through which Western, not Eastern, culture is cri-
tiqued (Montesquieu's *Persian Letters* and Goldsmith's *Citizen of the
World* for example).

Almost contemporaneous with the rise of Mormonism as a distinct religious community is a tendency to caricature the new religion.
Not coincidentally, one of the most pervasive forms this caricature took
was the Orientalization of Mormonism. Superficial parallels provided
the basis for a depiction that seemed to relegate Mormonism to the safe
realms of the primitive, the pagan. Even a casual perusal of American
fiction about Mormons reveals a pervasive appeal to comparisons with
Oriental religion. Sydney Bell paints a vivid portrait of "Joe Smith" ruling his "tens of thousands like an oriental despot."[16] Charles Clark
claims that the Mormon city of Salt Lake "wears a distinctly Oriental
appearance,"[17] and Jennie Switzer compares the "cruel wickedness of
the Mormon church" with Hindu practices.[18] Arthur Conan Doyle is
one of many who refer to Mormon harems, and James Oliver Curwood
calls one of his villains an "Attila of the Mormon kingdom."[19] Joseph
Smith and, later, Brigham Young are but "American Mohammeds";
even a popular text on the religion entitled *Mormonism: The Islam of
America* bears out this widespread practice.[20]

Science would participate in this same ethnic construction that
fiction did. In a meeting of the New Orleans Academy of Sciences in
1861, Dr. Samuel Cartwright and Prof. C.G. Forshey gave a paper using
parts of a report made by Assistant Surgeon Robert Barthelow of the
U.S. Army, "The Effects and Tendencies of Mormon Polygamy in the
Territory of Utah." The findings described characteristics of the new
racial type:

> The yellow, sunken, cadaverous visage; the greenish-colored eye;
> the thick, protuberant lips; the low forehead; the light, yellowish
> hair, and the lank, angular person, constitute an appearance so
> characteristic of the new race, the production of polygamy, as to
> distinguish them at a glance. The older men and women present
> all the physical peculiarities of the nationalities to which they be-
> long; but these peculiarities are not propagated and continued in
> the new race; they are lost in the prevailing type.[21]

In the case of Mormonism, however, such strategies of caricature
prove ineffective. For it is hardly consoling to construct the enemy as
alien if, as O'Dea reminds us, that enemy is indigenous. This situation,
I argue, has the consequence that this Orientalizing exhibits none of the
benign associations that have been often part of more traditional forms

of Orientalism. The pejorative nature of the comparison rather bespeaks a sense of outrage that what presents itself as "us" (Mormonism is, after all, a religion laying claim to being quintessentially American and Christian) is in reality more like "them," meaning Oriental in precisely those ways which are un-American and un-Christian.

By themselves, then, such strategies of caricature and physical containment are insufficient. The distance suggested by Orientalizing or otherwise reconfiguring the "other" is not, ultimately, a convincing one in the case of a group that continues to subvert or seduce its members from among the "us." It is my argument that Orientalizing the Mormons proves insufficient as a device to allay the dread of assimilation which motivates much anti-Mormon representation.

Violence as Mediation

Because heresy is contagion, options for dealing with the Mormon menace were usually seen as fairly absolute; "Exterminate—or be exterminated" reads the preface to one ant-Mormon work of the nineteenth century.[22] But as Richard Hofstadter has pointed out, even the paranoid style is usually employed by reasonable people who prefer other options.[23] So we find that even narrators of such vehemently anti-Mormon works as *The Mormoness*(1853) and *Frank Merriwell*(1897) are marked by a bizarrely conflicted voice, which depicts with horror and sympathy the anti-Mormon atrocities but exhibits an equal degree of consternation about the consequences of toleration. As well as being morally problematic, the recourse to violence against the Mormons was ultimately ineffective. Persecution and pogroms finally drove the Saints out of the United States in 1847, but the Church continued to thrive, missionaries spread throughout America and Europe, and the "Mormon Problem" became a social and political preoccupation for the next generation or two. In lieu of the solutions persecution and banishment offered, a rendering of Mormonism more efficacious than mere Orientalizing was employed to allay the anxiety of seduction so evident in works like the two mentioned above. Not surprisingly, both Russell and Standish find such a middle way, by which cultural conflict comes to be mediated by a particular fictive representation of violence.

One alternative to the construction of a comforting distance through attempted displacement (represented above by Orientalizing), is to insist that participation in the alien system could never be the result of the exercise of free will. And it is at this point that virtually all versions of the Mormon menace employ a generic structure that resolves this anxiety of conversion. Mesmerism, hypnotism, captivity, enslavement, bondage, kidnapping, coercion—these words and images pervade virtually the entire range of works in which Mormons figure as characters.

Switzer chronicles the Mormons' ill-defined "power over women,"[24] and Dan Coolidge portrays one of many victims "swayed [by a Mormon] . . . against her will by the touch of his hands and the power of his masterful eyes."[25] Standish and Coolidge concur in imputing to the Mormon leaders hypnotic power over women and men.[26]

Maria Ward's "true narrative" of her captivity among the Mormons explains that Joseph Smith "exerted a mystical magical influence over me—a sort of sorcery that deprived me of the unrestricted use of free will."[27] In fact, she claims, all Mormon elders were practitioners of this mesmeric technique, which had been obtained by Smith "from a German peddler, who, notwithstanding his reduced circumstances, was a man of distinguished intellect and extensive erudition. Smith paid him handsomely, and the German promised to keep the secret."[28] Maria Ward thereby spilled the beans on Mormonism's German peddler connection to an audience of more than 60,000 readers by 1866 (417).

Gazes of the serpent-charmer and mysterious influences abound, but even more frequent is out-and-out violence. Curwood describes an island kingdom is which the women are kept in line by whips and slave hounds. Zane Grey and Arthur Conan Doyle both draw Utah as a vast prison guarded over by avenging angels who track down escaping women.[29] And an early nickel-weekly paints Brigham Young as a despot who dispatches his minions on raids to provide Mormon harems with white slaves.[30]

The list is endless, and the psychology, I think, fairly transparent. The distance suggested by Orientalizing the "Other" is not, ultimately, a convincing one in the case of a group which continues to subvert or seduce its members from among the "Us." If identification with what is anathema is not precluded ethnically or geographically, one's sense of a stable, uncontaminated self can at least be assured by denying the function of choice in whatever assimilation by the "other" does occur. Supplementing the denial of such ongoing absorption by means of artfully contrived barriers, we find the insistence that those very practices which threaten to engulf (or seduce) us could never be the result of conscious choice.

The result is a representation of Mormonism in popular American fiction that functions rather like the lawyer's argument by alternative. Don't worry about Mormonism—it's too exotic to touch us. And even if it does claim a few victims, at least they don't go willingly. Ironically, then, violence becomes the fictive way of mediating radical difference, and caricature disarms anxiety by pretending to exacerbate it. We thus see a persistent erasure of agency, the elimination of will, in early representations of the Mormon experience. Only in the absence of volition was the phenomenon of conversion to such otherness thinkable.[31] Into the vacuum thus created, those familiar plot devices of mesmerism and bondage unfold. These literary practices, attempts to evoke the exotic and invoke the violent, represent two strategies to contain a threatening Other which proves resistant to both extermination and assimilation.

Contemporary Caricature: Genre as Mediation

Among contemporary works of fiction, some of the old Mormon caricatures continue to resurface in fairly generic ways. Popular romance writer Jennifer Blake, for example, can always invoke the foil of a "fanatic Elder Greer, who called his wanton desires the 'will of God,' " to contrast with her slightly more monogamous hero Ward Dunbar.[32] Mystery writer Tony Hillerman can exploit the Mormon figure in equally melodramatic ways. The mysterious entity behind strange happenings in *The Thief of Time* turns out to be Brigham (!) Houk, a schizophrenic triple murderer (of his mother and siblings) who tortures frogs and babbles about the devil and the angel Moroni.[33]

Perhaps surprisingly, in the academic world as well—as books like Paul Fussell's recent work remind us—selective bigotry continues to find intellectual respectability if the target is Mormons, fundamentalists, or other groups not yet beneficiaries of the "new tolerance." In his *BAD: The Dumbing of America,* Fussell suggests that "the creeping nincompoopism" that threatens to engulf our culture had its origins in the rise of Mormonism![34] One explanation for such continuing bigotry is offered by religious historian Martin Marty. "Fundamentalists," he notes, "seem to be one of the few groups that have no effective anti-defamation lobby."[35] (Ironically, he has himself been cited as an example of "the blatant prejudice against fundamentalists in American academe.")[36]

In the case of Mormonism, at least, an additional explanation offers itself. Through the nineteenth century, Mormonism lent itself readily to a political discourse largely preoccupied with questions of American identity. What values made the Union worth preserving? What criteria were relevant in the admission of a territory to statehood? How would the new Republican party define itself? Likening polygamy to slavery, as the first Republican Party platform did, comparing Brigham Young to an Asian despot, representing Mormon women as victims and frontier heroes from Captain Plum to Buffalo Bill as their saviors, accounting for the Prophet Joseph Smith's martyrdom as the penalty for his violation of the right to a free press—in these and many other scenes, Mormonism made available to the playwrights of the Great American Saga the heroes and antiheroes, the virtues and vices, of that dramatic self-creation.

The Center Doesn't Hold

Today the Mormon caricature has changed considerably, but so has the plot. Beginning in the 1950s, Mormonism entered a new era of respectability. Klaus Hansen has made a case for the "bourgeoisification" of Mormon culture,[37] evidence of which might be alleged in a variety of examples: Howard Hughes choosing Mormons as his personal aides, since they exemplify clean living and trustworthiness; the tendency of the FBI and the CIA to recruit heavily among the LDS population, exploiting their reputation for moral standards, patriotism, and family values; Mariott exemplifies the successful Mormon business ethic, and a Mormon apostle (Ezra Taft Benson) becomes one of the most popular cabinet members of President Eisenhower's administration. In 1992, two of Bush's most visible aides were prominent Mormons.

A perusal of contemporary novels reveals that the Mormon image in fiction has swung accordingly. Two writers dealing most explicitly with Mormon characters and setting reflect the new ambiguities and dilemmas facing modern caricaturists of Mormonism. Like many of his nineteenth-century predecessors, Edgar Award nominee Robert Irvine's perspective is shaped by his past affiliation with the church ("He comes from a prominent pioneer family," the book jacket advertises). Indeed, the most salient—and salacious—features of early anti-Mormon fiction are also present in his works; he has written several successful "Moroni Traveler" mysteries set in contemporary Utah, which presumably "give the reader a very compelling glimpse into this fascinating subculture" and reveal "telling details of its church-dominated region."[38] And what a subculture it is!

Church security is Orwellian, involving spies as young as twelve years old. Even public payphones are monitored by the church, hidden TV cameras are everywhere, and computers keep detailed records on all aspects of members' lives. And when Mormons aren't glutting their lust in polygamy, they're joining celibate male cults: "fifteen or twenty men dressed in black trousers and white home-spun shirts. All wore straggly beards that made them look like Orthodox Jews."[39] They don't wear zippered pants, since "They're an invention of the devil" (107). They are antiwomen and antisex, and engage in bizarre "touching" rituals.

Like Hillerman and Blake, Irvine makes a token gesture of distancing himself from anti-Mormonism by imputing the evils in his fic-

tion to fringe groups. Ultimately, however, he ignores his own dis-
claimers. Not only do the fundamentalist cults practice polygamy, but
in fact "a lot of Mormons around here, Mormons in good standing, have
more wives than the law allows."[40] When heinous murders occur, the
distinction between cultists and mainstream Mormons again evapo-
rates: "She'd been strung up by her feet and butchered. The Mormon
way" (*CH* 134). As with Zane Grey and Conan Doyle, the Danites, a secret Mormon terrorist organization with alleged ties to the church hierarchy, are suggested as likely suspects ("whatever their present-day
duties, membership was a closely guarded secret") (*CH* 14).

   With the fiction of Cleo Jones, also self-advertised as "an ex-Mor-
mon," the setting is equally horrific. In addition to deranged fanatics,
totalitarian church government, intrusive surveillance, and pervasive
polygamy, we find a cover-up of church involvement in Watergate, the
Bay of Pigs, and Kennedy's assassination.[41] To top it off, Mormons have
"five times the child murder rate!" and vividly described rampant child
abuse ("Her stomach was all puffed up and yellow and trembling like—
like . . . " [195]). Jones sees Mormon obsessiveness with sex reaching as
far as their famous icon, which she calls "the great phallic tabernacle
organ" (164).

   So far, these novelists sound like dredged-up hate mongers from
the Jacksonian period, writing in the familiar paranoid style. But these
modern caricatures of Mormonism are not without some surprising per-
mutations. For in the nineteenth century, heresy was self-explanatory as
an etiology of evil. Difference, especially radical difference, carried with
it its own taint of transgression. In contemporary representations, difference and evil are not at all synonymous; in a changed moral climate,
new grounds for censure clash jarringly with mechanically employed
stereotypes. Not surprisingly, novels like Irvine's and Jones's are rid-
dled with traces of this dissonance. Thus, we have Traveler's flash of insight: "For the first time, he truly understood . . . why Mormons still
swore temple oaths against the federal government" (*CH* 134). Unfortunately, the resurrection of this frequent nineteenth-century allegation
collides with a depiction of a society that he has already characterized
as patriotic to a fault. The Mormons, he reminds us in every one of his
novels, have taken over the once Catholic-dominated FBI; and as Jones
is at such pains to point out, BYU is the third largest supplier of army
officers (73), and the current prophet is dismissed as that "John Birch Society President" (192).

   Similarly, and even more revealingly, Jones and Irvine run into dif-
ficulties when they revive the single most ubiquitous charge against
Mormonism, in the face of their otherwise decidedly modern critique.
Both are fond of depicting polygamy in the traditional way—a thinly

veiled "justification for [Mormon] lust" (*GG* 25). Mormon villainy in another of his novels takes the form of a conspiracy between two men to drug and systematically rape virtually every woman in an entire community (*Called Home*). But when it comes to exploring the causes of Mormon depravity, Irvine and Jones fall into similar contradiction. An excessive devotion to conservative notions about sexual morality turns out to be the problem. Thus, in *Angel's Share*, we have the case of a crazed serial killer who thinks he is the reincarnation of Jack the Ripper. He hunts down and sexually mutilates his young victims. The culprit is known to be the head Mormon Apostle's son, but the explanation is discovered by the non-Mormon detective: "It's all my fault," confesses the fiancée of the murderer's friend. "I wouldn't sleep with Heber before he left for England. . . . But I now see that I was wrong" (*AS* 187). Such sexual deprivation makes Heber and his companion easy prey to a prostitute seductress, and the ensuing guilt drives one to celibacy and the other to madness.

In like fashion, in *Prophet Motive* ("Murder and Mystery—*Mormon Style*," as the cover blurb states), Jones depicts another deranged Mormon missionary, who she intimates is pushed over the brink by strict sexual standards and resultant sexual paranoia. Our "gentile" protagonist listens sympathetically to the lunatic's ravings: "I remember those missionary days when you weren't allowed to think of women" (26). By contrast, this same healthy, neurosis-free (and non-Mormon) chief of police knows enough to get out of these sexually repressed relationships. He leaves his Mormon wife because "you can sure get tired of being on top of a praying woman" (41). So Mormon polygamy is the institutionalization of unbridled lust, while at the same time the institutional repression of passion is ruining marriages, unhingeing missionaries, and creating serial killers.

Most telling of all, however, is Jones's explicit assessment of Mormonism's corruptive power. As her hero zeroes in on the crazed killer (who has, with fairly transparent symbolism, murdered her husband and concealed his body in a Mormon food storage bin), he describes the climactic confrontation:

> This is the true face of evil, I thought. But I knew immediately that that wasn't true either—that she was just a pudgy housewife before the high shelves of canned raspberries that told of her valiant effort to do right and strive for perfection.(186)

As the cover blurb makes clear, this book is marketed as an examination of "the extremes to which guilt and the quest for purity can drive ordi-

nary people." And there we have the irony of such contemporary caricatures. For if such people are meant to be taken as "ordinary," then obviously it is the norm itself that is in need of a vigorous reexamination.
And that is precisely the point. In the nineteenth century, any transgression of a sexual morality derived from Puritans was unquestionably
evil. To persist in depicting Mormons as sexually voracious carries little
or none of the original moral blemish in an era that has seen the politics
of AIDS move debate from sexual behavior to "homophobia" and, as a
consequence, attach a greater stigma to moralizing than to sexually
transmitted disease. The persistence of the stereotype shows the tenacity of literary paternity, but the contradictions it involves reveal a simple truth about caricature. The malleable features of any caricature must
be reconfigured anew as value systems change, if they are to elicit the
same derision as the early formulations. The above two authors, then,
are clear examples of caricature caught in anachronism. Funny hats and
unorthodox living arrangements no longer a villain make. But as they
also suggested, in however confused a fashion, the wrong kind of conformity may. And thus a new paradigm of caricature is now possible in
which too much, rather than too little, accommodation becomes a negative value.

It was once a simple matter to assume a norm for American culture and situate the Mormon well outside of it. But today, the Mormon
businessman not only has been assimilated into American society, he
has become American society. To borrow from Jones herself again, "BYU
is the third largest supplier of army officers. Mormons were Howard
Hughes's right-hand men. And so on. . . . " (73). Successful, white,
Anglo-Saxon, middle-class, suburban, one working parent in a traditional family with stay-at-home mother and five children. If Tom Clancy
wants a shorthand way of creating a young, clean-cut, and patriotic
guy-next-door he may simply refer to him as LDS, as he does with Ran-
dall Tait in *The Hunt for Red October*. (The fact that the Russians consider
him "a religious fanatic"[42] is presumably to his credit.) Similarly, his
hero in *Clear and Present Danger* refers to Mormons as "honest and hard-
working, and fiercely loyal to their country, because they believed in
what America stood for."[43] Once the target of a federal expeditionary
force under President Buchanan, charged with rebellion and sedition,
the Mormons are now the embodiment of public-spiritedness and "traditional values."

The meaning of this new role, however, is especially dubious in today's intellectual climate. It is now because Mormons occupy what used
to be the center that they fall into contempt. The embrace of ultracon-
servative values, not their flagrant rejection, is now construed as the

source of Mormon perfidy. For since Vietnam at least, employment in covert activities can suggest criminality as readily as it can be read by others as loyalty (as the case of Oliver North demonstrates), the nuclear family seems a distant relic (as Murphy Brown replaces Ozzie and Harriet),[44] and multiculturalism rather than melting pot is now the ruling paradigm. The repercussions of these developments for the Mormons are suggested by a 1971 *Ramparts* article by Frances Lang which faulted the church for providing to the FBI and CIA a steady supply of reliably conservative defenders of capitalist interests.[45] John LeCarré, from a British novelist's perspective, captures the irony, the simultaneous gain and loss, of Mormonism's new place in American society. When the CIA sends two agents to assist in a British operation, they are viewed as faceless twins, "Americans, so slight, so trim, so characterless," whose "Mormon cleanliness I found slightly revolting."[46]

It is as if Mormons had effaced all traces of otherness only to discover that the model of "Americanism" they now appear to embrace has become the new antihero of the Great American Saga currently playing. This is because we have now reached a point in contemporary intellectual culture where the politics of the periphery are working to devalue the center. Indeed, the politics of marginalization and collective guilt as they operate today make it clear that status as an oppressed group is not without its political advantages.[47] The furious storm of opposition to Hirsch's "Cultural Literacy" project, the desperation and rejection of Pat Buchanan's 1992 Republican National Convention speech in which a beleaguered, fading majority sought to consolidate its stewardship of cultural values, suggest that a word like "mainstream" may soon be as obsolete as it is already becoming opprobrious.

In this new climate where the center seems to be fading and the margins acquire new vitality and worth, difference acquires new value. If we return briefly to Russell's account of Mormonism, we see the way in which a particular value system is almost immediately invoked as the context for the action about to unfold. Russell, torn between hostility and toleration, revealed the self-interested nature of both when he framed his critique of Mormonism in the context of repeated references to "our institutions" (55, 69, 71) and to the themes of American toleration and pluralism, yet such toleration is only demonstrable in the face of acutely felt difference: "the Jew, the Mahometan, the Pagan, and even the atheist" are its beneficiaries. The precondition for one's claim to this American virtue is therefore the designation of an unorthodoxy which is situated outside of it. In other words, the values that constitute the ground of narrative authority emerge in the context of an "other" they presume to embrace. Therefore, to exaggerate difference, to demonize

the other, is necessarily and by the same degree to valorize one's tolerance as the generous embrace of such difference. This is the root of the
tension characteristic of that nineteenth-century literature of the hostile
imagination which does not entirely capitulate to the paranoid style,
caught as it is between xenophobia and the need for self-presentation as
a tolerant, law-respecting American.

As diversity becomes more highly valued than conformity, and
multiculturalism rather than melting pot the ruling paradigm of American society, the ideological investment in exaggerating difference becomes even more important than it was for Russell. Thus we have the
case of a recent television episode that featured a Mormon seemingly
caught in an incestuous liaison with his daughter.[48] The case unfolds to
reveal not incest but clandestine polygamy as the aberration. One horror is substituted for another, and the dramatic interest is thereby
heightened by the fictive transgression of not one but two societal
taboos. With shock and repugnance at an appropriately high level, the
ensuing courtroom scene plumbs the complexities of this conflict of religious conscience and law, challenging the viewer to reconsider this
sympathetically portrayed "difference."

Two Mormon-affiliated stations, in Utah and Washington, pulled
the series in protest, even though the writers had incorporated a disclaimer that made clear the Mormon church no longer officially sanc-
tions polygamy. So the piece could not be accused of misrepresenting the
Church, and the Mormon was in fact a fairly likable character; what was
the problem? The point, of course, is not merely that juxtaposing Mormonism and polygamy has a semiotic force that no disclaimer can really
temper. More seriously, the network, like Russell, used deviance as a
mirror in which the viewer's tolerance and generosity of spirit may be
reflected—or at least interrogated. Difference has not, however, really
been embraced—it has been prostituted to the parading of pluralism.

Genre as Mediation

In the nineteenth century, literature could be deliberately and irrespon-
sibly inflammatory and provocative. Often, however, it enacted violence in such a way as to effectively mediate irreconcilable difference.
At present, the higher cultural value assigned to diversity, as well as the
movement of Mormonism toward the mainstream, have disarmed
much of the anti-Mormon rhetoric typical of the nineteenth century. In
addition, the mediational function which the represention of violence
had in the fiction we have surveyed has now come to be served, to some
extent, by generic categories themselves. Rhetoric and representation

are constrained by the way in which culture has come to divide up discourse generally. In 1890, Zane Grey could get in his shots against the Mormons, newspapers from New York to California could call for their extermination, and Senator Noell could cite Artemus Ward in Congressional testimony to the same end, without this strange melange of sources and forums devoted to a common political end jarring anyone's sensibilities. It may be no easier today than in the nineteenth century to sort out hysterical hate mongering from objective reporting of the facts when a new and threatening presence appears on the American cultural or religious scene. But if fact and fiction are still slippery labels, we find a kind of intellectual refuge in generic distinctions, and control discourse that way.

To measure the distance we have come, we could examine the novelette *Bessie Baine* (1876), about a young Quaker girl who is desired as Elder Russell's fifth wife. When she declines, she is kidnapped, drugged, and dragged to Utah, with the "husband" explaining to curious witnesses that he is returning his daughter to an asylum. The horror eventually weakens her mind, and by the time she arrives at the institution, she is trying to convince herself she is not insane.[49] Still resistant to Elder Russell's advances, she is admitted to a regimen of head shavings, whippings and beatings, torture, and the unremitting echoes of cries and screams through the labyrinthine passages. The narrator informs us that this punishment lasts until the inmates "promise obedience or [are] driven insane" and is "still used by the Mormon leaders as a prison for refractory women"(20).

This author's insistence on the veracity of her story's horrors is typical of most of those novelizing the Mormon theme. That they were taken at their word is evident from that fact that such an important debate as that surrounding the Cummins Bill was largely informed by "facts" garnered from "reliable sources" that turn out, on inspection, to be the novels and exposeés we are examining. In his testimony of 18 May 1870, Senator Cragin quotes liberally from works by John Hyde (*Mormonism: Its Leaders and Designs* [1857]), Catherine Waite (*The Mormon Prophet and His Harem* [1866]), and numerous others he does not name ("I have read of some women . . . ") to impute to the Mormons corruption, licentiousness, and occasional assassinations. Some of the charges he recites appear to have been too bizarre for novelists to even attempt adapting (human sacrifice and a system of polyandry "only privately talked of in secret circles").

Reciprocally, many of the undocumented themes he introduces into his testimony are by that time already or soon to become mainstays of anti-Mormon fiction for the next generation. He alleges that women were driven insane by the "plurality," that others were "hunted" down for rebelling; he alleges private passageways and secret subterranean torture chambers in Brigham Young's apartments (where he "punishes his refractory wives"), a white slave trade, and thousands of officially sanctioned murders. Analogies as well as charges will resurface in fictive accounts. His evocation of Juggernaut, infant sacrifice, and suttee, for example, will be echoed in Switzer's *Elder Northfield's Home* (1882).

Even blatant satire was taken at face value. In February of 1867, the House was debating women's suffrage. Some critics of Mormonism felt that the vote would give the women of Utah Territory a weapon with which to free themselves from the burden of polygamy. In lending his support to the bill, Representative T. E. Noell never mentions such a motive explicitly. But he does represent a humorous anecdote about Mormon polygamy from Artemus Ward's *Travels* as having been an actual experience of Ward while in Utah. In his account, a group of polygamous widows propose en masse to a wealthy bachelor. The point of Noell's reference is more comic relief ("they were pretty enough, . . . it was the muchness of the thing that he objected to") than persuasive evidence of the "base prostitution" he is alleging.[50] But the use to which he puts the story is beside the point. It is the status accorded the account that is striking. "When Artemus Ward was in Utah . . . " may serve to introduce a tall tale or a deadly serious episode, and maybe politicians are especially vulnerable to confusing the two. But the pervasiveness of this disregard for generic distinctions gives a universalizing quality to anti-Mormon rhetoric that is especially resistant to rebuttal. How does one refute a joke? What discourse is appropriate to challenge a plot structure that transcends any particular text?

No wonder, then, that "documented" case histories found credible audiences, such as happened with *The Fate of Madame La Tour*.[51] A novelized account of life in Utah, its impressive format included an appendix with affidavits alleging the discovery of mass-burial pits containing "rawhide thongs" and the battered skulls of large numbers of children, as well as numerous other atrocities perpetrated against rebellious members.

Such legalistic accoutrements might win popular belief even today. But frequently these "affidavits" have a rather dubious twist to them. In 1872, for instance, citizens opposed to Utah's petition for statehood filed with Congress a "Memorial . . . Against the admission of that Territory as a State." Dozens of affidavits were included, attributing all manner of crime and criminality to the Mormon people. But the following phraseology is typical of the line before the signature: "About the endowment house oaths and the rest she sincerely believes to be true" (70); "Affiant further says that he has read Bill Hickman's book about murders and other crimes, and he believes it true, . . . Affiant believes that Brigham Young and the leaders commanded murders and robbery" (61); "Affiant further says that he has read the affidavits of Abraham Taylor, James Ashman, and John P. Lloyd, on Mormon matters, and he knows the contents thereof, and he believes each one to be true" (72); "Affiant further says that he has read 'Bill Hickman, the Danite Chief's Book,' and he believes it true; also, Beadle's book, and he believes that true: also Mrs. Ward's book, and he believes that true" (79).

We may wonder if such a reading list is meant to substantiate or discredit the force of the complaint, if the testimony is buttressed by or merely parroted from such accounts. Affidavits cite affidavits, memoirs cite affidavits, and affidavits cite memoirs. But the contrast with today's generic scrupulousness is unmistakable. It is not merely that genres have proliferated. For clearly old forms fade out (satyr plays, epic poetry, and sonnets) as new forms develop (sitcoms, sound bites, and the academic novel). Perhaps what *has* changed is the extent to which generic distinctions have come to pervade public discourse in general, and not so much to demarcate *how* an object is represented as to constrain the claim such a representation makes upon us. Such discursive categories serve more as functional indices of authorization than as guides to form. Thus, authority and legitimacy displace nineteenth-century persuasiveness and moral fervor as operative rhetorical criteria. Credentials are more important than eloquence; a kind of propriety in the author–audience and author–subject matter relationships assumes an importance not known since Horace.

As a consequence, literature of intolerance currently finds its institutional forum almost uniquely in sectarian publishing houses and fringe hate groups. Newspapers have become elaborate reports on crime and economic indicators which relegate controversial editorializing to a clearly demarcated section. Pulp fiction is quite happy to occupy its niche of profitability and intellectual disrespectability, with neither inclination nor credibility enough to engage in social polemics. (And the omnipresent formulaic disclaimer about names and events would be necessary even in a less legalistic milieu.)

Certainly, persistent forms of prejudice and stereotyping will invariably trickle through the media, from television sitcoms to Harlequin romances to letters to the editor. But whether or not history is likely to repeat itself, the appropriation of, say, the popular novel to wage a campaign of disinformation and hate-mongering against a new ethnic group or religious sect is improbable simply because fiction has lost its stature as moral champion and arbiter of American values to televangelists and political grandstanders (and, increasingly, prime-time television).

There are, of course, exceptions. Contemporary satire, for example, certainly blurs the gates of ivory and of horn, but, like the *roman à clef*, this very obfuscation is its *raison d'être*, not an incidental blemish. Historical fiction forewarns by its very label that the poet "nothing affirmeth." When fiction presumes to claim the authority of history, as when Hollywood increasingly usurps the role of journalism, a category like "docudrama" immediately emerges to contain the new area of transgression.

These distinctions can, of course, cut both ways. In the observance, they mediate cultural violence as we have argued. But in the breach, they become a rhetorical ploy by which fiction is endowed with an unwarranted claim to referential validity. And we have seen, in fact, the persistence of anti-Mormon fiction which *does* make a claim to historical truth. The Moroni Traveler mysteries are marketed as "a very compelling glimpse into this fascinating subculture" revealing "telling details of its church-dominated region." Therefore, the channeling of cultural violence into particular forums has not disabled such violence altogether. But in the absence of a literary counterpart to "docudrama" which would generically condone such dabbling, new grounds must be invented to constitute narrative authority when moral fervor alone is no longer sufficient. The latest strategy for such a move is made possible under the aegis of the postmodern turn to ethnography. From Black Studies to Women's Studies to multicultural curricula, fiction has been embraced as the key to newfound appreciation for diversity and difference. Political morality, the embrace of diversity, and a new academic cosmopolitanism thus become means of empowering discourse with a referential value it would otherwise lack. And so we are not so far removed from the basis for nineteenth-century representations after all. Moral fervor again becomes the ground for trespassing discursive categories that would work to restrain representation. Whether we read the novelist Chinua Achebe to understand Ibo culture or watch an episode of *Picket Fences* to catch an appreciative glimpse of a heterodox religious group, whether clad in the lofty liberalism of a prime-time television show or the well-intentioned multiculturalism that too often can invite pseudo-anthropology, representing the other-fashioning will continue to be the road to self-fashioning.

In all of this, we hear the eerily familiar ring of a nineteenth-century author who revealed the close kinship of those representations which demonize the other to relieve cultural anxieties and those which appropriate the other with more benevolent intentions. In *John Brent* (1862), two male heroes are stymied when they learn the Mormoness they wish to free is not seeking a liberator.

> [She was] clutched by this foul ogre [the Church], and locked up in an impregnable prison. And we two were baffled. Of what use was our loyalty to woman? What vain words . . . our knightly vow to succor all distressed damsels. . . . did [they] wish to escape? No.[52]

So they respond in a way that echoes the efforts of nineteenth-century antipolygamy crusaders trying to galvanize the uninterested Utah women: "She must be saved, sooner or later, whether she will or no" (185). But not because *her* welfare demands it. The author makes clear what is at stake—what, in fact, has been at stake all along in these renderings of the Mormon as alien. The liberation of the nineteenth-century Mormons, like their acceptance within a pluralistic culture in the twentieth, are but different means to the same end—*America's* self-definition. As the not-to-be-thwarted heroes of *John Brent* remind their audience, it is America, after all, that has given to the "Old World . . . tobacco, woman's rights, the potato" (313).

Notes

1. Sen. Aaron Harrison Cragin (New Hampshire), Debate on the Cummins Bill, *Congressional Globe,* 41st Congress, 2d session, 18 May 1870, 3577.

2. Thomas deWitt Talmage, *The Brooklyn Tabernacle, A Collection of 104 Sermons* (New York: Funk & Wagnalls, 1884), 37.

3. Although they are not grouped together by category, most occurences of the Mormon character in fiction will be found in the Chad Flake's comprehensive *Mormon Bibliography 1830–1930* (Salt Lake: University of Utah, 1978).

4. Archibald Maxwell, *A Run through the United States during the Autumn of 1840* (London: H. Colburn, 1841), I: 24. Further references cited parenthetically.

5. John Evans, *History of All Christian Sects and Denominations; Their Origin, Peculiar Tenets, and Present Condition,* 2d ed. (New York: James Mowatt, 1844).

6. John Winebrenner, *History of All the Religious Denominations in the United States,* 2d ed. (Harrisburg, PA: 1848), table of contents.

7. For his remarkable story, see William L. Stone, *Matthias and His Impostures: Or, The Progress of Fanaticism* (New York: Harper, 1835).

8. David Meredith Reese, *Humbugs of New York: Being a Remonstrance against Popular Delusion; Whether in Science, Philosophy, or Religion* (New York: Taylor, 1838), 265.

9. Susan L. Fales and Chad J. Flake, *Mormons and Mormonism in U.S. Government Documents* (Salt Lake City: University of Utah Press, 1989).

10. Leo Tolstoy's reputed opinion that Mormonism was the quintessentially American religion is cited second hand in a number of Mormon sources, as well as by Harold Bloom (*The American Religion: The Emergence of the Post-Christian Nation* [New York: Simon & Schuster, 1992]), who claims "there is something of Joseph Smith's spirit in every manifestation of American religion" (43). See also Leland A. Fetzer, "Tolstoy and Mormonism," *Dialogue: A Journal of Mormon Thought* 6.1 (1971), 13–29.

11. Thomas O'Dea, "Mormons," *Harvard Encyclopedia of American Ethnic Groups*, ed. Stephan Thernstrom (Cambridge: Harvard University Press), 720.

12. One of the most prevalent of the many stereotypes of Mormon converts held that they were drawn from the dregs of American and European society. Objective accounts of such observers as Charles Dickens were quite to the contrary. The novelist visited an emigrant ship about to sail for America, and wrote of the Mormons, "I should have said they were, in their degree, the pick and flower of England" (William Mulder and A. Russell Mortensen, *Among the Mormons* [New York: Knopf, 1958], 337).

13. John Russell, *The Mormoness; or, The Trials of Mary Maverick* (Alton, Il.: Courier Steam Press, 1853), 38. Further references will be cited parenthetically.

14. Following an extermination order by Missouri Governor Lilburn Boggs, an armed mob massacred eighteen or nineteen men and boys at the small Mormon settlement of Haun's Mill in October 1838. The standard LDS account is that of survivor Joseph Young, recounted in volume 3 (183–186) of Joseph Smith's *History of the Church of Jesus Christ of Latter-Day Saints* (Salt Lake: Deseret, 1973).

15. "Author of Frank Merriwell" [Burt L. Standish], "Frank Merriwell among the Mormons: or, The Lost Tribes of Israel," *Tip Top Weekly* (19 June 1897), 2. Further references cited parenthetically.

16. Sydney Bell, *Wives of the Prophet* (New York: Macaulay, 1935), iv.

17. Max Adeler [Charles Heber Clark], *The Tragedy of Thompson Dunbar, A Tale of Salt Lake City* (Philadelphia: Stoddart, 1879), 10.

18. Jennie (Bartlett) Switzer, *Elder Northfield's Home: or, Sacrificed on the Mormon altar* (New York: J. Howard Brown, 1882), 115.

19. Sir Arthur Conan Doyle, *A Study in Scarlet* (New York: Burt, n.d. [London, 1888]), 129; James Oliver Curwood, *The Courage of Captain Plum* (Indianapolis: Bobbs-Merrill, 1908), 97,261.

20. Bruce Kinney, *Mormonism: The Islam of America* (New York: Revell 1912).

21. Stanley Ives, "Notes on Mormon Polygamy," *Western Humanities Review* 10 (Summer 1956), 238.

22. Such is the remedy suggested by "An American" [William Loring Spencer], author of *Salt Lake Fruit: A Latter-Day Romance* (Boston: Rand, Avery, 1884). In his preface, he insists that anti-Mormon legislation (such as the Cummins Bill) is not the solution. Hope will come only if, "in her might, Liberty puts her heel on the serpent's head, and crushes it. No intermediate legislation will avail. Exterminate, or be exterminated" (iii, v). This, we have seen, was governor Bogg's exact prescription.

23. Richard Hofstadter, *The Paranoid Style in American Politics and Other Essays* (New York: Knopf, 1965).

24. Switzer, *Elder Northfield's Home*, 274.

25. Dan Coolidge, *The Fighting Danites* (New York: Dutton, 1934), 182.

26. Standish, "Frank Merriwell," 12; Coolidge, *Fighting Danites*, 131–32.

27. Maria Ward [pseud.], *Female Life among the Mormons. A Narrative of Many Years' Experience among the Mormons . . .* (London: Clarke, 1855), 65.

28. Ward, *Female Life among the Mormons*, 417.

29. See, for example, Zane Grey, *Riders of the Purple Sage* (New York: Harper, 1910); and Doyle, *A Study in Scarlet*.

30. "Author of Buffalo Bill" [Prentiss Ingraham], "Buffalo Bill and the Danite Kidnappers; or, The Green River Massacre," *The Buffalo Bill Stories: A Weekly Devoted to Border History* (1 February 1902).

31. A similar strategy seems to operate today with those sects that have displaced Mormonism as a threatening "cult," such as the Unification Church and Scientology. Opponents of both groups have charged that coercive persuasion deprives members of any choice in their conversion. The Supreme Court of California, in *Molko vs. Holy Spirit Association for the Unification of World Christianity* (252 California Reporter [Calif. Supreme Ct. 1989], 122–156), went so far as to validate one such allegation that "brainwashing" rendered its members "incapable of exercising their own will" (122). Similarly, the 1993 confrontation with Branch Davidian "cultist" David Koresh spawned news coverage that referred to his "wizardry," the "mystic spell" he cast over members, and his "magnetism." See "Intimidation, Wizardry Marked Tiny Cult's Rule," *Richmond Times-Dispatch*, 3 March 1993, A8.

32. Jennifer Blake, *Golden Fancy* (New York: Fawcett, 1980), cover blurb.

33. Tony Hillerman, *A Thief of Time* (New York: Harper Row, 1988), 196.

34. Paul Fussell, *BAD: The Dumbing of America* (New York: Summit, 1991), 197.

35. Martin E. Marty, "Explaining the Rise of Fundamentalism," *Chronicle of Higher Education,* 28 October 1992, A56.

36. Terry J. Christlieb, letter, *Chronicle of Higher Education,* 2 December 1992, B5. The criticism was a response to Marty's essay on Fundamentalism.

37. Klaus J. Hansen, *Quest for Empire: The Political Kingdom of God and the Council of Fifty in Mormon History* (Ann Arbor: Michigan State University Press, 1967), 247.

38. Gerald Petievich and an anonymous critic describing Irvine's work, cited in the blurb to Robert Irvine, *Called Home* (New York: St. Martin's, 1991). *Called Home* henceforth cited parenthetically, by page number, as *CH.*

39. Robert Irvine, *The Angel's Share* (New York: St. Martin's, 1989), 105. Henceforth cited parenthetically as *AS.*

40. Robert Irvine, *Gone to Glory* (New York: St. Martin's, 1990), 135. Henceforth cited parenthetically as *GG.*

41. Cleo Jones, *Prophet Motive* (New York: St. Martin's, 1984), 73. Henceforth cited parenthetically.

42. Tom Clancy, *The Hunt for Red October* (Annapolis: Naval Institute Press, 1984), 200.

43. Tom Clancy, *Clear and Present Danger* (New York: Putnam's Sons, 1989), 480.

44. According to a report by the Population Reference Bureau, "The 'Ozzie and Harriet' model of 1950's television fame—a breadwinning husband and a wife who stayed home with the children—once was the dominant pattern in America. Now, one in five married couples with children fits in." Cited in an AP story in the *Richmond Times-Dispatch,* 25 August 1992, A2.

45. Frances Lang, "The Mormon Empire," *Ramparts* 10 (September 1971), 40.

46. John LeCarré, *The Russia House* (New York: Bantam, 1989), 211.

47. A recent *Time* editorial makes the same point: "The assimilation of Hispanics is news because two allied groups of political operators are trying to pretend that it isn't happening. Leaders of ethnic communities fear the success of their communities because it makes special favors unnecessary and deprives leaders of their status as favor brokers." See Richard Brookhiser, "The Melting Pot Is Still Simmering," *Time,* March 1993, 72.

48. *Picket Fences,* CBS (originally aired 22 January 1993).

49. M. Quad, *Bessie Baine: The Mormon's Victim* (Boston: G. W. Studley, 1898 [1876]), 13.

50. T. E. Noell (Missouri), "Equality of Suffrage" *Appendix to The Congressional Globe*. 39th Congress, 2d session, 11 and 18 February 1867, 111.

51. Mrs. A. G. Paddock, *The Fate of Madame La Tour* (New York: Fords, Howard, Hulbert, 1881).

52. Theodore Winthrop, *John Brent* (New York: Lovell, 1862), 177, 164.

8

Destruction, Revolution, and Cultural Nihilism

Tonglin Lu

An iconoclast par excellence, Lu Xun, the May Fourth radical writer, spent his entire life fighting against the idols in Chinese tradition, considering them the source of numerous problems existing in Chinese society. Ironically, he was my childhood idol, and his way of thinking still has a strong impact on me and on some Chinese intellectuals of my generation. To a certain extent, the present essay may be perceived as an attempt to imitate Lu Xun's iconoclastic gesture, namely, to hold our idol—in this case, Lu Xun himself—responsible for our current problems.

Thanks to their author's pessimistic view of Chinese culture and a lucid reflection on the dead end to which destruction motivated by cultural nihilism will lead, Lu Xun's works can be perceived as a mirror of Chinese intellectual radicalism of this century. On one hand, as a Chinese intellectual deeply rooted in his culture in spite of his better judgment, Lu Xun could not help searching for a higher value, an ideological Big Other, that would justify his participation in a rally of destruction of the past. On the other hand, his lucidity forced him to see the fallacy of such a higher value, whatever form it might take. Lu Xun complained very often in his writings of his inability to communicate with the oppressed, who belonged either to the laboring class or to the second sex. Despite his lack of communication, this May Fourth writer sincerely but somehow unsuccessfully tried to avoid the trap of using the other as a proof of his higher value system and as a way out of his cultural and ideological dilemma.[1] Obsessed with the idea of destruction, oscillating between hope and desperation, Lu Xun's works exemplify the path taken not only by the May Fourth intellectuals but also, to a large extent, by their followers at the end of this century with its contradiction, hopelessness, and suffering. Lu Xun was no doubt one of the modern Chinese intellectuals who were best versed in traditional Chinese culture. At the same time, he was also one of the most radical iconoclasts of the same culture. Furthermore, his lucidity—or "self-dissection," as he put it—allows us to understand the insoluble dilemma faced by a modern Chinese intellectual. Lu Xun did not attempt to criticize Chinese culture as an outsider. Even in his most vehement attacks on this culture, he always included himself as partly its product and not simply a detached observer. Because of this unique combination of various contradictory qualities, Lu Xun's works powerfully and tragically testify to the failure of the practice of sociocultural destruction supported by cultural nihilism.

Cultural nihilism in modern China has alternatively been expressed by two forms of cultural absolutism. In one form promoted by modern radical intellectuals including Lu Xun, China must transform its old cultural identity into a completely new one in order to survive in the modern world. In the other, Chinese culture is so superior in the eyes of its defenders that it does not need to engage in any dialogue with other cultures. The first form still prevails among a number of contemporary Chinese intellectuals in search of a Westernized identity. The second, however, can count among its supporters certain Sinologists in China as well as in the West.[2] Despite appearances, these two forms are not contradictory but rather overlapping and complementary. As versions of the same inferiority complex, this cultural absolutism has hindered modern China from engaging in genuine and equal dialogues either internally, among different groups, or internationally, with other cultures.

Dead Fire as an Image of Revolution

For the majority of leftist intellectuals of Lu Xun's generation, revolution or radical change was considered a vague hope for ending the agonizing and humiliating situation of China for which they blamed the "evil" Chinese tradition. This may explain the intimate and intricate connections between the New Culture Movement (*xin wenhua yundong*), in which most progressive intellectuals of the 1920s and 1930s participated, and the socialist revolution led by the Communist Party. In fact, the May Fourth Movement is considered one of the main sources for the formation of the Chinese Communist Party.[3] Chen Duxiu, one of the three leaders of the May Fourth Movement and the founder of the leading literary journal of this movement, *New Youth (xin qingnian)*, in 1915, was also the founder of the Communist Party in 1921. In his youth, Mao Zedong himself not only was an avid reader of *New Youth* but also published an article in this journal.[4] As Maurice Meisner states: "A young

Mao Zedong was the intellectual product of the first cultural revolution, and an aging Mao was the political promoter of the second."[5] During the 1930s, a large proportion of prominent left-wing writers, participants in the New Culture Movement, such as Mao Dun, Rou Shi, Ding Ling, and Xiao Jun, joined the Communist Party.[6]

Although Lu Xun himself was never a member of the Communist Party, his name has been used on both sides of the Taiwan Straits as a symbol of "literary revolution" *(wenxue geming)*. Mao Zedong on many occasions praised Lu Xun as a model for Chinese revolutionaries. In his "Talk at the Yan-an Forum on Literature and the Arts," the article which established the literary conventions of socialist realism in China for more than four decades, Mao Zedong again enthusiastically endorsed this May Fourth radical writer.[7] Thanks to Mao's promotion, the author of *Call to Arms*, whose mind was supposedly "in communion with" Mao's own, has been sanctified and worshipped as a national hero in socialist China since 1949. On the other side of the Taiwan Straits, Lu Xun was regarded for similar reasons such a dangerous enemy that his works were censored for decades.

On one hand, Lu Xun's uncompromising critique of traditional society made him a perfect fellow traveler of the Communist Party, which embodied a destructive force par excellence as a dissident party. On the other hand, this fellow traveler could not follow the party to the end, because Lu Xun's hope, which was very often equated with revolution in his writings, was by nature negative or destructive, whereas the Communist Party claimed to work toward a teleologically conceived future.

This difference is exemplified by Lu Xun's metaphor "dead fire" *(sihuo)* for hope or for revolution in contrast to the metaphor "raging fire" *(liehuo)*, which is used in socialist realism as a different vehicle for the same tenor.

> This was dead fire. Despite its blazing appearance, it remained perfectly immobile. It was completely frozen—in the form of branches of coral. There was coagulated dark smoke at the end of each branch; the dead fire was shrivelled as if it had just come out from a burning hell. The fire was mirrored on all sides of the icy wall, which in its turn reflected back and forth; its image was transformed into numberless shadows, coloring the icy valley with a coral red.

> During my childhood, I loved to watch the foam and waves left by swift ships and raging flames darting out from a blazing furnace. Not only did I love to watch them, but I also wanted to retain clear pictures of them. Unfortunately, they changed every

second, never stabilizing their shapes. Although I gazed and gazed, they never left any distinct trace.

Dead fire, I have finally seized you![8]

Dead fire embodies the longings of the narrator in his childhood and the dreams of the adult poet. Dead fire is characterized by two contradictory qualities: a stable or even static form combined with an extremely dynamic force, or the image of death saturated with life. In other words, life, no longer measured by temporality, is spatialized and finalized in the form of an aesthetic object through death. One may say that Lu Xun also hoped for this impossible combination, a finalized change or a change so constant that it finally becomes unchangeable. Lu Xun's relationship to revolution can be illustrated by this poetic image of dead fire as a finalized image of change. Dead fire can only preserve its dynamic form in congelation, thus losing its dynamic force. The eternal congelation will soon make the dead fire "perish."[9] This aesthetization of a dynamic, changing, and destructive force suggests an aspiration for an ivory tower—confining Lu Xun's subversive drive within the realm of a harmless aesthetic game. Nevertheless, like the dead fire in the narrator's dream, Lu Xun preferred immediate destruction to this slow death by congelation. The image of this immediate destruction invokes the action of revolution in its radical negativity, as the conversation between the narrator and the dead fire demonstrates:

"I would like to bring you out of the icy valley so that you will never be frozen again but will remain burning forever."

"Alas, I will burn out!"

"I would feel sorry for you if this happened. Well then, let me leave you here."

"Alas, I will be frozen to death!"

"So, what can we do?"

"How about yourself, what would you do?" The fire asked me.

"I have told you, I would get out of this icy valley . . . "

"So let me burn out."

The dead fire suddenly jumped up like a red comet, taking me along out of the icy valley. A big stony car unexpectedly ran toward me; I was finally crushed under its wheels. Before I had time to see that car I fell into the icy valley.

"Ha-ha, you will never meet dead fire again!" I laughed triumphantly, as if this were what I had wished.[10]

The dead fire's choice is also the narrator's choice in his dream, namely, to destroy the self along with the surrounding world, regardless of the consequences. Like the dead fire, Lu Xun faced a dilemma. On one hand, he would have liked to destroy traditional society perceived as the source of China's problems. On the other hand, this destruction could not avoid a certain implication of self-destruction, since Lu Xun belonged to the world that he intended to destroy just as the dead fire belonged to the icy valley. Lu Xun's concept of revolution was as elusive as his childhood image of burning fire, consisting of a destructive force which ceaselessly renews itself in death. Nevertheless, this image of dead fire originating in Lu Xun's childhood memory also entails a return to a forsaken past. This return endows the image with a slightly nostalgic undertone. Like a child's game, this image is aimless. It may be projected into a past but not into the future. Revolution in Lu Xun's terms is thus a futureless destructive game. Choosing revolution is tantamount to choosing destruction and self-destruction with a devilish laughter—like that of the narrator dying along with the dead fire. The past is finished, and so is the destroyer as part of this past that he must destroy.

If the narrator equates dead fire with hope, the icy world represents society. The fire in this icy world can only play a decorative role by coloring the otherwise colorless world. The fire cannot have any impact on the world unless it is destroyed along with part of the frozen world. The narrator's happy laughter in his dream is a laughter of death which represents the last step in a desperate rebellion. Death can be perceived as the failure of the rebel, since it marks the end of his rebellion. However, it can also be considered the mark of his victory, since the world against which he rebels can no longer exercise any power over him. This mark of victory illustrates the pessimism in Lu Xun's writings, where rebellion is presented more as a hopeless gesture of destruction than as any teleologically constructive act.

The Madman as Revolutionary

It was not surprising that a large number of May Fourth intellectuals ended their ideological wandering by anchoring themselves in communism. Despite their radically iconoclastic attitude toward Confucianism, the ideological world of most intellectuals of this period was still implicitly influenced by the Confucian training of their formative years. The nihilistic attitude toward the Chinese cultural heritage prevailing among the May Fourth participants did not necessarily help them overcome the effects of their cultural heritage. On the contrary, by repressing their connection to the past, they were even more haunted by the ghost of this heritage, since they had not settled accounts with their personal share in the Chinese cultural tradition. Lu Xun, for example, suggested to the younger generation that they should completely ignore classical Chinese literature.[11] At the same time, only in classical Chinese could he write the diary by means of which he expressed some of the most intimate details of his personal life. The option of classical Chinese as the language of his diary shows that Lu Xun remained a "Native" of this culture. The connection between the May Fourth iconoclasts and the Confucian tradition can be found in their commonly shared belief in collectivism. Confucianism, as a collective ideology, emphasizes the social responsibility and moral mission of each individual. For Confucius and his disciples, an individual existed mainly as an embodiment of the social relations and functions implied by his titles: father, son, minister, and so forth.[12] As a Western collectivist ideology, communism was particularly attractive to these May Fourth intellectuals who urgently wanted radical change for their nation but were nevertheless unable to eradicate the ideological makeup of their formative years.

Despite his similarities to this generation of radical intellectuals, Lu Xun still represents an exception among them. Most May Fourth intellectuals who joined the Communist Party believed in the function of collective salvation. Lu Xun, however, occasionally perceived communism as a hope mainly because he associated the Communist Party, the most powerful dissident organization, with negation. In the same vein, Lu Xun identified revolution with hope not because he believed that revolution was hopeful but because he considered hope as illusory as revolution.

Lu Xun is not the only pessimistic writer among the May Fourth radicals. The works of a large number of writers of the May Fourth movement—such as Ba Jin's *Family (Jia)*, Yu Dafu's *Sinking (Chenlun)*, and Rou Shi's *February (Zaochun eryue)*—demonstrate the same kind of pessimism concerning the constructive function of any individual action. In the eyes of these writers, the individual is a powerless victim of society, so that society must take the blame for what happens to him and his surroundings. This image of a powerless individual facing a powerful society further entails that the individual subject does not need to be truly responsible for what happens to both his objective and subjective world. Lu Xun's attitude, however, differed from that of most of his contemporaries. For him, destruction was not only a passive outcome of the subject's victimization but also an active choice in which the rebel's subjectivity was constituted. Lu Xun's rebellion might very well have been aimless and fruitless, but it was not irresponsible. Despite his sense of disorientation, the rebel must assume the responsibility for his choice as well as for the outcome of his unavoidable failure. In this sense, Lu Xun's pessimism gains a tragic dimension.[13]

Most of the radical writers of his generation attributed their personal desperation to the political and economic situation of their nation. For them, the destruction of the evil tradition would solve their personal as well as national problems.[14] This may partly explain the appeal of communism for a large number of Chinese radical intellectuals of the May Fourth Movement, who considered the Russian Revolution an example of collective salvation. By contrast, collective salvation was never truly part of Lu Xun's agenda. The reason is not too complicated: in his opinion, traditional Chinese society was hopeless not only because of its oppression of individuals but also because corrupted or corruptible individuals were the products and carriers of this tradition. Lu Xun's protagonist in "The Madman's Diary" provides a good example of an individual rebel limited by his own connection with his subverted object, traditional society. In this story, the hero radically protests against the practice of cannibalism at the risk of being declared insane by other submissive members of society, including his family. However, his protestations do not prevent the madman from joining the group of "eaters of human beings" in traditional society, since the hero regains his sanity by becoming a potential member of officialdom *(houbu dao-tai)*.[15] The madman's rebellion does not substantially shake the foundations of traditional society. On the contrary, it finally turns into a journey toward his own integration with, and submission to, this evil society.

If the madman, initially a determined rebel, in the final analysis cannot save himself from participating in the cannibalism practiced by traditional society, how can we expect such rebels to save us from the same tradition? The madman's transformation from a determined revolutionary to a member of officialdom reveals Lu Xun's skepticism regarding the notion of collective salvation. A savior who is beyond traditional society and free from the present power structure does not exist in reality. At the same time, no one (including the author himself) is spared this contamination by an evil tradition.

Lu Xun was revolutionary to the extent that revolution was transformed into a synonym for negation—ceaseless negation of both the objective and the subjective world. This double negation distinguishes Lu Xun's view of revolution from the teleological notion of a construc- tive revolution promoted by the Communist Party. Ironically, the myth of Lu Xun as a great revolutionary created by Mao Zedong and his party contributes to cancelling out his subversive or revolutionary potential which largely depends on this double negation, namely, the negation of the world and of the self.

The Uncertainty of Negation

In 1925, Lu Xun wrote to his student and wife-to-be, Xu Guangping:

This fantasy cannot be proved as fantasy with any certainty. Con- sequently, it may be taken as a consolation, as God in the eyes of his believers. You seem to read my works very often, but they are too dark. Although I constantly sense that only "darkness and ni- hility" do "truly exist," I still cannot help resisting them desper- ately. As a result, my voice sounds rather radical. Very likely, this belief may have something to do with age and experience and may not be true, since finally I am unable to prove that only darkness and nihility truly exist.[16]

Lu Xun's hope results from his inability to negate hope with cer- tainty, since the existence of the opposite pole of hope, that of darkness and nihility, cannot be proven. Like Pascal, who based his faith in God on an intellectual bet on providential existence in order to preserve his own possible salvation in the future, Lu Xun preferred to take refuge in a fantasy of hope. Although he understood his own desperate situation and that of his nation, Lu Xun did not want to sink into darkness and nihility prematurely, in case the future were not as dark as he had imag- ined. His hope was then the winnings on his bet, conditioned by a fail- ure to find substantial justification for his desperation.

At the end of "My Old Home," Lu Xun presented hope as a beau- tiful dream, beautiful precisely because it was unreal.

While lying down, I listened to the water rippling beneath the boat, and realized that I was following with my own path. I thought: although Runtu and myself had become so distant, our next generation could still communicate with each other, right now was Honger not thinking of Shuisheng? I hoped that they would not like us become distant in the future. . . . At the same time, I also did not hope that in order to maintain their closeness, they would have toiled restlessly like me; nor would they have toiled to the point of stupefaction like Runtu; nor would they, like others, have toiled for the sake of dissipation. They should be able to enjoy a new life, a life we have never experienced. . . .

I thought about hope and suddenly felt frightened. When Runtu wanted to keep the incense burner and candlestick, I was secretly laughing at him. He always worshipped idols and could not forget them for a single moment. Now, what I called hope was it not also the idol that I myself created? The only difference was that his wish was close and tangible, whereas mine was distant and elusive.

With my dreamy eyes, I saw a stretch of emerald green sand which bordered the ocean and extended under the golden full moon in the dark blue sky. One cannot be certain whether hope exists or not. This is just like roads in this world. Originally, there was no road on earth. Only because a great number of people have passed by, have roads taken form.[17]

After twenty years of wandering, the narrator returns to his home town in order to move his family away from his old home. Despite the gloomy atmosphere in his childhood home which has already been sold to a new owner, the narrator arrives with the hope of seeing a childhood friend, Runtu, a peasant of his own age. The childhood friendship with Runtu seems valuable to the narrator especially because this single relationship beyond class segregation in the narrator's life represents for him the hope of overcoming the lack of humaneness engendered by the traditional social hierarchy. The encounter with the adult Runtu, however, brings only disillusionment. As a prematurely aged peasant and the father of five children, Runtu, burdened by poverty, natural disasters, and taxation, has become an *ordinary* peasant, and respectfully calls his childhood playmate "master." When the narrator's mother asks him why he does not call the narrator by his nickname, as in the past, Runtu replies that as a child he did not understand the "rules" *(guiju)*. This conventionalization of the relationship between the two childhood friends from different social backgrounds shatters the narrator's hope based on a romanticized past. Having witnessed his nephew and Runtu's son befriending each other as a reenactment of his and Runtu's own formerly egalitarian relationship, the narrator nevertheless ends his short story with an image of new hope. However, it is no longer possible to sub-

stantialize this hope, be it in his past memory or in the conceptualiza-
tion of an idealized future. It becomes "dreamy" *(menglong)*, "distant
and elusive" *(mangyuan)*.

Before the narrator meets the adult Runtu, his hope can be epito-
mized by the image of a twelve-year-old boy in the middle of "a stretch
of emerald green sand which bordered the ocean and extended under
the golden full moon in the dark blue sky."[18] Following the narrator's encounter with the true peasant, this portrait of "the little hero" becomes
"blurred."[19] The vanished image of the past Runtu in the middle of a limitless natural world has been replaced at the end by another image of
hope, a similar image of the natural world which nevertheless excludes
any human being. This empty image of nature exemplifies the narrator's
hope in its total negation. Hope will emerge only after the destruction of
the current world, as the point of departure, or the degree zero.

The idealized image of the Runtu remembered as a child in a sense
deprives him of a subjective voice, since he is primarily the outcome of
the narrator's subjective projection. Like the beloved lady in the romance of courtly love, the peasant Runtu, as the representative of the laboring class, becomes an empty sign onto which the narrator may
project his subjectivity.[20] In the final scene which summarizes the narrator's hope for a classless society, even this empty sign must be excluded. However, Runtu, the representative of the Other, is not the only
one to be excluded—the narrator himself, as the author's spokesman in
the story, is also denied access to this world of hope. The final description of beautiful nature, as a reconfiguration of hope at the end of the
narrator's journey, refuses entrance to any inhabitant of the old world.

What should this new life look like? The narrator's description of
this new life, "a life we have never experienced," consists of three neologisms which negate the existing modes of life: it should not be like the
narrator's own life, "toiling restlessly" *(xingku nianzhuan)*, nor like
Runtu's, "toiling to the point of stupefaction" *(xingku mamu)*, nor like
others', "toiling for the sake of dissipation" *(xingku ziwei)*.

The three neologisms offer a fresh perspective from which various
lifestyles in society may be perceived. This perspective, independent of
the conventional symbolic system, marks the relative autonomy of the
narrator's axiology. Lifestyle is reclassified and reevaluated by an invention of three expressions that grant the narrator a critical distance
from the conventional language as the basis for social discourse. Due to
their idiosyncratic nature, the three expressions are self-referential
within the context of the story and will become meaningless once displaced into a context of common language. As a somehow idealistic reformer who is determined to fight against social hierarchy and at the

same time is unable to escape from the determination of the same social structure, the narrator's mode of life described in the story endows the first expression with a vivid image. The image of Runtu, with his wooden face and emotionless language, the worn-out middle-aged peasant, makes the second expression true to life. By means of her vulgar but colorful language and greedy but amusing manner, Beancurd Xishi convincingly illustrates the third expression. At the same time, one cannot accurately describe these images invoked by the three neologisms verbally. "Toiling" *(xingku)*, as the first two Chinese characters of each expression, serves as a critique of society in general. By repeatedly using this term, the narrator seems to imply that every member of society toils uselessly, regardless of his or her social origin and ideological belief. His refusal to use any expression existing in conventional language may be interpreted as a mark of protest against the hierarchical society inherent in this language. In other words, the term *xingku* puts people of different social classes on an equal footing—sharing the same negative position as a somewhat aimless slave in relation to society. On one hand, this equalization of people of different origins expresses hope, hope for a utopian equality. On the other hand, this gesture also expresses desperation, since the rebellion is realized only in language— a negative language of fiction.

However, Lu Xun's invention of the three neologisms is largely based on his mastery of classical Chinese. As in classical Chinese poetry, the concision of these expressions and their structure free of any conjunction, create a highly suggestive effect, and invoke a dreamy image of what the narrator calls hope. Like these three neologisms, hope in Lu Xun's writings can hardly be translated or explained by any intelligible terms of conventional language. At the same time, the connection with word formation in classical Chinese tinges the image of hope created by the three neologisms with a nostalgia for a golden past.

A Spiritual High Wall

In his "Preface to the Russian translation of 'The Official Story of A Q,' " Lu Xun wrote:

> Although I have tried, I am still not certain about my own ability to draw a truly accurate spiritual portrait of our fellow citizens. For others, I am unable to learn with certainty. But for myself, I seem always to sense the existence of a high wall that separates each of us from others. This wall isolates us and makes communication impossible. This is because our intelligent ances-

tors, called sages, divided people into ten different categories, each of which was classified in a hierarchical structure presumably in accordance with its degree of superiority. Nowadays, although we no longer use the same titles, the ghost of this hierarchy is still alive. Moreover, this isolation has developed further so that it has even extended to the different parts of the human body so that the hands even become contemptuous of the feet. The creator of human beings was already ingenious enough to make us insensitive to others' physical pain. Our sages and their disciples even further perfected this creation by making us insensitive to others' emotional pain.[21]

On one hand, Lu Xun considered this spiritual high wall the source of many social problems in modern China. On the other hand, he also realized that he himself, as the product of traditional culture, was a prisoner of this wall. Like most of his contemporaries, Lu Xun was haunted by the ghost of the traditional hierarchy. But unlike most of them, Lu Xun understood that it was not enough to destroy the social hierarchy in order to establish a new society, since this social hierarchy was inherent in everyone's subjective world, including his own. How could one pretend to destroy any trace of the past without destroying along with it the rebel's subjective world, if the rebel was part of this past? At the same time, if this destruction affects not only society but also the rebelling individual, who will be left to construct a less hierarchical society in the future? Admitting that someone will be left after total destruction, will he be able to escape the ghost of the traditional hierarchy? In other words, even destruction was perceived as a suspicious act, since it was initiated by individuals who belonged to a world subject to destruction. Lu Xun differed from his contemporary iconoclasts because he did not believe that one could purify his subjective world by drawing a line between the self and society. At the same time, he was still no less obsessed by the urge to free the world completely from its evil past. He was lucid enough to understand that totality or purity did not exist, since any clear-cut category, including the one dividing old and new, was artificial and conventional. But he was unable to give up his dream of a new society which can emerge only after the total destruction of the old. The keen awareness of the impossibility of his dream and the persistent unwillingness to give up this impossible dream made Lu Xun the most original and at the same time the most tragic writer of modern China.

Lu Xun's short stories are very often told from the perspective of a first-person narrator. This narrator always presents certain striking autobiographical elements. Furthermore, despite his position as an observer, this first-person narrator usually feels a deep compassion for the victims of society, be they members of the oppressed sex or laboring class. At the same time, the compassion expressed in the stories never succeeds in overcoming the gap between the first-person observer and his objects of observation. Lu Xun's narrator is emotionally and physically distant from lower-class victims to the point that any genuine communication between the two parties is impossible.

Marston Anderson points out that the narrator's attitude toward Sister Xianglin in "The New Year Sacrifice" is similar to Lu Xun's attitude toward Qian Xuantong in Lu's preface to *Call to Arms*.[22] Sister Xianglin, the protagonist of Lu Xun's story, is a laboring-class woman. A mere commodity, she is sold as a child bride to a family. After the death of her first husband, she is sold by her mother-in-law to her second husband, with whom she conceives a baby. After the death of both her second husband and their son, she returns to the household of the narrator's uncle in order to resume her past job as maid. Perceived as unchaste since she was married twice, and as a bearer of misfortune since both of her husbands died, sister Xianglin is treated as the unwelcome underdog in the narrator's home town. When the narrator meets her on the street, she has already become a beggar. On the verge of death, Sister Xianglin asks the narrator if there is an underworld where the souls of dead people meet. The narrator, taken by surprise and frightened by the prospect of becoming responsible for what happens to her in the future, offers an ambivalent answer: "I don't know for sure" (*wo shuo bu qing*).[23] Despite his belief in social equality and his compassionate description of her life, the narrator cannot communicate with her, since the only words he can articulate are a mark of the failure of communication. This mark further suggests a condescending attitude—the educated male narrator should not tell the truth to the uneducated female protagonist in order to protect her from deep disillusionment. To this extent, the high wall that separates them is also of the benevolent narrator's own making. In spite of his position as reformer, deep in himself the narrator still does not believe that a laboring-class woman can communicate with him as an equal partner. As a result, any genuine communication between them becomes impossible. Therefore, Sister Xianglin is never granted an individual voice, and, like her body, her language has been commodified in the story.

As an activist in the New Culture Movement, Qian Xuantong, however, was neither uneducated nor a woman, and Lu Xun held him in a much higher regard than he did the women in his stories. Lu Xun did not want to explain to Qian his own disbelief in the effectiveness of

their activities, mainly because he tried to avoid passing his "bitter lone-
liness" on to "these young dreamers."[24] As in the case of the narrator's
conversation with Sister Xianglin, Lu Xun condescendingly tried to protect the reformers from the truth concerning the futility of their effort.
Lu Xun could not engage in genuine communication with Qian Xuantong and his comrades, because the author of *Call to Arms* believed that
truth was beyond their grasp and too painful for them to bear.

The Preservation of Hope by Means of Illusion

The condescendingly benevolent attitude toward more naive reformers
did not prevent Lu Xun from occasionally laughing openly at their
naiveté. Very often, the revolutionaries in his writings appear as lu-
natics, idiots, and losers, misunderstood by the ignorant and miserable
masses for whom they intended to work. In "The Shrew, the Fool, and
the Slave," for example, the fool wants to help the slave open a window
in his suffocating room. The slave, however, frightened by the boldness
of his well-intended savior, denounces the fool to the master. As a result,
the master severely punishes the fool for his transgression and rewards
the slave for his loyalty.[25] In his preface to *Call to Arms*, Lu Xun compared China to an iron house in which the inhabitants would sooner or
later die of suffocation. Revolutionaries are compared to the few awakened people who try to wake the sleeping crowd in order to destroy the
apparently indestructible iron house.[26] In this case, revolution is meta-
phorically identified with the action of opening a window in a suffocating house. Revolutionaries are thus associated with the naive fool,
whose good intention only reveals that he is completely out of touch
with reality.

   Qian Xuantong, as the friend who "forced" Lu Xun to write short
stories, is described by the author in his preface to *Call to Arms* as an ide-
alist who, much like his fool, would also like to destroy the walls of the
iron house. By "obeying" his order, Lu Xun willingly and deliberately
identified with a naive fool—or a revolutionary.[27] By means of this half-
hearted identification, Lu Xun reluctantly joined the group of revolutionaries. One may say that Lu Xun was a revolutionary to the extent
that he and other revolutionaries were equally the objects of mockery in
his fictional world for their hopeless idealism and lack of any effective
action:

   Since I did not write directly out of a faith in literary revolution,
   for what reason did I start writing? I remember now, it was mostly

because of my compassion for the enthusiastic people. I thought, even in their solitude these warriors had some good ideas. Thus, I should make some noise to cheer them up. Initially, this was the only reason. Naturally, in the meantime, I also hoped to be able to expose the source of illness in traditional society in order to attract attention with the hope of finding a certain cure. For the realization of this hope, I needed to keep up pace with the forerunners. As a result, I suppressed darkness, pretended to laugh, and embellished my works with happiness in order to brighten them.[28]

On the surface, Lu Xun must pretend to believe in the success of the revolutionary action of his forerunners in order to support them by writing his stories. In reality, however, Lu Xun also needed their naive perspective in order to break his own silence. Only through this perspective could Lu Xun perceive a faint light which made him doubt the certainty of darkness and nihility. Had he acquired this certainty, Lu Xun would no longer have had any reason to write. To this extent, the naive perspective saved Lu Xun from total silence or intellectual death. He wrote out of desperation, but only through hope could he justify his act of writing. For a moralistic and nationalistic May Fourth writer like Lu Xun, to write was tantamount to hoping for his nation, even if hope might mean merely a hope for negation. To this extent, Lu Xun needed the revolutionary community and a simulacrum of faith in revolution in order to survive in his lonely world of desperation. Although Lu Xun understood the futility of their cause, without these fellow revolutionaries his life would have been composed only of darkness and nihility.

Thanks to the perspective of his naive comrades, Lu Xun could indulge himself in an illusion of hope which his usual intellectual keenness would have denied. At the same time, since this optimism was based on other people's perspectives, Lu Xun could also easily mock their naiveté. Oscillating between the naive hope of his fellow traveler and his own pessimism, Lu Xun's writings constantly recreate and destroy hope. Hope emerges, disappears, and reemerges through dream, disillusionment, and the recreation of illusion. Lu Xun was indeed a collectivist to the extent that he had to rely on a collective illusion, revolution, to negate his own destructive and self-destructive drive, although revolution as a collective ideology in China exemplified destruction for the May Fourth writer. Moreover, this collective illusion was doubly necessary especially because it allowed Lu Xun to express his personal disillusionment. For him, revolution as a collective illusion justified his act of writing by means of which he could analyze the futility of such an

illusion. To a large extent, this dialectic of belief and disbelief was responsible for the complex and very often self-contradictory nature of Lu
Xun's works.

Solitude as Its Shadow

At the end of "My Old Home," Lu Xun wrote: "Despite my conviction,
I could not erase hope, since hope lies in the future."[29] Since hope cannot
be judged according to the criterion of true and false, hoping may be considered similar to dreaming. In Lu Xun's writings, the possibility of hoping lies precisely in this illusory nature, or indeterminacy. Hope wanders
on the margins of reality between the possibilities of its realization and
its destruction, just as in Lu Xun's prose poem "The Shadow's Farewell"
the shadow wanders between daylight and darkness:

> In the heavens, there is something I resent, so I am unwilling
> to go there. In the underworld, there is something I resent, so I am
> unwilling to go there. In your future golden world, there is some-
> thing I resent; I am unwilling to go there.
>
> However, you are the one I resent.
>
> Friend, I am unwilling to follow you any more; I am unwill-
> ing to stay.
>
> I am unwilling!
>
> Alas, I am unwilling. It would be better if I could wander in
> a no-man's land.
>
> I am only a shadow, which will soon part from you in order
> to sink into darkness. Darkness, however, will engulf me, whereas
> light will dispel me.
>
> I do not want to wander between darkness and light, so it
> would be better if I sank into darkness.[30]

Lu Xun's hope can be represented by this image of a leave-taking
shadow that constantly refuses any definitive destination. Only in darkness or the no-man's land can the shadow find its hope or its freedom,
even if it were at the price of its own disappearance. This freedom *is* its
disappearance, since, detached from the body on which its existence depends, the shadow can only disappear. Like the shadow, Lu Xun also
hopes for the same kind of freedom, freedom from traditional society,
from the high wall that isolates each individual, and from the power

structure that makes each person choose between the role of victim and that of victimizer. This freedom for Lu Xun, however, can be realized only in destruction and self-destruction, since the individual who hopes for the destruction of all these negative aspects attributed to traditional society is also the product of the same society. As the shadow cannot survive without its body, the individual rebel cannot be completely detached from the evil tradition without eliminating its product, namely, himself.

By dissociating itself from "*your* future golden world" *(nimen jianglai de huangjin shijie)*, the shadow, as the author's spokesman, also denies any connection with a teleological vision. Hope in Lu Xun's writings is not only illusory but also aimless, since it cannot be projected into the future. Lu Xun's hope subverts the commonly accepted notion of hope to the extent that he hoped to deny, if not to destroy, what others hoped for the future, a representation of the golden world.

Nevertheless, although he did not believe in the existence of "*their* future golden world"—a future his leftist fellow traveler would create by means of revolution—Lu Xun might also invent a faint image of *his* own golden world. This golden world, paradoxically for a modern reformer like Lu Xun, is very likely situated in a bygone past. As in "My Old Home," the only possible happiness in Lu Xun's writings always existed in a remote past, such as childhood. Only as children can the narrator and Runtu enjoy a humanized relationship untouched by the inhuman hierarchical society in "My Old Home." Only a child can be innocent in a society where people practice cannibalism as in "Madman's Diary." Furthermore, the "diary" ends with a hopeful appeal, "Save the children" *(Jiujiu haizi).*[31] The difference between Lu Xun's golden world and the revolutionaries' is also a matter of temporality. Lu Xun located his hope in an irrevocable past, whereas his leftist friends projected theirs into a revolutionary future. The past can no longer be changed, whereas the unknown future can be arranged and rearranged in accordance with an ideal. This may partially explain why Lu Xun's hope offers a much gloomier image than that of his revolutionary friends, despite their common ground.

Like the shadow, Lu Xun's subjectivity could not be rooted in any fixed intellectual and ideological ground. Although he did not believe in the effectiveness of any collective salvation, Lu Xun could not give up his sense of social responsibility, remaining an intellectual still implicitly determined by the rejected Confucian training of his formative years. In the Confucian tradition, the best scholar is supposed to become a mandarin who "must feel concerned before the entire world did, and feel happy after the world did" *(Xiang tian xia zhi you er you, hou tian xian zhi le er le).*[32] The leave-taking shadow knows perfectly well that there will be no place for him, but cannot give up searching. After examining the heavens and the underworld, light and darkness, the shadow can only find a "no-man's land" or the "land of nothingness" *(wudi)*. For someone like Lu Xun, who was torn between his deep resentment for and close ties to the Chinese tradition, this land of nothingness may also be taken as his intellectual destination.

In this no-man's land, hope can be preserved only by a playful but at the same time desperate rebellion; playful because the rebel does not believe in the effectiveness of his action, desperate because the rebellion aims mainly at destruction.[33] This playful and desperate rebellion is Lu Xun's gift to his readers, as seen in the shadow's words:

> You are still expecting a gift from me. What can I offer you? If you insist, I will still offer you the same darkness and nihility. Nevertheless, I hope that it is only darkness which may disappear in your daylight; I hope that it is only nihility which will not take any space in your heart.[34]

Although Lu Xun repeatedly stated that he was finally also unable to prove the existence of darkness and nihility, his shadow has left a unique gift to his readers—darkness and nihility. The only hope of diminishing this radically pessimistic vision is to separate these two negative entities. In other words, darkness without nihility or nihility without darkness may be less overwhelming so that the reader whom Lu Xun's shadow addresses may have a slightly greater chance of escaping the oppression of the objective world. In this sense, the gift of darkness and nihility is also an appeal to resist them. Since for Lu Xun's shadow darkness and nihility are more substantial than daylight, this resistance becomes its own aim and its own hope by means of its destructive potential. In this sense, the gift of darkness and nihility is an expression of hope, a hope for the future generation which will be awakened from the world of darkness and nihility and will search for daylight. For Lu Xun and his shadow, the daylight only dispels them since, despite their awareness of darkness and nihility, they also belong to the same world subject to negation. Therefore, this is a negative gift par excellence, a gift of daylight from someone who is unable to welcome it.

The shadow who belongs to the world of darkness and nihility is proud of its solitude. As for Lu Xun's shadow, despite the suffering it might cause, solitude for Lu Xun was also a mark of distinction. As the shadow seeks solitude, it says:

I will engage in a long journey to darkness alone, leaving not only you behind but also other shadows. There will be only me sinking into darkness; the entire universe will belong to me.[35]

As a rebel against the well-to-do class of Chinese society to which he still belonged, Lu Xun had chosen a marginal position in his own class. At the same time, his rebellion did not provide him with access to the oppressed class, for which he intended to work. As an alien among the laboring class, he also felt misunderstood and unable to communicate with the people for whom he would like to speak. Like the leave-taking shadow, Lu Xun detached himself from the social body on which he was supposed to depend. At the same time, he could neither belong to the group of people who were supposed to be his kind. Like his shadow, Lu Xun did not belong anywhere, whereas the entire universe of solitude and darkness belonged to him.

Notes

1. Regarding the benevolent sexism of certain radical writers, including Lu Xun, see Yue Ming-bao, "Gendering the 'Origin' of Modern Chinese Fiction," in *Gender and Sexuality in Twentieth-Century Chinese Literature and Culture,* ed. Lu Tonglin (Albany: SUNY Press, 1993).

2. Simon Ley, the Belgian Sinologist, for example, constantly expresses in his writings a desire to preserve intact traditional culture, as if China would be better off as an immense museum of its precious past.

3. Arif Dirlik states: "The Laying of the foundations of 1920 meant for the Communists the reorganization of the May Fourth legacy" (*The Origins of Chinese Communism* [Oxford: Oxford University Press, 1989], 12). At the same time, the National Government in Taiwan blamed the May Fourth literature for their loss of the mainland, since it extended the influence of the Communist Party (Peng Ruijin, *The Forty Years of the New Literature Movement in Taiwan* [Taipei: Zili wanpaoshe wenhua chubanshe, 1991], 65).

4. Maurice Meisner, *Mao's China and After: A History of the People's Republic* (New York: Free Press, 1989), 14.

5. Ibid., 16.

6. Mao Dun (1896–1981), author of *Midnight* (1933) and other literary and critical works. Rou Shi (1901–1931), author of *February* (1929) and other stories, executed by the Guomindang Government in Longhua with four other writers and some Party members. Ding Ling (1907–1986), author of "Miss Sophia's

Diary" (1927), *The Sun Shines over the Sangkan River* (1949), and other works. Xiao Jun (1908–present), author of *Village in August* (1942) and other works.

7. Mao Zedong, "Talk at the Yan'an Forum of Literature and the Arts" (Yan'an zuotanhui shan de jianhua), in *Lun wenxue yu yishu* (Beijing: renmin wenxue, 1960), 81. My translation.

8. "Dead Fire," in *Wild Grass,* in *Lu Xun quanji* (Beijing: People's Literature Press, 1956), 2: 195.

9. Ibid., 196.

10. Ibid., 196.

11. Lu Xun wrote to the Chinese Youth: "I believe that you should read very few, if any, Chinese books, and read more foreign books" ("The Books Young People Must Read," in *Collection of Misfortune* [Huagai ji], in *Lu Xun quanji*, 3: 12).

12. See Confucius's notion of the "five relationships" *(wulun).* I use the masculine singular third-person pronoun instead of both masculine and feminine to refer to the individual either in the Confucian or the May Fourth context. Admitting that unlike Confucius, the misogynistic defender of the patriarchal order, Lu Xun and his generation of radical intellectuals were the benevolent advocates of women's emancipation, women nevertheless have not truly gained subjective voices in their works. As in the case of the women's emancipation promoted by the Communist Party, women were the *objects*, not the *subjects*, of this movement. Concerning this problem, see Yue Ming-bao's "Gendering the 'Origin' of Modern Chinese Fiction."

13. See Tim Reiss, *Truth and Tragedy: Study in the Development of a Renaissance and Classical Discourse* (New Haven: Yale University Press, 1980).

14. At the end of his short story "Sinking," Yu Dafu's protagonist blames the weakness of China for his own failure in sexual relationships ("Sinking," in *Modern Chinese Stories and Novellas: 1919–1949,* ed. Joseph Laugh et al. [New York: Columbia University Press, 1981], 141).

15. "The Madman's Diary," in *Call to Arms,* in *Lu Xun quanji,* 1: 422.

16. "Letter to Xu Guangping," in *Letters between Two Areas* (Liangdi shu), in *Lu Xun quanji,* 11: 20–21.

17. "My Old Home," in *Lu Xun quanji,* 1: 435.

18. Ibid., 477.

19. Ibid., 485.

20. See Eugene Vance, "The Châtelain de Coucy: Enunciation and Story in Trouvère Lyric," in *Marvelous Signals* (Lincoln: University of Nebraska Press, 1986), 51–85.

21. Preface to the Russian Translation of "The Official Story of AQ," in *Lu Xun quanji,* 7: 81.

22. See Marston Anderson, "The Morality of Form: Lu Xun and the Modern Chinese Short Story," in *Lu Xun and His Legacy* ed. Leo Ou-fan Lee (Berkeley: University of California Press, 1985), 41.

23. "New Year Sacrifice," in *Wandering* (Panghuang), in *Lu Xun quanji,* 2: 7.

24. Preface to *Call to Arms,* in *Lu Xun quanji,* 1: 419–20.

25. "The Shrew, the Fool, and the Slave," in *Wild Grass,* in *Lu Xun quanji* 2: 216.

26. Preface to *Call to Arms,* in *Lu Xun quanji,* 1: 419.

27. Ibid., 419.

28. Preface to *Self-Selected Works,* in *Collection of Southern Accent and Northern Intonation* (Nanqiang beidiao ji), in *Lu Xun quanji,* 4: 455–56.

29. Preface to *Call to Arms,* in *Lu Xun quanji,* 1: 419.

30. "The Shadow's Farewell," in *Wild Grass,* in *Lu Xun quanji,* 2: 165.

31. "The Madman's Diary," in *Lu Xun quanji,* 1: 433.

32. Fan Zhongyan (989–1052), "Rhapsody on Yueyang Mansion" *(Yueyang lou fu),* in *Guwen guanzhi* (Beijing: Zhonghua shuju, 1959), 419.

33. He wrote to his wife, Xu Guangping: "In conclusion, my method of preventing sadness is devoting myself to make trouble for the oncoming suffering. Then, I take this scoundrel's performance as a sign of victory and force my voice to sing the triumphal song as if this were a pleasure" (*The Letters between Two Areas,* in *Lu Xun quanji,* 11: 16).

34. "The Shadow's Farewell," in *Lu Xun quanji,* 2: 166.

35. Ibid., 166.

9

Murder as Play: Conrad Aiken's *King Coffin*

Mihai Spariosu

Preliminary Intellectual, Historical, and Literary Background

With the advent of modernism, homicide becomes a rather common literary theme and is linked as a rule to the larger, modernist question of the uneasy relation between aesthetics and ethics. In turn, this question has its modern roots in the libertine, Romantic, and Postromantic traditions of the eighteenth and nineteenth centuries (present, for example, in the literary productions of Choderlos de Laclos, the Marquis de Sade, E.T.A. Hoffmann, Pierre-François Lacenaire, Thomas Griffiths Wainewright, Thomas De Quincey, Edgar Allan Poe, Théophile Gautier, Marcel Schwob, Robert Louis Stevenson, Villiers de L'Isle-Adam, Oscar Wilde, and of many lesser representatives of the decadent and the art-for-art's-sake movements), but can ultimately be traced back to the ancient quarrel between philosophy and poetry initiated by Socrates in Plato's *Republic*. During the beginning stages of the Romantic movement, Kant takes up this quarrel again, in his third *Critique*, and attempts to resolve it by proposing an aesthetical foundation for his ethics; Kant nevertheless eventually subordinates art to morality, which for him becomes the higher purpose of purposeless art.[1]

Thomas De Quincey, among others, challenges Kant's subordination of aesthetics to ethics, and he does it precisely in terms of an ironical transvaluation of homicide as a form of artistic play, in a series of essays entitled *On Murder Considered as One of the Fine Arts*. In reversing the Kantian relation between ethics and aesthetics, De Quincey becomes a precursor of Nietzsche, who transforms philosophy itself into a fine art, through his notions of the "artist-metaphysician" and the aesthetic transvaluation of all values. But Nietzsche goes even further, in his *Birth of Tragedy*, when he claims that existence itself can be justified only in aesthetic terms and that all process can have only aesthetic meaning: "a kind of divinity, if you like, God as the supreme artist, amoral, recklessly creating and destroying, realizing himself indifferently in whatever he does or undoes, ridding himself by his acts of the embarrassment of his riches and the strain of his internal contradictions." This god is not Christian but Hellenic (Dionysus), and by proclaiming his return to the modern world, Nietzsche intends to "resist to the bitter end any moral interpretation of existence whatsoever."[2]

The aestheticist or "decadent" movement at the end of the nineteenth century equally rebels against the Kantian notion of art as a higher form of morality and develops the counterconcept of "art for art's sake." This concept leads, in turn, to the realization that art goes back to an older, pre-Platonic version of mimesis, which can no longer be interpreted as a tame imitation of reality but as an archaic form of play, creating and destroying this reality at will. In Hellenic epic and drama, an archaic world transpires in which might makes right and in which the gods themselves are "amoral," playing arbitrarily with men, their delightful toys.[3] In many modern "decadent" writers, art thus returns to its origins in archaic play, or in play as an innocent and unashamed manifestation of power. Homicide as a "fine art" becomes naturally a nexus of this whole problematic because it is the most blatant and radical form of moral transgression: Once it is stripped of its ethical and legal (that is, rational) guises, it emerges as a pure, unrepressed form of archaic, violent play. In much decadent, modernist, and postmodernist fiction, then, homicide as play is presented as a creative act that shatters the normal (middle-class) boundaries of everyday reality and contributes to fashioning a new life, based on Dionysian, tragic principles, where pleasure and suffering commingle indifferently in a joyful, ecstatic affirmation of all that is.

On the other hand, in much anti-aestheticist fiction at the end of the nineteenth and the beginning of the twentieth century, homicide as play is often also employed to confront the prevailing rational and ethical values of modern Western culture, but without the violent, transgressive solutions envisioned by its decadent counterpart. Rather, this confrontation is often presented in terms of a perennial literary theme: the gap between art and life, illusion and reality, thought and action, freedom and necessity.[4]

In this context, homicide as play turns out to be an illusion (from the Latin *in-lusio*, literally "in play") engaged in by the protagonist. By the end of the narrative, however, the protagonist often discards it as delusion and returns to the "real" world of morality and prevailing values. Should he refuse this return, he is promptly isolated from or cast out of his fictional community. This is the case in much popular fiction, including a host of detective novels where both the murderer and the detective play a cat-and-mouse game which, far from being subversive, ends up by reestablishing the social and moral status quo.

But in the most interesting of the anti-aestheticist narratives dealing with homicide as play, the "real" world of middle-class morality remains by no means unproblematic, and a desideratum of radical, *nonviolent* change in prevailing values is often implied by the end of the story. Conrad Aiken's *King Coffin* is one such anti-aestheticist narrative that points to the highly ambiguous nature of Western ethical norms, suggesting indirectly a radical reexamination of these norms.

Murder as Play in *King Coffin*

Conrad Aiken has a relatively solid reputation as a poet, but his fiction is either entirely ignored or too easily dismissed. Yet this fiction is quite sophisticated by both American and European standards, engaging some of the major themes of modernity, and has had no small impact on other novelists, notably on Malcolm Lowry. One of Aiken's most intriguing novels is *King Coffin*, which was inspired by the famous Leopold–Loeb case that shook Chicago in the 1920s. According to Clarence Darrow and Benjamin Bacharach, the defense attorneys in that case,

> The civilized world had been startled out of its routine complacency on May 31, 1924, by the amazing confession of these two youths of nineteen and eighteen respectively, of the kidnapping and murder of a young neighbor and acquaintance of Richard Loeb, fourteen-year-old Bobby Franks, purely for the thrill and adventure. The wealth of the three families, their prominence in the community of Chicago, the bizarre and apparently motiveless homicide, and the instantaneous newspaper notoriety which was given the crime from every conceivable angle, aroused public interest throughout the entire civilized world in the fate to be meted out to the young murderers.[5]

The Leopold–Loeb case inspired several works of fiction, including Patrick Hamilton's play *Rope's End* (on which Alfred Hitchcock based his motion picture *Rope* in 1948) and Meyer Levin's *Compulsion*; but Aiken's novel is perhaps the most interesting because it places its subject in a long novelistic tradition, developing it in terms of the notion of "pure murder." Although Aiken borrows certain superficial features from the case, he goes well beyond his source of inspiration or model, concentrating on the apparent "irrationality" of Leopold and Loeb's motives for committing the crime.

The plot of *King Coffin* is fairly simple, and readers who look for a fast-paced, sensational thriller need to turn elsewhere to find it, although Aiken's story does contain a final twist. Jasper Ammen, a young man of independent means, has associated himself with a group of anarchists operating in Boston. But Ammen becomes disillusioned with the petty goals of this group and decides to follow a path of his own. A great admirer of Nietzsche, whose death mask is one of the few adornments of his "chaste and epicene" room, he considers himself an Overman and proposes to live beyond the morals of the crowd. In practice, this largely amounts to cutting off his friends or visiting them at three o'clock in the morning and reading their private diaries. In order to raise himself above the herd, Ammen decides to commit "pure murder"—for him, an act beyond good and evil. After considering the possibility of killing one of his friends, he discards the idea because it lacks "purity"— by selecting a friend as victim he would act upon a personal motive. Instead, Ammen chooses at random a complete stranger whose name, appropriately enough, turns out to be Jones.

Ammen studies the habits of Jones for several weeks, managing at the same time to keep his friends interested in his secret life. He learns about their reactions by stealthily reading the diary of his neighbor, the law student Toppan. Jasper also makes an alliance of sorts with Gerta, the young woman who is in love with him, sharing with her as much of his project as he considers safe to disclose. Moreover, he encourages her to get sexually (but not emotionally) involved with Sandbach, a Jewish anarchist, so that his own relationship with her would remain "pure." To Toppan he presents his plan of murdering a complete stranger as a purely theoretical problem to be made into the subject of a novel entitled *King Coffin*. Gerta becomes more and more concerned about his odd behavior, while Toppan grows more and more suspicious. Finally, an anonymous letter is sent, presumably at Gerta's instigation, to Ammen's father, informing him of his son's criminal intentions. A new complication arises from the fact that Jones's wife has a stillborn child. Ammen secretly attends the funeral, and instead of killing Jones, he tries to kill himself by turning on the gas in his apartment, but not before sending a letter to Gerta so that she could arrive in time to save him.

Several critics have seen Aiken's novel as no more than a psychological casebook. For example, Vincent McHugh describes the work as the "crisis-chart of a paranoid psychosis, complete with narcissism, megalomania, sexual symbols and a psychopathic inheritance."[6] Likewise, Frederick J. Hoffman writes: "If I seem to be overlong in describing Aiken's failures, it is only with the aim of setting the stage for a discussion of his major failure—in fiction, that is. All of the contrivances, half-starts, hollowness and thinness of characterization culminate in the novel *King Coffin*. Its hero, Jasper Ammen, descends from Dostoevski, Poe and Nietzsche; and in each case he loses much of the inheritance. . . . On the edge of Harvard Yard, Ammen plots the 'perfect crime'. . . . He is the Emersonian soul gone sour, an Ahab turned Raskolnikov, with the motive of neither for planning his acts."[7] Hoffman in effect blames *King Coffin* for not being the kind of Fosterian novel of manners it was never meant to be. He seems to take the narrative at its face value, ignoring the fact that it is presented from Ammen's point of view and consequently failing to perceive the ironical standpoint of the narrator. Hoffman also fails to inform his reader that Ammen never kills anyone but rather attempts suicide, thus missing the final ironic reversal in the narrative.[8] But apart from several factual inaccuracies, Hoffman fails to address what seems to be a major issue, at least from the standpoint of his kind of New Critical approach. Although Ammen descends from Poe, Dostoevski, and Nietzsche—and one could add another dozen names to the list—the question remains whether Aiken's novel is merely a lame, self-conscious imitation or an instance of the conscious use of a literary tradition toward an original artistic end. In *King Coffin*, Aiken takes up the literary problematic of the "perfect crime," and by linking it to an individualistic notion of self, he carries it to its logical conclusion: In order to commit a perfect crime—or, rather, "pure murder"—the protagonist chooses as victim a perfect stranger. In the end, however, this stranger turns out to be himself. Furthermore, Ammen never commits, but only *plays* at, murder (so he can hardly be accused of being a psychopathic killer), and the ending of the novel remains deliberately ambiguous.

We should first draw a distinction between Hoffman's "perfect crime," which belongs to the tradition of the detective novel, and what Ammen calls "pure murder," which belongs to the tradition of the aestheticist novel. A "perfect crime" is a legalistic concept, implying a deed that cannot be detected because it cannot be traced back to an apparent motive. A "perfect crime" is both a challenge to and a triumph of rationality or logic; it is a mathematical problem. "Pure murder," on the other hand, is ultimately more of an aesthetic question than a logical or rational one. As Ammen observes to himself, once he has decided to look for a possible victim, "the terribleness of the deed must be kept pure: the problem had become a problem in art-form" (328). On one level, the two concepts are diametrically opposed; on another, they overlap. Whereas both concepts defy the normal ethical standards, a perfect crime suspends the question of ethics, whereas a "pure murder" is explicitly directed against it. As Jasper Ammen points out to Toppan,

> "To injure or destroy is natural, it's life itself: to deny that is to deny life. Well, you know it's right, and I know it's right, but society won't agree with us, will it? . . . Consequently what ought to be a public action, and done openly has to be private or secret: unless you make up your mind to go the whole hog and *do* it openly and take the social consequences. That's the way it ought to be, to be perfect, it ought to take place in *sunlight*."[9]

A perfect crime is perfect only as long as it remains undetected, whereas pure murder remains imperfect *unless* it is committed in broad daylight as Ammen and the surrealists argue.[10]

Most importantly, the two concepts point to different mentalities in Western culture: aristocratic (or archaic) and median. Through pure murder Ammen claims to revive an archaic world in which might makes right, whereas a perfect crime largely belongs to a rational mentality in which might is separated from right. But since Ammen lives in a median culture, he is fully aware that pure murder must also be a perfect crime, and, indeed, the two notions overlap in several respects. For one, they overlap because of their "purity." Thinking of his insane brother, Kay, Ammen rejects the possibility of his own madness by arguing that "purity is not insanity. An action could have the purity of a work of art—it could be as abstract and absolute as a problem in algebra" (319). In other words, the two concepts overlap because they are both ludic in nature: A perfect crime involves a game of hide-and-seek between the perpetrator and the detective, while pure murder involves a cat-and-mouse game between the aggressor and the unsuspecting victim.

Ammen is fully aware of the pleasurable, playful quality involved in choosing his victim at random, tracking it down—what Ammen calls "detection for the *sake* of detection" (326)—and eventually annihilating it. Telling Gerta about King Coffin, the name of a physician he had seen on a sign somewhere in Boston or Saint Louis, he exclaims: "I'd *like* to play King Coffin. . . . It seemed to me a very good, and very sinister name for a doctor—it sounds a little supernatural. It might not be a *man* at all, but a sort of death-principle" (320). Ammen repeatedly uses the cat-and-mouse analogy in order to describe his playing King Coffin: "As he stood still by the corner, observing first one face and then another , one hand jingling pennies in his pocket, the other holding his unlighted pipe, it occurred to him that a cat must feel something like this:

a cat alone in a cellar, sitting perhaps on the top of a flour barrel, and watching the naive and unconscious antics of mice" (310).

The other common analogy Ammen uses for his game is that of the puppeteer pulling the strings of his puppets at will. Once he chooses Jones as the intended victim, he resists the impulse of calling up Gerta to say that "I've found a man, a stranger, and I have him on the end of an invisible cord, a cord three miles long, and with this cord I shall slowly but surely kill him, I shall dangle him there like a puppet, like Punch or Judy, until I want him" (343). Ammen likewise thinks of Gerta and his other friends as puppets to be manipulated to his own ends: "They, as much as Jones, were his own creation, they were falling into their grooves, they no longer had any freedom of will. To all intents, they had become [his] puppets" (363).

Ammen sees his game as pure because it has no material object, it is simply a game that enhances his feeling of power for its own sake. Looking over Boston at sunset, the protagonist feels that the surrounding world is "all Jasper Ammen, a singular magnification or distillation of his own essence, it was himself gone abroad for the greater exercise of his subtlety and power. The tower was his strength, the trees were his strength, the evolving and changing of light were merely, as it were, the play of his thought over an earth everywhere his own" (300). Killing for the sake of killing is part of this feeling of power, which seeks to expand beyond all boundaries, beyond good and evil. In this sense, pure murder can equally succeed as a perfect crime because its object is transcendental and therefore impossible to trace back to any material motive.

For Ammen, purity also means lack of emotional involvement beyond even the sheer pleasure of the hunt. As he reasons with himself, the victim must be a stranger,

> someone to whom one could be completely indifferent. He must be neither attractive nor unattractive, not to be loved or pitied, nor hated or feared, someone whose strangeness and anonymity (in the sense that one knew nothing about him and *felt* nothing) was pure. The face must be quite ordinary, just a face, the bearing and gait must be neither offensive nor enviable, the clothes of a sort of universal characterlessness. In short it must be simply "a man." (332)

But as Ammen finds out soon enough, everyman does not exist except in the realm of thought, and therefore he cannot kill Jones outside this realm and still preserve the "purity" of the deed. In the practical realm, no deed is "pure." He gets emotionally involved in Jones's petty existence just as he had become emotionally involved at the meeting with his fellow anarchists, an emotional involvement that he again visualizes through a ludic metaphor:

> The affair of the meeting [with Sandbach and the other anarchists] had been certainly only a partial success, it was in some measure because he had gone there with his plans unformulated, with nothing but his anger and contempt, and therefore it had got beyond his control: or at any rate, his control had not been quite perfect. This remained tethered to him, as by threads or eyebeams, as if himself, the puppeteer, had become subtly and dangerously entangled in the threads of his own puppets, could not quite escape from them, found their voices still at his ears, like gnats. (314)

In this respect, Ammen's very motive for commiting murder is impure, because it is "polluted" by his rage for purity itself. His object is to separate himself from the crowd by which he feels "contaminated." For instance, he explains angrily to Gerta why he does not want a sexual relationship with her:

> "I won't be contaminated any longer, by you or anyone else. That's something the exceptional man must learn sooner or later, and I've learned it. Nietzsche speaks of it in *Beyond Good and Evil*. The exceptional man is subject to one great temptation—a sort of desperateness—a sudden weak-kneed longing for the society of the commonplace and orderly, the good little parasites. He thinks he gets a kind of healing from it. It's a flight from himself, from his loneliness. The same with sex." (317)

By killing one of the "good little parasites," Ammen hopes to raise himself above the herd: "He was going to *do* something, he must *do* something, there must be the final action by which he would have set the seal on his complete freedom. To escape the company of rats, to express the profundity of his contempt—to *kill* a rat—!" (309). But Ammen's need to separate himself from the crowd is precisely what makes him one of the crowd. A cat does not need to separate itself from the rats to become a cat. A cat is a cat *before* it kills a rat, not *because* it kills one.

Ammen's feelings of hate for the crowd, therefore, clearly contradict his idea of purity. Of course, he defines "hate" in a Nietzschean manner, as a dispassionate means of achieving distance from the herd, but he quite obviously fails to live up to this definition, for example, when he associates hate with the impure, physical aspects of humanity.

The idea of murder occurs to him "precisely at the moment when the mere physical nearness of a stranger's human body was beginning to oppress and stifle him, making itself felt as an unwarrantable and disgusting intrusion. The feeling of hatred, intolerable hatred, had come like a flash and had revealed to him as never before the rightness of the *deed*. . . . [T]he mere presence of the human body had shown him not only what he wanted but exactly why he wanted it" (310).

Moreover, if purity means retreat into the "kingdom of thought," how can one achieve it through a "deed," that is, by moving in the opposite direction? Ammen attempts to solve this dilemma theoretically by expanding his self over the entire world so that the outside object becomes part of the subject. In practice, however, Ammen preserves a distinction between self and world, thought and action:

> Between his world and the world outside, a peculiar division had now arrived, and if time still existed importantly for himself, it had no longer any important existence elsewhere: in his own kingdom, the kingdom of thought, he could move as rapidly as he liked, stay as long as he liked, the outside world would meanwhile stand still, and he could rejoin it whenever he wished, and exactly at the point at which he had left it. (310)

Ammen's assumption that the outside world will stand still until he chooses to rejoin it reveals the nature of his problem: In spite of his interest in a cosmic expansion of the self, he never questions the dualistic notion of subject and object that controls his mode of thought and behavior. In order to unite himself with the world-object, he has to act. But by acting he becomes part of the world-object (rather than the object part of himself), and therefore, instead of gaining his freedom, he loses it. Ammen knows with half his mind that he is omnipotent only in the "kingdom of thought" as long as his idea remains pure, i.e., does not become fact. (This knowledge, incidentally, distinguishes him from the clinical paranoid and makes possible the final dramatic reversal in the narrative.) For instance, Ammen has the feeling that his idea of pure murder has been "deranged" when he first sets eyes on Jones and instantly chooses him as a victim: "This was no Joseph Kazis [a name Ammen had picked at random from the telephone directory], no abstraction, nothing so remote as a name in South Boston, and in that sense it was already possible to feel an acute disappointment, a definite derangement of the basic idea" (335). By the end of the narrative he also admits that "vision is one thing, action or speech another" (402).

The same derangement of the idea of purity in the face of outside reality is present in Ammen's relationship with Gerta. In order to gain complete freedom, he wants to disentangle himself emotionally from her. In keeping with his subjective view of the expansion of the self (and ironically anticipating his suicide attempt), he reasons, commenting on a Zarathustrian maxim: "Take care lest a parasite ascend with you! But the parasite was actually, in such a case, simply oneself. . . . [T]he cause of one's hatred was not without but within; it was not therefore a question of getting rid of Sandbach or Gerta, not at all, but of getting rid of one's *need*" (305). But Ammen miscalculates again his—and Gerta's—capacity for purity or living in the absolute. He loves Gerta, though he rejects this love in order to build a new, "pure" relationship with her, in which he would allow her to share his feeling of power. In this he follows again a Nietzschean precept: "The happiness of man is: I will. The happiness of woman is: he wills." But when Gerta takes him at his word and gets sexually involved with Sandbach, Ammen is visibly hurt and feels betrayed.

The dialectic of subject and object reaches its crisis in the narrative when, like Oedipus, Ammen discovers that, ironically, the stranger is himself. This is the logical outcome of his subjectivism, the ironical clarification of another Zarathustrian maxim: "But remember, if thou gazest into the abyss, the abyss will also gaze into thee." Early on, Ammen sees Jones as the obscenity of the world and himself as the "destructive positive." By the end, Jones as the obscenity of the world has become part of himself or his double—a sort of Mr. Hyde or picture of Dorian Gray. It is in this sense that Jones, the victim, now threatens to kill his aggressor. Ammen's contemplated suicide is thus consistent with his notion of pure murder, becoming ironically the "conscious end of the conscious world." Suicide is the only possible actualization of pure murder in a rational world, because it presupposes a closed circle in which the murderer becomes his own victim. But also, from a subjectivist standpoint, to commit suicide means to annihilate the whole world, negating its fundamental principle, the Schopenhauerian will to live.

The duality of subject and object is moreover closely connected with the problematic of mimesis-imitation that one can trace through *King Coffin*. There are two anthropological notions of mimesis in the narrative, operating in terms of a dialectic of subject and object, or aggressor and victim. There is a good mimesis in which the subject identifies or becomes at one *with* the object (love) and a bad mimesis in which the subject attempts to *identify* the object and distance himself from it in order to control, or even annihilate, it (hate).[11] As we have seen, Ammen practices mostly the bad kind, and this becomes again obvious in his attitude toward Jones: "The stranger had been identified—hadn't he—as Jones, and as such could thus be destroyed: the *strangeness* in Jones had been recognized, with its terror and its pure desirability; it had been observed carefully and inimically as the thing-that-wants-to-be killed; it could be killed. There is no compromise with the object, no placid or reasoned acceptance of it. It is seen, understood, and destroyed" (403).

Once Ammen is motivated by hate, he no longer plays, he imitates. Of course, as we have seen, he attempts to employ the Nietzschean Overman's technique of avoiding mimetic conflict by ceaselessly increasing the distance between himself and others. But instead of keeping aloof from his fellow humans, he actually goes to great lengths to spurn them, constantly engaging in a bad mimetic relationship with them. When he finally identifies with Jones, he does so in terms of hate rather than love. It is true that he experiences something like "love" for Jones when he tries to protect their "special" relationship of aggressor and victim against the "others" (Gerta, Sandbach, and Toppan) who try to stop him. But this illusory "love" dissipates when he no longer feels threatened. Ammen does not escape the dialectic of aggressor and victim, but eventually sees himself as a victim, or as Jones's double. Now it is he himself, the strange creature who has failed to rise above the ethics of pity and become an Overman, who must be destroyed. Appropriately, when Ammen looks at himself in the mirror, his face momentarily becomes that of Jones or the stranger. This face "was as surprising and as mean, as vital and objectionable, as definitely something to be suspected and distrusted and perhaps destroyed, as some queer marine creature which one might find on overturning a wet rock by the sea. . . . It might have to be killed" (404).

Ammen, however, takes only half-hearted steps toward killing himself. Instead he chooses to turn his suicide into a game. He now appears to rely on the chance that Gerta will receive his letter in time to come and rescue him. In this sense, one could argue that the situation is reversed again and that Ammen's recognition of his strangeness has become a false one. Having discovered the advantages of being a victim, he refuses to give up his game of power and attempts to manipulate Gerta through her need to help him.

But by leaving his novel open-ended, Aiken also allows for a completely different interpretation of Ammen's final action. One could argue that by giving himself up to chance, by putting his own existence on the line, Ammen is at last beginning to turn away from his mentality of hate. Throughout the novel, Aiken presents Ammen as literally moving between two incommensurable modes of thought and behavior, or two radically different models: Nietzsche and Buddha. His "chaste and epicene" room contains not only the bust of Nietzsche, but also that of Buddha, which is repeatedly referred to at key junctures in the narrative.

The bronze Buddha is mentioned for the first time at the beginning of the novel when Ammen looks at himself in the mirror, admiring his own face: "Yes, it was a noble face, and fine, as Gerta had said—the conscious end of the conscious world. The room was grey and pictureless, there was no ornament save a small bronze Buddha on a scarlet shelf. This he could see behind him in the mirror as he began passing the comb backward through the dark luxury of his hand" (306). In fact, throughout the narrative the statue is never confronted by Ammen directly but always through a mirror or an ambivalent play of shadow and light. But of crucial importance here is the phrase "the conscious end of the conscious world." On the one hand, this phrase can be read paranoiacally as Ammen's belief that through his person the conscious world has reached its "end" in the teleological sense of entelechy or full development. On the other hand, it can be read ironically and prophetically (in view of Ammen's suicide attempt by the end of the narrative) as a loose citation from Schopenhauer's *The World as Will and Representation*, referring to the will's coming to understand, through consciousness, the necessity of denying itself.

In a sense, then, Aiken establishes in *King Coffin* a dialogue between Nietzsche and Schopenhauer about the will, self, and consciousness. It is Nietzsche himself who had initiated this dialogue, not only in the *Birth of Tragedy*, but also, most importantly, in *Beyond Good and Evil* and the *Genealogy of Morals*, books that inform Ammen's thinking and, to some extent, behavior. When the Buddha reappears in Aiken's narrative one page later, we learn that for Ammen it had meant "a brief experiment with the hardening doctrine of yoga, the deep breathings, the concentration on the thought of drowning, the concept of the individual" (307). We are allowed to infer that this brief phase in Ammen's intellectual development was replaced by the Nietzschean doctrine of the will to power, just as Nietzsche had succeeded Schopenhauer in the history of Western thought. The implied question that the novel sets out to answer, therefore, is whether this development constituted a form of progress or regress in that history. Let us briefly review Nietzsche's and Schopenhauer's philosophical positions in order to understand how they correspond to Ammen's ambivalent frame of mind in the narrative. According to Schopenhauer, being can best be understood as a "will to live" (*der Wille zum Leben*). This will is immanent in the cosmos as well as in humans, but humans can adopt two contrary attitudes toward it: affirmation or denial. The affirmation of the will means involvement in the physical world of becoming, violence, and death. All life, at bottom, means striving, suffering, and perishing. The will to live is therefore involved in a "delusion," and injustice and cruelty are signs of deep entanglement in that delusion. Conversely, moral virtues such as justice and philanthropy are signs that "the appearing will is no longer firmly held in [its] delusion, but that disillusionment already occurs."[12] Clinging to life and its pleasures will now "make way for a universal renunciation," which also brings about a denial of the will. This denial is demanded by human intelligence itself, which "can only be reaction to the will; but since all willing is error, the last work of intelligence is to abolish willing, whose aims and ends it has hitherto served" (*The World as Will*, 610). Hence Schopenhauer's positive valuation of the religious teachings of Buddha and Christ, which seem to him to start from a denial of the will to live. For him, the Buddhist and the Christian renunciation of the will is the highest manifestation of philosophical consciousness in its heroic, if ultimately futile, attempt to transcend itself. It is what, in *King Coffin*, Ammen ironically refers to as "the conscious end of the conscious world," and it is precisely the protagonist's journey from the affirmation of the will to its denial that Aiken traces in his narrative.

For Schopenhauer, moreover, philosophical knowledge must ultimately give way to mystical or "true" knowledge. If mystical knowledge begins where philosophical knowledge ends, then it must begin with nothingness. But from the standpoint of the mystic, nothingness can be described positively as a "consciousness of the identity of one's own inner being with that of all things, or with the kernel of the world." This holistic consciousness is the opposite of the consciousness leading to the affirmation of life expressed through "the phenomenal world, diversity of all beings, individuality, egoism, hatred, wickedness" (*World as Will*, 610).

Nietzsche both subscribes to and revises Schopenhauer's philosophy of the will. He replaces Schopenhauer's philosophical principle of *Wille zum Leben* with that of *Wille zur Macht*, the will to power. As in the case of the will to live, the will to power is immanent in the cosmos, and humans can adopt only two attitudes toward it: affirmation or denial. In contradistinction to Schopenhauer, however, Nietzsche advocates the affirmation of the will to power at all costs, that is, the affirmation of the world of becoming, multiplicity, and individuality— a world that equally includes violence, suffering, death, and the void. Consequently, for Nietzsche the denial of the will is a sign of weakness, of physical and cultural decadence rather than one of strength or supreme self-knowledge. Hence his highly ambiguous, mostly negative valuation of Buddhism and Christianity as manifestations of a perverted will to power.

At the beginning of the novel, we find Ammen adopting a definite Nietzschean stand. If the world is "a kind of phantasm," he argues, then "how could there be rights or wrongs or obligations? or injuries or thefts?" (305). If all is as "scattered and meaningless as that, as intangible, or almost intangible, then the only course was to extend oneself violently outward, to thrust everywhere, to occupy the world entirely with one's own length" (306). What Ammen describes here is Nietzsche's will to power which, as presented in the *Genealogy of Morals,* avoids the void or nothingness at all costs (but it was already Aristotle who defined power as that which abhors the vacuum and seeks to fill it). Yet, by the end of the novel, Ammen comes to see this will as a bitter delusion. In a Schopenhauerian manner he renounces his desire to dominate and control, giving himself over to the play of chance and the void. This development is underscored in the narrative by the frequent recurrence of the image of the Buddha, which always hovers at the back of Ammen's consciousness, coupled with the protagonist's distaste for violent action which ought to signal to all but the most obtuse reader that Ammen is no psychopathic serial murderer. For example, early on in the narrative, he proves incapable of hurting even a cat: "[Ammen] remembered first his impulse to drop the cat out of the window, and the curious repugnance which had seemed to rise as if from his hands; then the relief with which he had driven the cat out into the corridor" (329).

King Coffin charts the development of Ammen's consciousness from violently experiencing the fear of nothingness as hate to accepting this nothingness at least conditionally as a first step toward a different mode of thought and behavior. If at the beginning of the narrative Ammen declares that "the essential thing in life is hate" (327), he ends by implying, in his last letter to Gerta, that the essential thing in life could be love. Once he realizes that Jones's stillborn child is, in fact, a symbol of his own aborted project of pure murder, he is confronted with himself as a stranger, and then as nothingness. In other words, he experiences a dissolution of the self. But nothingness now becomes a positive state, in the Buddhist or Schopenhauerian sense, as that which allows access to a new mode of being and a new kind of self, or to what Schopenhauer describes as the *irenic* "consciousness of the identity of one's own inner being with that of all things, or with the kernel of the world." This transformation is suggested in the novel by Ammen's experiment with the air currents in his apartment a few hours before turning on the gas.

Looking for another way of manipulating Gerta, Ammen believes he can employ the flow of air into and out of his apartment to create the appearance of a bona fide suicide attempt. The steady currents in his living room and bedroom are quite suitable for his purpose. To his disappointment, however, the draft in the kitchen, where his source of gas is, proves unsatisfactory: "But the kitchenette, presumably because its window was shut, or simply because it was out of the path of the main currents, was a disappointment: the movement of the [cigarette] smoke [exhaled by Ammen], whether at floor or ceiling, was scarcely perceptible, sluggish, equivocal. In fact it would go exactly where propelled" (402). Given the fact that the gas will flow only slowly out of the kitchen where he would have to sit if his suicide attempt were to be credible, Ammen realizes that the case is altered: Instead of being completely in control, he would now *have* to gamble with his own life.

It is also at this moment that Ammen realizes the liminal nature of his newly discovered playground: "It was like the backwater of a river: it was stagnant; and looking at it he became abruptly aware of the profound nocturnal silence. It was that moment between night and morning when the traffic is stillest, the brief interval between the end of the night life and the beginning of the day—the hour when life is at its ebb" (402). Once he decides to carry out his plan, Ammen has relinquished control, staking his own being in the game. Will Gerta arrive in time to save him? The novel ends on this equivocal note, suggesting that Aiken is fully aware that his protagonist would have to sojourn in a no-man's land, between life and death, before he could reemerge from this experience with a transformed self.

Far from being a mere psychological casebook or a failed novel of manners, therefore, Aiken's *King Coffin* is the conscious end of a long aesthetic tradition, standing out as a complex and path-breaking literary work in its own right.

Notes

1. See Mihai Spariosu, *Dionysus Reborn: Play and the Aesthetic Dimension in Modern Philosophical and Scientific Discourse* (Ithaca: Cornell University Press, 1989), 33–52.

2. See Friedrich Nietzsche, *The Birth of Tragedy*, trans. Francis Golffing (Garden City, New York: Doubleday, 1956), 9–10. For a full discussion of Nietzsche's project of aesthetically transvaluating modern ethics by returning to a "heroic" mentality, see Spariosu, *Dionysus Reborn*, 68–99.

3. See Mihai Spariosu, *God of Many Names: Art, Play, and Power in Hellenic Thought from Homer to Aristotle* (Durham, NC: Duke University Press, 1991).

4. An attempt to understand murder as an aesthetic phenomenon, in terms of a Romantic interplay of art and life extending into American pop culture, can be found in Joel Black, *The Aesthetics of Murder: A Study in Romantic Literature and Contemporary Culture* (Baltimore: Johns Hopkins University Press, 1991).

5. Clarence Darrow and Benjamin Bacharach, Introduction to Maureen McKernan, *Amazing Crime and Trial of Leopold and Loeb* (Chicago: Plymouth Court Press, 1986 [1924]), vii.

6. See Vincent McHugh, *Primer of the Novel* (New York: Random, 1950), 34.

7. Frederick J. Hoffman, *Conrad Aiken* (New York: Twayne, 1962), 53–54.

8. Hoffman is equally cavalier in his treatment of Aiken's short story "Smith and Jones," a sort of prototype for *King Coffin*. He states that Jones kills Smith, again missing the final ironic reversal, in which Smith, the supposed victim, kills Jones.

9. Conrad Aiken, *King Coffin*, in *The Collected Novels of Conrad Aiken* (New York: Holt, Rinehart and Winston, 1964), 326–27. Further page references will be to this edition.

10. The violent, archaic kind of play which Ammen envisages and in which might makes right is equally shared by the surrealists. See, for example, André Breton's desideratum of shooting real pistol bullets, at random, into a live audience; or Antonin Artaud's project of stabbing a fellow actor on stage in order to implicate the audience in ritual murder, thereby recovering the "sacred" origin of drama in sacrificial victimage. Georges Bataille's secret society, the *Acéphale*, belongs to the same ludic category: the members of this society were reportedly looking for a volunteer to be sacrificed in a scapegoat ritual. Apparently, a willing human victim was found, but no willing executioner, and the members ended up sacrificing a ram instead. Ammen would have certainly been embraced by the surrealists as a kindred spirit.

11. For detailed theoretical background, see Karl Eckhardt, "Concepts of Mimesis in French and German Philosophical and Anthropological Theory," in *The Play of the Self*, ed. Ronald Bogue and Mihai I. Spariosu (Albany: State University of New York Press, 1994), 67–86.

12. See Arthur Schopenhauer, *The World as Will and Representation*, trans. E. F. Payne (New York: Dover, 1958), 2: 610. Further page references are to this edition.

10

Contest vs. Mediation: Innovative Discursive Modes in Postmodern Fiction

Marcel Cornis-Pope

The fairy tale of the 'realistic' novel whispers its assurance that the world is not mysterious, that it is predictable—if not to the characters, then to the author—that it is available to manipulation by the individual, that it is not only under control but that one can profit from this control. The key idea is verisimilitude: one can make an image of the real thing which, though not real, is such a persuasive likeness that it can represent our control over reality. This is the voodoo at the heart of mimetic theory that helps account for its tenacity.

—Ronald Sukenick, *In Form* (3–4)

The metamorphosis of immediate power configurations into mediated, representational ones often results in both a repression of and a nostalgia for origins. On the one hand, rational mentality represses its prerational counterpart, labeling it "savage," "barbarian," "primitive," precisely because prerational power presents itself in a naked, unashamed and violent form. On the other hand, rational mentality experiences the transition to mediated forms of power as a loss of presence and a yearning for (absolute) authority.

—Mihai I. Spariosu, *Dionysus Reborn*, 11

Postmodern Critiques of the Power Configurations of Narration

The above two quotations, one from an innovative writer's digressions on the act of fiction, the other from a theoretical analysis of Western discursive practices, highlight a common concern with the conditions and power configurations of narrative articulation. With different discursive tools (novel and essay, in the first case, philosophic-semiotic analysis in the latter), Ronald Sukenick and Mihai Spariosu have undertaken a critique of mimetic representation, exploring the sociopolitical and existential circumstances that have made this paradigm so dominant. Both remind us that mimesis is wedded to power and control, constructing its own axioms of existence and rules of acceptability rather than supplying us with a simple scale model of reality. Against a mimetic tradition that has subordinated fiction to a concept of synecdochal representation, to processes of manipulation and control through "plot," "character," and "symbol," Sukenick has proposed a "generative" concept of fiction based on narrative improvisation and a revisionistic exercise of cultural imagination. This concept is akin to Spariosu's performative semiotic which mediates conflictive sides of discourse.

Criticism has been slow in recognizing the sociocultural significance of an innovative concept of fiction such as Sukenick's, discussing it chiefly as a formalistic exercise rather than as an ideological response to the crisis of credibility undergone by the novel in the postmodern age.[1] Until recently there has been little focus on what Jerome Klinkowitz has called the "extraliterary causes" of innovative fiction. The "inhibiting conditions of living, loving, teaching, writing" in postindustrial America, and the "wooden convention of genre-based and industry-controlled publishing," have probably had as much impact on Sukenick's theory and practice of fiction as other specifically literary circumstances.[2] Because of its involvement with the "extraliterary forces of its circumstance," Sukenick's generative fiction is revisionistic, questioning our perceptual and discursive systems, reinventing the rules by which reality is projected. This type of fiction "does not aspire to the factuality of history," being *recreation* in both senses of the word, i.e., a self-conscious act of articulation "not different from that of composing one's reality."[3] But this recreation moves beyond the formalistic "autoreferentiality" usually imputed to it.[4] Experience is neither avoided nor deprived of its "substantiality" but confronted on several levels (social, rhetorical, and cultural), submitted to a transformative consciousness.

Critics of postmodernism have recognized this revisionistic impulse in "surfiction" (Sukenick, but also Walter Abish, Raymond Federman, Madeline Gins, Steve Katz, Clarence Major, Ursule Molinaro, Ishmael Reed), but have often misread its purpose. According to Alan Wilde, the "fragmented and randomized surface" of reflexivist fiction conveys little besides the author's self-image," which, substituting for an engagement with the world of invention, validates only its own identity.[5] As a result of a "scriptural behavior that pulverizes plot and character, scrambles traditional narrative elements, and relentlessly plays with coherence by means of disorienting typographical tricks," this fiction "proclaims the nonreferential or reflexive nature of writing in general" (*Middle Grounds*, 44–45). The problem with such an interpretation is that it reduces innovative fiction to an "either-or" logic that opposes deconstruction to articulation and self-reflection to "true mimesis." But, as I have argued elsewhere,[6] surfiction and other projects of narrative innovation (feminist, postcolonial, etc.) refuse this binary logic, submitting each term to a critical reevaluation. Such fiction is neither naively experiential nor entirely scriptural: Concerned with the recreative interplay of "invention" and "reflection," formalism and realism, innovative fiction upsets and reformulates both poles. The point that a "surfictionist" like Sukenick has been making is not that the world exists "wholly within the word"[7] but that our versions of reality depend on limiting conventions of narrative and linguistic articulation. It is, therefore, the writer's responsibility to challenge and rewrite the given representational frames and to imagine better aesthetic and sociocultural syntheses, just as it is her concern to prevent her articulations from rigidifying into a new dogma.

To be sure, not all pronouncements of the act of fiction are as culturally aware as my opening Sukenick quote. Innovative writers share with their critics some of the responsibility for their own misrepresentation, often describing their tasks in formalistic rather than political terms: "The elements of the new fictitious discourse . . . must be digressive from one another—digressive from the element that precedes and the element that follows. . . . Rather than being a stable image of daily life, fiction will be in a perpetual state of redoubling upon itself. It is from itself, from its own substance that the fictitious discourse will proliferate—imitating, repeating, parodying, retracting what it says."[8] More recently, in reappraising "Self-Reflexive Fiction" for the *Columbia Literary History of the United States*, Raymond Federman ascribed narrative reflexivity a stronger ideological function in extricating the novel "from the postures and impostures of realism and naturalism."[9] By replacing a conventional mimesis of "content" (stable myths and symbols) with a subversive "mimesis of form" that renders "concrete and even visual in its language, in its syntax, in its typography and topology" the differential energy of American experience, self-reflexive fiction creates a disorder in the traditional socialization of reality, disentangling the discourse of the individual subject from "official discourse." Innovative fiction, Federman argued further, departs from the "linear movements and sequential logic" (1152) of traditional cultural narratives, denouncing their structure of clichés and silent agreement with "the official discourse of the State." The "critifictions" of Abish, Gins, Federman, Katz, Major, Molinaro, Sorrentino, and Sukenick attack—out of ideological necessity, not formalistic self-indulgence—"the very vehicle that expressed and represented that [American] reality: discursive language and the traditional form of the novel" (1155). Since many of the mechanisms that create injustice and domination are demonstrably found in language, self-reflexive fiction is justified in pursuing a critique of novelistic/cultural articulation. The novel takes on an important ideological function, that of renewing social imagination and expanding the available modes of narrative articulation so as to allow individuals to take hold of their own life-stories.

Reappraisals such as Federman's rehistoricize innovative fiction, inscribing literary aesthetics within the framework of a cultural politics that both asserts and problematizes the sociocultural value of narrative experimentation. But they continue to hesitate between two theoretical descriptions of innovation: One explains the novelist's task in deconstructive terms, as a "purification" of language by "rendering [it] seemingly irrational, illogical, incoherent, and even meaningless" (1156); the other emphasizes the socially relevant task of reformulation, arguing that "the techniques of parody, irony, introspection, and self-reflexiveness directly challenge the oppressive forces of social and literary authorities" (1156). The first evaluation tends to confine postmodern fiction to a "disruptive complicity" with its medium, to an aesthetics of "negativity" identified with Beckett, cited as "the ultimate model for most serious fiction written during the 1960s and 1970s" (1157). The second evaluation credits innovative fiction with a rearticulative capacity: Its role is not simply to "neutralize the fiasco of reality and the imposture of history" but also to create a space for the affirmation of the repressed, imaginative qualities of experience.

At the root of this theoretical hesitation between two concepts of innovation is a dissociative model of narration in which deconstruction and rearticulation, improvisation and analysis, are often at odds. Derived from a simplified understanding of Jacques Derrida's deconstruction, or of Michel Foucault's and Jean-François Lyotard's critiques of the falsely universalizing discourses of modernity,[10] this model emphasizes divisiveness and incompleteness in narration. The role of postmodern theory and practice, as Lyotard sees it, is to challenge traditional epistemologies, laying bare the comprehensive modes of assemblage and self-legitimation that societies resort to in order to minimize risk and unpredictability. These modes are most often narrative, legitimizing "first-order" practices of inquiry within a broader totalizing metadiscourse that makes "an explicit appeal to some grand narrative such as the dialectics of Spirit, the hermeneutics of meaning, the emancipation of the rational or working subject, or the creation of wealth" (*The Postmodern Condition*, xxiii). Postmodernism is encouraged to undercut these powerful metanarratives, replacing them with a "discontinuous, catastrophic, nonrectifiable, and paradoxical" order of *pétits recits* that recognize "the heteromorphous nature of the language games" and of reality (60, 66). These fractured local stories promote experimentation and differentiation; they also prevent a comprehensive view of the cultural system they are part of. Therein lies both the strength and the limitation of the postmodern order envisioned by Lyotard. Society, for Lyotard, is an "interweaving of heteromorphous classes of utterances" (65) in which individuals participate as nodes that mediate several discourses but lack the purview of the whole. His view of culture as heteromorphous and nontotalizable accentuates the fragmentation of contemporary discourses, "de-theorizing" and depoliticizing them.[11] In the absence of any comprehensive analysis of local beliefs and narrative strategies, we are left with a fragmented but also bureaucratized cultural scene, enslaved to its conflicting sets of norms.

There is, finally, little difference between Lyotard's "grand" and "smallish" narratives: They all participate in an economy of self-legitimation and contest. The "construction and choice of one story over others" can be shown to be governed by "a will to power," "a desire *not* to hear certain other voices or stories."[12] As makers and breakers of order, all narratives involve a paradoxical mix of experimentation and self-regulation. To quote Foucault, "There is nothing more tentative, nothing more empirical (superficially, at least) than the process of establishing an order among things; nothing that demands a sharper eye or a surer, better-articulated language."[13] Like other postmodern discourses, experimental fiction finds itself trapped within this fundamental paradox: Even as it undercuts the totalizing practices of traditional narration, postmodernism legitimates its own discursive preferences and displacements, creating a new mastery system. Hence the need felt by most postmodern writers to "think in fragments," in "heterogeneous" modes of discourse; but also their critical awareness that no act of fiction, however innovative, can entirely escape a self-regulating "will-to-mastery." But if, as Jane Flax has argued, postmodern writers "are not free from a will to power whose effects they trace elsewhere," they have at least attempted to "construct an alternative narrative whose rhetorical force is to displace the traditional self-understanding of mainstream Western thought."[14]

Contest vs. Mediation: A Critical-Integrative Model of Discourse

The task of constructing an alternative model of Western discursivity that would reconcile the subversive, deconstructive side of postmodernism with the goals of rearticulation has been pursued theoretically by postdeconstructionist and feminist theorists. Feminism's challenge, according to Sandra Harding, is to articulate a gender-specific epistemology as a defense against male claims of "objectivism/universalism," on one hand, and self-denying relativism ("interpretationism"), on the other.[15] For this particular task, Lyotard's "agonistic theory of language and paralogistic theory of legitimation cannot serve as basis."[16] The tendency of a more radical brand of postmodernism to put everything "under erasure" undermines important cross-cultural concepts such as those of knowing subject, gendered agent, feminine experience. As Nancy Fraser and Linda J. Nicholson insist, feminism still requires these concepts or "at minimum large narratives about changes in social organization and ideology, [as well as] empirical and social-theoretical analyses of macrostructures and institutions."[17] Feminist fiction needs to articulate strong, coherent narratives of "women's real life" in order to counterbalance the many misrepresentations of femininity in patriarchal literature.

But this effort is not without problems: As long as it stays within the framework of "classic" realism, feminist fiction risks perpetuating some of the "androcentric" gestures inscribed in that tradition: the search for strong causal explanations, the subordination of contingency to abstract generalization, the suppression of "other stories," and so on. Therefore, as Nicholson argues, feminism must simultaneously articulate and critique its own "large narratives" about women's historical struggle against male domination, submitting them to a postmodern revisionistic dynamic.[18] Postmodern deconstruction and feminist articulation can collaborate toward "an epistemology and politics which recognizes the lack of metanarratives and foundational guarantees but which nonetheless insists on formulating minimal criteria of validity for our discursive and cultural practices."[19]

A similar attempt to integrate these conflicting tasks into an alternative model for Western discursive practices can be found in Mihai Spariosu's work, from *Literature, Mimesis and Play* (1982) to *Dionysus Reborn* (1989) and *God of Many Names* (1991). Drawing on a revisionistic reading of Hellenic thought, post-Nietzschean philosophy, and cultural anthropology, Spariosu has introduced a much-needed interdisciplinary perspective in the current debate concerning the philosophic and ideological underpinnings of signification. Spariosu broaches the problem of signification from two related perspectives: On one hand, he highlights the stubborn mimetic tradition underlying Western discourses, its dependence on a violent, conflictive notion of difference between "model" and "copy," signifier and signified; on the other hand, he tries to advance a countermodel of semiosis based on *mediation* (sociolinguistic, cultural, political).

Spariosu's successive books can be read as stages in a "larger cultural historical project that attempts to define the relationship of literature to other modes of discourse in Western thought by focusing on the notions of play, mimesis, and power."[20] The history of these interrelated terms is recapitulated in the form of a bifurcated narrative that has as one plot the gradual suppression/regulation of anarchic play through mimesis. As redefined by Plato and Aristotle, mimesis subordinates poetic performance to metaphysical truth and translates the power principle underlying discourse from a "spontaneous, free, [and] arbitrary" mode of existence, into a principle of "reason, Ideal Form, and Eternal Order."[21] A counterplot emerges subsequently with Kant and other representatives of German idealism who begin the "uneven, and by no means irreversible process or restoring play to its pre-Platonic high cultural status" as "an indispensable cognitive tool" (*Literature, Mimesis and Play*, 9, 22). Literature is informed by these two conflicting plots, one that controls the differential play of reality through mimesis, the other that recovers the subversive potential of play, participating in the "creation and establishment of certain states of affairs (power configurations)" (10).

In his two subsequent books, *Dionysus Reborn* and *God of Many Names,* Spariosu refines his two-pronged narrative, highlighting the areas where these plots overlap, cooperating or questioning each other. According to him, the development of our "proto-logo-rational" mode of thought followed from the start a paradoxical path between power and play: The ethos of play contained in it both epiphanies of violence and the germs of a countermodel that harked back to a nonviolent, performative concept of play. This double-constituted notion of play and power has become an intrinsic part of our spiritual heritage, generating divergent evolutionary plots: rationalistic and authoritarian through the age of the Enlightenment, emphasizing play as the ordering activity of Reason; and antirationalistic, reviving a more archaic concept of play as the willful, irrational power of nature itself, in Nietzsche and the "artist-metaphysicians" following him (Heidegger, Fink, Gadamer, Deleuze, Derrida).[22] Literary mimesis is a product of this process of double constitution, reflecting the "conflictive . . . nature of Western humans and their play: gentle, reasonable, and peace-loving on the one hand, and competitive, intractable, and warmongering on the other" (*Dionysus Reborn*, xiv).

At the same time, however, Spariosu invites us to see these alternative plots (and the concepts that underlie them) as "polytropic," interacting and transforming each other. Thus power often contaminates play, repressing and restricting its subversive manifestations; and play complicates and problematizes the scene of the struggle, taking heterogeneous forms "such as agon, chance, necessity, play as freedom, mimicry, and simulation" (*Dionysus Reborn*, xiii). For example, the oppositional terms constructed by Plato (mimesis as imitation vs. mimesis as play) and Aristotle ("speculative art" related to knowledge and truth vs. "mimetic art" related to logo-rational pleasure) continue to contaminate each other (*God of Many Names*, 202). In Aristotle's *Poetics*, the devalued categories of the emotive and performative return to haunt Aristotle's discussion of catharsis and of the higher forms of pleasure afforded by philosophy and tragedy (*God of Many Names*, 213). In Plato's dialogues, Socrates often mimics the arguments and strategies he purports to undo, delighting in the contradictions he thereby creates. By presenting both sides of the argument, "Plato makes it possible, at least theoretically, to conceive of a third alternative" (142) welcomed by Spariosu: a nonconflictive model of signification that would mediate between philosophy and poetry, rationality and play, turning away from the power contest. Spariosu rediscovers aspects of this third model in the post-Nietzschean philosophic direction that has fed into postmodernism. Whether conceived as "the groundless grounding principle of truth" and Being in Heidegger and Fink or as the performative movement of Gadamer's hermeneutics or as an affirmation of the totality of chance and difference in Deleuze and Guattari, play is reinscribed in all these discourses both as the suppressed Other and as the condition of possibility of Being, Reality, World, Meaning (*Literature, Mimesis and Play*, 41).

Spariosu's analysis of Western discursive practices with their paradoxical interplay of contest and mediation, inscription and transcendence of power, has immediate relevance for a discussion of the performative semiotic of postmodernism. Spariosu highlights for us the bifurcated nature of postmodernism's discursive heritage while also illustrating its mediative-utopian impulse in his own philosophic project. He begins by urging us to move beyond "an agonistic mode of thought" and "our mentality of power as a whole" (*God of Many Names*, xviii). Parting with Nietzsche and his modern heirs, Spariosu argues that "power is only one of the ways, and not necessarily the best way, in which human beings can construct their world or relate to it" (xvi). "Al-

ternative ways to mimetic thinking" can at least be imagined, and that
has been the "background desideratum" of Spariosu's own writing
since *Mimesis in Contemporary Theory*,[23] a collection of essays he edited
in 1984 in response to the philosophic impasse created by the postmodern contest between realists and reflexivists. Though well aware of the
underlying problems of the anthropological and onto-phenomenologi-
cal projects (Heidegger, Adorno, Fink, Girard) that propose to transcend
the historical bifurcation of subject and object, sign and image, Spariosu
has contributed his own game plan in "the utopian manner," imagining
a language that would give up "hierarchy and segregation" and "the
power principle with its faithful instruments, good and bad mimesis."[24]
His concept of nonconflictive language, as we shall see, resembles surfiction's notion of a nonmimetic "stream language," or feminism's non-
phallogocentric *écriture*; like them, it remains a hypothetical project,
critically aware of its own utopianism. By comparison to other attempts
to move from mimetic struggle back into a prehistory (with Adorno) or
a posthistory (with René Girard) of "non-dividual" semiosis, Spariosu's
version of linguistic utopia is carefully qualified: What he envisions is
not the eradication of difference from cultural transactions but a performative, participative economy of differentiation that resists an ap-
propriative dialectics.

　　Whether this economy of differentiation can entirely escape the
mimetic paradigm is a complicated question. As Spariosu concedes,
even the self-reflexive foregrounding of the compositional process allows the reappearance of mimesis "in an occult form, as production,
rather than re-production, of Nature on the analogy of the 'infinite I
AM': the subject reappropriate[s] and reconstitute[s] the object, in a sort
of reversed mimesis."[25] And yet, as a form of "liberated bad mimesis,"
as a game of *as if* that exercises the "free constructive activity of the in-
ventive faculty,"[26] self-reflexive fiction can both expose and transcend
the given constructions of reality. Other modes of innovative fiction (political metafiction, surfiction, the feminist novel) take this process a step
further, revising simultaneously the power configurations of "reality"
and of their own narration. These narratives expand our linguistic and
ideological awareness, engaging us in a process of reformulation both
at the level of poetics and that of cultural ideology.

Contest and Mediation in Recent Innovative Fiction

We could thus argue that the task of constructing a discursive model
that would no longer depend on a rigidly mimetic (and therefore conflictual) economy of signification has been more successfully pursued

in the practice of fiction. The solutions advanced, for example, by surfiction and the feminist novel parallel closely Spariosu's search for an
alternative model of nonconflictive, open-ended articulation, while
avoiding the suggestion of semiotic idealism. Ronald Sukenick has used
improvisational techniques to destabilize hierarchical narrative codes,
replacing a power-oriented representational language (figured as an
"art of rape") with a process-oriented language of experiencing, "inseparable from the body and its physical existence."[27] Sukenick's concept of "generative fiction" departs polemically from both mimetic
realism and self-reflexive formalism. As a "beneficial form of counter-
feit," the novel is an experiential, recreative medium: "Its truth is poetic:
a statement of a particular rapport with reality sufficiently persuasive
that we may for a time share it" (*In Form,* 31). This rapport, Sukenick's
essays suggest, has to be conceived outside the traditionally static terms
of mimesis. Innovative fiction must restructure and historicize the referential relation in order to realign the "truth of the page" with the
"truth of experience" (*In Form,* 211). Its task is to pursue "liberation in
thought" rather than "bondage to fact" (82), but in a way that will enhance the "individual sense of experience" as against "official versions
of reality" (67).

It is important to note that Sukenick's critical target is not narrative reference in general but conventional mimesis whose static typifi-
cations suppress the lived-world, substituting it with a production of
abstract likenesses. The mimetic-referential relation is not simply dis-
carded but rather submitted to a critical revision that upsets its dual
structure, rendering its oppositional terms (model/image, mimesis/
poesis, fiction/reality) problematic. "Representation" is reconceived as
a dynamic interplay of subject, object, and language. Its purpose is to
immerse fiction in life, bridging the "schizoid" division between them
and reclaiming segments of experience obfuscated by the exclusionary
techniques of conventional realism:

> [Surfiction is] an attempt to get at the truth of experience beyond
> our fossilized formulas of discourse, to get at a new and more in-
> clusive "reality," if you will. This is a reality that includes what the
> conventional novel tends to exclude and that encompasses the va-
> garies of unofficial experience, the cryptic trivia of the quotidian
> that help shape our fate, and the tabooed details of life—class, eth-
> nic, sexual—beyond sanctioned descriptions of life. It is an orien-
> tation that is distinctly democratic in tendency, which may explain
> some of the hostility it meets.[28]

Sukenick's "generative fiction" continually reformulates its styles of articulations, "push[ing] out to the edge of culture and of form" in order to "allow more reality into the work" (*In Form*, 135). This effort can be read as another instance of the post-Nietzschean drive to "free prerational mentality of its rational bonds and . . . reaffirm . . . prerational values in modern culture" described by Spariosu (*Dionysus Reborn*, 11). As such, it partakes of some of the problems attending a move back to the experiential, playful, and performative. While Sukenicks' surfiction capitalizes on the performative-recuperative dynamic of narration, it cannot erase the underlying dichotomies of representation, maintaining a productive tension between them. The inconsistencies that criticism has imputed Sukenick (his wavering between a conception of nonrepresentational and self-contained language, on one hand, and a notion of art as a liberating experiential medium, on the other) can be viewed as competing claims within a representational dynamic that, as Wolfgang Iser has contended, remains open ended because it generates "mutually exclusive positions":

> Representation arises out of and thus entails the removal of difference, whose irremovability transforms representation into a performative act of staging something. This staging is almost infinitely variable, for in contrast to explanations, no single staging could ever remove difference and so explain origin. . . . Representation is first and foremost an act of performance, bringing forth in the mode of staging something which in itself is not given.[29]

Surfiction also emphasizes the performative, "infinitely variable" play of narrative representation, suggesting that narration cannot escape its contradictory dialectic as long as it wants to remain "reflexive" in a philosophic sense and articulate a significant world. The only other alternative is some mythic lingo like "Bjorsq," the visceral nonlanguage of "growls squeaks farts gargles clicks and chuckles" imagined in *98.6*. Sukenick's narrators dream every so often of a nonrepresentational "stream language," but their better efforts go to "stitching together" the novel's "bungled fragments" (*98.6*[30]), exploiting the irreconcilable poles of the narrative "field of action."

In redefining the novel as "a field of action" (*In Form*, 13), surfiction rehistoricizes narration. In this view, representation is no longer an "imitation" of something preexisting "whose ontological status is more stable and assumed, more grounded and foundational," but a process of imaging-forth, a "proleptic" performance that produces objects "whose condition is historical mutability."[31] The "open field" of the novel modifies whatever enters it: events, agents, objects. What the sur-fictionist seeks is not rhetorical and ideological unity but a provisional balance between competing claims and styles of articulation. In Sukenick's fiction, for example, an elusive-cryptic discourse that creates the expectation of a hidden "message" collides with a self-reflexive rhetorical style that problematizes the hermeneutic movement of the text. Between the suggestive-cryptic and the minimalist-disconnected prose that repeats without accumulating, one can sometimes find an in-stantaneous, "phenomenological" style that retraces the contradictory movements of life, the "feel" of a Brooklyn street, the wanderings of var-ious characters from one mysterious "meet" to another.

Imaginative *metamorphosis* (idea adapted from Emerson—see *In Form*, xix) is Sukenick's response to the postmodern existential and cul-tural fragmentation. The "metamorphic power of imaginative lan-guage" expands the experiential possibilities of the novel, enriching its ontological space. At its best, the "feverish," "disordered imagination" of Sukenick's narrators creates transformative connections between disparate facets of life. This metamorphic, projective technique can be recognized already in *Up* (1968), a novel that starts conventionally as a first-person narrative but then switches unawares to a narrative-inside-narrative ("The Adventures of Strop Banally") which remains sketchy, delineating only potential story situations. As a character-reviewer in *Up* complains, this book "is just a collection of disjoined fragments. You don't get anywhere at all. Where's the control, where's the tension?"[32] Chronology is messed up, character motivation is dubious, fiction and historical "documentary" often merge. But beyond this surface disorder there is an acknowledged effort to "work out the essentials of our fate" (223). The frequent shifts in plot, character, and genre free experience from preformulated stories, providing a dynamic narrative space wherein author, character, and reader can renegotiate a "favorable rap-port" with reality. The narrative is propelled ahead not by a preexisting concept of mimetic form but by a series of recursive acts, by a process of mediation/rewriting: "Form is when you look back and you see your footprints in the sand."[33]

An even better example of this kind of mediative/reformulative work can be found in Sukenick's *98.6* (1975). The novelist's effort "to get at the truth of experience beyond our fossilized formulas of discourse" ("Autogyro," 294) begins with a deconstructive rereading of the "Frankensteinian" features of contemporary society (cultural violence, sexual domination, psychological stagnation). Then, in the second part of the novel, entitled "The Children of Frankenstein," Sukenick rearticulates the cultural scene around new narrative propositions. Ron, the intradiegetic author-character, initiates a social experiment (a utopian settlement in California) in order to provide his novel-in-process with a riveting theme. The book he is writing traces the shortlived history of this utopian project, turning a failed social experiment into a relatively successful textual production. Yet the novel we are reading under the title of *98.6* is not celebratory but ironic of the Rousseauistic idealism that infuses both the social experiment and the narrator's own effort to turn his novel into "something organic, an addition to nature."

The last part of the novel, "Palestine," picks up again the themes of cultural and narrative reformulation, taking a more pragmatic view of them. This part illustrates the strengths and limitations of *utopian-subversive* fiction. Sukenick's narrative imagination revises both collective history and individual autobiography, promising "composure grown out of ongoing decomposition" (*98.6*, 167). By way of a few chance "connections" (his identity of name with the discoverer of the Dead Sea Scrolls, his misread references to the "Mosaic Law" of fiction), the authorial narrator finds himself in a land of new possibilities, a postmodern "zone" constructed through imaginative "misattribution."[34] "Improbabilities of the unknown" expand the real, rewriting political events to create a more acceptable world (Robert Kennedy has not been assassinated, Jews and Arabs have negotiated a lasting peace, etc.). As a paradigmatic utopia, "Palestine" is the "fantastic product of [a] creative practice," of a "fictionalizing process" that both pluralizes and neutralizes reality.[35] At the same time, the last part foregrounds the dramatic tensions between reality and utopia. The voice that articulates this utopian vision is increasingly theoretical and self-controverting, splitting into several identities, one of which is again that of Dr. Frankenstein. Through him, Sukenick calls attention to our Janus-faced postmodern culture, wavering between utopia and farce, violent assertion and denial of power. The novelist's own art illustrates this paradoxical Frankensteinian condition, seeking composure in its own internal decomposition, moving its contradictory realities and modes of articulation (historical and imagined, comic and utopian) toward a moment of "Luminous Coincidence." In this dialogic vision, innovation is a progressive "loosening of tongues,"[36] a struggle to "decontrol" and rewrite a culture's narratives.

Surfiction shares this dialectic of unwriting/rewriting with innovative feminist fiction. Feminist fiction has made consistent use of "differential" gender thinking in order to disrupt the traditional system of "phallogocentric" representations, creating new discursive and narrative structures more responsive to women's experiences. Women's

interests have been traditionally controlled through complicated rhetorical processes of displacement and subordination. "The whole artistic
endeavor," Donna Przybylowicz has argued in a study of Henry James,
"involve[d] the repression of the private message of the fantasy through
the mediating processes of condensation and displacement, thus involving the substitution of form for the immediate gratification of wish-
fulfilling content."[37] Feminist fiction has had to renegotiate a balance
between its desire to articulate new experiential contents and its need to
deconstruct the falsely "universalizing" discourse of traditional fiction
which has often repressed women's real needs. Predictably, "the first
wave of feminist fiction dealt primarily with the 'content' of feminist in-
sights within fairly traditional structures. . . . [B]ut it quickly became obvious to a number of important female authors that the basic
assumptions and conventions underlying realistic fiction—its reliance
on reason and causality, . . . its requirements for a dramatic action in
which conflicts could be resolved, its implications about what constituted 'heroism' and 'significant' action—were inherently male-defined
and hence in many ways inadequate to convey the most salient features
of women's lives."[38] As a consequence, the earlier phase of content accommodation was followed beginning in the mid-1970s by radical forms
of innovation, from surreal deconstruction to feminist political utopias.

In challenging the symbolic order of traditional realism, feminist
fiction has not had to give up the task of articulating an interpretation
of present-day culture. On the contrary, as many innovative novelists
have found, their rearticulative effort is better served by the introduction of anti-authoritarian and collaborative discursive relations such as
those theorized, for example, by Julia Kristeva or Hélène Cixous.[39] Their
poststructuralist notion of a feminist semiotic helps us move outside the
traditional framework of representation, pitting a dialogic form of narration which encompasses differences and contradictions against the
fixed truths of androcentric realism. This vision has appealed to experimental women novelists, but they have not failed to recognize its
utopian disposition. Feminist fiction continues to take a circumspect
view of language and its capacity to shed the vestiges of "phallocentric"
mastery. As Madeline Gins confessed in *Word Rain*,[40] "The saddest thing
is that I have had to use words." Yet, just as with surfiction, the feminist
novel cannot entirely forgo narrative language for a surrealistic-
naturalistic babble like "Bjorsq." A better alternative is that of linguistic-
ideological reformulation: making revisionistic use of representational
codes for a new narrative articulation; or proposing alternative modes
for "seizing the language" that would break with the phallogocentric
tradition of fiction. Therefore, as Nicole Brossard has cogently argued,

the art of feminist writers must remain *experimental* (trying to under-stand the processes of writing) and *exploratory* (searching for new dis-cursive and sociocultural frameworks).[41] It must also be subversively erotic, capable of engaging a broad exchange of energy between the body of writing and the body politic. The focus on the "body" will help feminist writing revalorize "marginal" experiences, deprogramming the dominant cultural codes and making "space for the unthought [women's subjectivity and experience]"(p. 81).

The interplay of these complementary tasks is best illustrated in Toni Morrison's *Sula* (1973), a novel that achieves not only a "figural breakthrough"[42] but also a significant revision at the level of narrative poetics. Described by Morrison as a novel about black women's inti-mate companionship, *Sula* endeavors to "repossess, re-name, re-own"[43] a space for feminine experience within an androcentric tradition. Criti-cism has also perceived this novel as "anomalous" and disruptive in re-lation not only to conventional realism but also to the traditions of black fiction, focusing "less on conventionally defined 'protest' than on a depiction of the black experience"—but an experience that is at once "rebellious" and "*anti*traditional . . . disputing the communalistic, socio-centric claims and 'verities' of much African-American literature."[44] What I have argued[45] is that the rebellious character of Sula—a woman who refuses the traditional role of mother-wife, living for herself rather than "for others"—becomes possible precisely because of the revision-istic work undertaken at the narrative and thematic level. After a false start (the book begins with a male character and a historicist framework that suggests a chronicle novel), *Sula* refocuses on a number of highly individual women and their absorbing relationships. Room for this new focus is created through a shrewd process of narrative elimination/ restructuring. The few male figures that count in the novel are bodily or mentally "curtailed." They are upstaged by strong, independent women like Eva and her daughter Hannah and granddaughter Sula, who gain increasing freedom through a process of self-"amputation": giving up a leg, a son, marriage, traditional domesticity, and replacing them with an undissimulated enjoyment of their newly gained free-doms. Accosted by four Irish boys, Sula slashes off the tip of her finger with a paring knife: "If I can do that to myself, what do you suppose I'll do to you?"[46] Later, in a partial reversal of this castrating gesture, she learns how to use "the cutting edge" of her sexuality in order not to tran-scend her being in a union with the male but to savor "her own abiding strength and limitless power" (122-3).

A similar restructuring goes on at the narrative level: *Sula* evokes images that seem to reinforce known symbolic frameworks (historical, socioethnic, metaphysical, mythic), but these orders are emptied of their conventional content and refilled with the fluid reality of "femaleness." For example, the motif of adolescent initiation is torn away from the patriarchal site and restructured around the experiences that the two female protagonists, Sula Peace and Nel Wright, share with each other. The traditional, male-oriented specularity of fiction is likewise disturbed to make room for women in the position of focalizers and rewriters of traditional stories: One-legged Eva enjoys some power as "overseer" of the community from her top-floor bedroom; Sula watches dispassionately her mother die in flames or herself making love; Nel beholds, mesmerized, in an ironic reversal of the androcentric Oedipal scenario, Sula's naked body interacting "aesthetically" with that of her own husband, Jude.

One of the most important mythic-narrative traditions that *Sula* revisits, according to Elizabeth J. Ordóñez, is "a heretofore buried or subversively oral matrilineal tradition, either through inversion or compensation—of alternate mythical and even historical accounts of women: Sula's Eva implicitly recalls her Biblical foremother, then shifts our perspective away from the authority of the Biblical text toward matrilineal autonomy and bonding."[47] By disrupting the formal and mythic-symbolic frameworks of fiction, *Sula* creates space for this alternative narrativization of women's experience. But this process of restructuring remains ideologically open ended. No single narrative perspective or concept of selfhood is allowed to dominate: the novel plays the voices of order against those of anarchy, heterosexuality against homosexuality, power against powerlessness, without settling their conflict. The intimate companionship between Sula and Nel empowers both girls, enabling them to "see old things with new eyes" (95); but their fresh semiotic valorizing female interactions and desires cannot entirely displace the patriarchal symbolic order. *Sula* remains an interesting postmodern project text that interplays disruption and rearticulation, contest and mediation, in order to create a new, albeit "unfinished" concept of womanhood and feminine narration.

The rearticulation of our "cultural destiny" in both surfiction and the feminist novel thus depends on a rewriting of the power relations and mastery mechanisms of narrative discourse. As modes of "radical rethinking & reinvention of expression," they apply their capacity for reformulation both to intradiscursive relations and to the extralinguistic contexts that govern discourse, illustrating Erica Hunt's concept of "oppositional poetics."[48] Such works as *98.6, Sula,* or (to use Hunt's own examples) Morrison's *Beloved* and Primo Levi's *Survival* are effective socioculturally precisely because they respond to "extremely violent [cultural] conditions" with complex narrative strategies of "resistance," mediation and rearticulation. Naturally, our list of examples could be expanded to include other innovative texts written by political metafictionists, postcolonial writers, ecofeminists, and so on. These writers respond to a common need to ground "radical statements" in innovative discursive choices, reconnecting the "arts and letters" to their "community's struggle."[49] But they also share an understanding of the complexities of literary discourse which needs to retranslate sociocultural conflict into the transactional terms of narration. A literary imagination that simply reflects the power configurations of contemporary society, communicating in ideological abstractions, leaves us "nerve dead" and "life dumb." As Sukenick further argues in his most recent "Avant-Pop" narrative, literary imagination must return us to the fluid nonpolarized contingencies of life, those ubiquitous "leftovers of reality" that "make another kind of sense, a sense that you don't, can't, or don't want to see" (*Doggy Bag*, 65, 66).

Notes

1. As Ronald Sukenick remarked in an interview with Joe David Bellamy, "One of the reasons people have lost faith in the novel is that they don't believe it tells the truth anymore, which is another way of saying that they don't believe in the conventions of the novel. . . . People are surrounded by all sorts of information coming in to them through all sorts of media, and the novel, on that level, doesn't have anything to say to them." Bellamy, *The New Fiction: Interviews with Innovative American Writers* (Urbana: Illinois University Press, 1972), 56, 59–60.

2. Jerome Klinkowitz, "The Extra-Literary in Contemporary American Fiction," in *Contemporary American Fiction*, ed. Malcolm Bradbury and Sigmund Ro (London: Edward Arnold, 1987), 19–20, 28.

3. Ronald Sukenick, *In Form: Digressions on the Act of Fiction* (Carbondale: Southern Illinois University Press, 1985), 206, 208.

4. Linda Hutcheon (*The Politics of Postmodernism* [New York: Routledge, 1989], 27) prefers to see "both American surfiction and the French texts of *Tel Quel* . . . as extensions of modernist notions of autonomy and autoreferentiality and thus as 'late modernist.' " Alan Wilde (*Middle Grounds: Studies in Contemporary American Fiction* [Philadelphia: University of Pennsylvania Press, 1987], 18) includes Sukenick in the group of "reflexivists" (together with Gass, Federman, and Barth) whose "concern is entirely and wholeheartedly with 'writing about writing.' "

5. Wilde, *Middle Grounds*, 20.

6. See "Postmodernism beyond Self-Reflection: Radical Mimesis in Recent Fiction," in *Mimesis, Semiosis and Power,* ed. Ronald Bogue (Philadelphia: John Benjamins, 1991), 127–55; "Narrative Innovation and Cultural Rewriting: The Pynchon–Morrison–Sukenick Connection," in *Narrative and Culture,* ed. Daniel R. Schwarz and Janice Carlisle (Athens: University of Georgia Press, 1993), 216–37.

7. Wilde, *Middle Grounds*, 124.

8. Raymond Federman, "Surfiction—Four Propositions in Form of an Introduction," in *Surfiction: Fiction Now . . . and Tomorrow,* ed. Raymond Federman, 2d ed., enlarged (Chicago: Swallow Press, 1981), 11.

9. In *Columbia Literary History of the United States,* ed. Emory Elliott (New York: Columbia University Press, 1988), 1146. Page numbers cited hereafter parenthetically in text.

10. See Michel Foucault, *The Order of Things: An Archaeology of the Human Sciences* (New York: Pantheon Books, 1970), particularly chaps. 2, 3, and 5; Jean-François Lyotard, *The Postmodern Condition: A Report on Knowledge,* trans. Geoff Bennington and Brian Massumi (Minneapolis: University of Minnesota Press, 1984).

11. See Seyla Benhabib, "Epistemologies of Postmodernism: A Rejoinder to Jean-François Lyotard," in *Feminism/Postmodernism,* ed. Linda J. Nicholson (New York: Routledge, 1990), 112.

12. Jane Flax, *Thinking Fragments: Psychoanalysis, Feminism, and Postmodernism in the Contemporary West* (Berkeley: University of California Press, 1990), 195.

13. Foucault, *The Order of Things,* xix.

14. Flax, *Thinking Fragments,* 192, 195.

15. Sandra Harding, "Feminism, Science, and the Anti-Enlightenment Critiques," in *Feminism/Postmodernism,* ed. Linda J. Nicholson (New York: Routledge, 1990), 87–88.

16. Benhabib, "Epistemologies of Postmodernism," 122.

17. Nancy Fraser and Linda J. Nicholson, "Social Criticism without Philosophy: An Encounter between Feminism and Postmodernism," in *Feminism/Postmodernism,* ed. Linda J. Nicholson (New York: Toutledge, 1990), 26.

18. Nicholson, introduction to *Feminism/Postmodernism,* 6.

19. Benhabib, "Epistemologies of Postmodernism," 125.

20. Mihai Spariosu, *God of Many Names: Play, Poetry and Power in Hellenic Thought from Homer to Aristotle* (Durham: Duke University Press, 1991), x.

21. Mihai Spariosu, *Literature, Mimesis and Play: Essays in Literary Theory* (Tübingen: Gunter Narr Verlag, 1982), 21–22.

22. Mihai Spariosu, *Dionysus Reborn: Play and the Aesthetic Dimension in Modern Philosophical and Scientific Discourse* (Ithaca: Cornell University Press, 1989), x, 15–16.

23. Mihai Spariosu, ed., *Mimesis in Contemporary Theory*, vol. 1, *The Literary and Philosophic Debate* (Philadelphia: John Benjamins, 1984), xxii.

24. Mihai Spariosu, "Mimesis and Contemporary French Theory," in *Mimesis in Contemporary Theory*, 99.

25. Mihai Spariosu, Editor's Introduction, in *Mimesis in Contemporary Theory*, ii.

26. For an analysis of Hans Vaihinger's philosophy of "Als Ob" (As If), see Spariosu, *Dionysus Reborn*, 246–58.

27. Sukenick, *Doggy Bag* (Boulder, CO: Black Ice Books, 1994), 72.

28. Ronald Sukenick, "Autogyro: My Life in Fiction," vol. 8, *Contemporary Authors Autobiography Series*, ed. Mark Zaderzny (Detroit, MI: Gale Research, 1989), 294.

29. Wolfgang Iser, "Representation: A Performative Act," in *The Aims of Representation: Subject/Text/History*, ed. Murray Krieger (New York: Columbia University Press, 1987), 228, 232.

30. Ronald Sukenick, *98.6* (New York: Fiction Collective, 1975), 187–88.

31. Thomas Docherty, *After Theory: Postmodernism/Postmarxism* (New York: Routledge, 1990), 97, 200.

32. Ronald Sukenick, *Up* (New York: Dial Press, 1968), 222.

33. Ronald Sukenick, *Out* (Chicago: Swallow Press, 1973), 164.

34. For a discussion of this procedure in constructing alternative postmodern ontologies/geographies, see Brian McHale, *Postmodern Fiction* (New York: Methuen, 1987), 45–58.

35. On the features of utopianism, see Louis Marin, *Utopics: The Semiological Play of Textual Places*, trans. Robert A. Vollrath (Atlantic Heights, NJ: Humanities Press International, 1990), 54.

36. Ronald Sukenick, *Long Talking Bad Conditions Blues* (New York: Fiction Collective, 1979), 29.

37. Donna Przybylowicz, *Desire and Repression: The Dialectic of Self and Other in the Late Works of Henry James* (University: University of Alabama Press, 1986), 6.

38. Larry McCaffery, "The Fictions of the Present," in *The Columbia Literary History of the United States,* ed. Emory Elliott (New York: Columbia University Press, 1988), 1170–71.

39. See, for example, Julia Kristeva, "The Subject in Signifying Practice," *Semiotext(e),* 1.3 (1975), 22, 24–25; Hélène Cixous, "The Laugh of the Medusa," trans. Keith and Paula Cohen, *Signs* 1 (Summer 1976), 875–99.

40. Madeline Gins, *Word Rain* (New York: Grossman, 1969).

41. Nicole Brossard, "Poetic Politics," in *The Politics of Poetic Form: Poetry and Public Policy,* ed. Charles Bernstein (New York: The Segue Foundation/ROOF books, 1990), 79.

42. Hortense Spillers, "A Hateful Passion, a Lost Love," in *Feminist Issues in Literary Scholarship,* ed. Shari Benstock (Bloomington: Indiana University Press, 1987), 181.

43. Sandi Russell, "It's OK to Say OK," interview with Toni Morrison, *Women's Review* 5 (March 1986), 22–24; rpt. in *Critical Essays on Toni Morrison,* ed. Nellie Y. McKay (Boston: G. K. Hall, 1988), 45, 46.

44. Robert Grant "Absence into Presence: The Thematics of Memory and 'Missing' Subjects in Toni Morrison's *Sula,*" in *Critical Essays on Toni Morrison,* ed. Nellie Y. McKay (Boston: G. K. Hall, 1988), 90–102.

45. See Cornis-Pope, "Narrative Innovation and Cultural Rewriting," 227–30.

46. Toni Morrison, *Sula* (New York: New American Library, 1987 [1973]), 54–55.

47. See Ordóñez, "Narrative Texts by Ethnic Women: Rereading the Past, Reshaping the Future," *Multi-Ethnic Literature of the United States* 9 (1982), 17, 19.

48. Erica Hunt, "Notes for an Oppositional Poetics," in *The Politics of Poetic Form,* ed. Charles Bernstein (New York: The Segue Foundation/ROOF Books, 1990), 198.

49. Catharine R. Stimpson, "Literature as Radical Statement," in *Columbia Literary History of the United States,* ed. Emory Elliott (New York: Columbia University Press, 1988), 1073.

Contributors

Ronald Bogue is Professor of Comparative Literature at the University of Georgia. He is the author of *Deleuze and Guattari* (London: Routledge, 1989) and editor of *Mimesis, Semiosis and Power* (Amsterdam: John Benjamins, 1991) and *The Play of the Self* (with Mihai Spariosu; Albany: SUNY Press, 1994).

Elisabeth Bronfen is Professor at the English Seminar, University of Zürich, Switzerland. She is the author of *Over Her Dead Body: Death, Femininity and the Aesthetic* (Manchester/New York: Manchester University Press/Routledge, 1992) and editor of *Death and Representation* (with Sarah McKim Webster Goodwin; Baltimore: Johns Hopkins University Press, 1993).

Stanley Corngold is Professor of German Languages and Comparative Literature at Princeton University. He is the author of *Forms of Feeling: Tensions in German Literature* (Lincoln: University of Nebraska Press, forthcoming), *Borrowed Lives* (with Irene Giersing; Albany: SUNY Press, 1991), *Franz Kafka: The Necessity of Form* (Ithaca: Cornell University Press, 1988), and *The Fate of the Self: German Writers and French Theory* (New York: Columbia University Press, 1986).

Marcel Cornis-Pope is Professor of English at Virginia Commonwealth University. He is the author of *Hermeneutic Desire and Critical Rewriting: Narrative Interpretation in the Wake of Poststructuralism* (New York: St. Martin's 1992; London: Macmillan Press, 1991) and editor of *The Comparatist.*

Susan Derwin is Assistant Professor of German and Comparative Literature at the University of California, Santa Barbara. She is the author of *The Ambivalence of Form: Lukács, Freud, and the Novel* (Baltimore: Johns Hopkins University Press, 1992).

Terryl Givens is Assistant Professor of English at the University of Richmond. His articles on theories of representation and on nineteenth- and twentieth-century literature have appeared in *Comparative Literature Studies, European Romantic Review, Luso-Brasilian Studies,* and *Hispanófila.*

Jerry Herron is Professor of English at Wayne State University. He is the author of *Afterculture: Detroit and the Humiliation of History* (Detroit: Wayne State University Press, 1993) and *Universities and the Myth of Cultural Decline* (Detroit: Wayne State University Press, 1988).

Albert Liu is a doctoral candidate in the Humanities Center at the Johns Hopkins University. His dissertation focuses on intersections between science and literature in the late nineteenth and early twentieth centuries. He has published in *American Literature, Genders, Lusitania, Modern Language Notes,* and *The Semiotic Review of Books.*

Tonglin Lu is Associate Professor of Asian Languages and Literatures at the University of Iowa. She is the author of *Rose and Lotus: Narrative of Desire in France and China* (Albany: SUNY Press, 1991) and editor of *Gender and Sexuality in Twentieth-Century Chinese Literature and Society* (Albany: SUNY Press, 1993).

Mihai Spariosu is Professor of Comparative Literature at the University of Georgia. He is the author of *God of Many Names: Play, Poetry, and Power in Hellenic Thought from Homer to Aristotle* (Durham: Duke University Press, 1991) and *Dionysus Reborn: Play and the Aesthetic Dimension in Modern Philosophical and Scientific Discourse* (Ithaca: Cornell University Press, 1989). He has also edited several collections, including *Building a Profession: Autobiographical Perspectives on the History of Comparative Literature in the United States* (with Lionel Gossman; Albany: SUNY Press, 1994).

Index